planet
HOME

planet HOME

Conscious Choices for Cleaning and Greening the World You Care About Most

Jeffrey Hollender

with Alexandra Zissu

Clarkson Potter/Publishers
New York

MELCHER MEDIA

The book was designed by
Melcher Media, 124 West 13th Street, New York, NY 10011
www.melcher.com

Publisher: Charles Melcher
Associate Publisher: Bonnie Eldon
Editor in Chief: Duncan Bock
Senior Editor: Holly Rothman
Editor and Project Manager: Megan Worman
Production Director: Kurt Andrews
Production Assistant: Daniel del Valle

Library of Congress Cataloging-in-Publication Data
Hollender, Jeffrey. Planet home / Jeffrey Hollender.
1. Conduct of life. 2. Human ecology. 3. Home economics.
I. Title. BJ1581.2.H615 2010 640–dc22 2010028312

ISBN 978-0-307-71664-4

Printed in the United States of America

10 9 8 7 6 5 4 3 2 1

First Edition

Acknowledgments

from Jeffrey Hollender:

My deepest gratitude goes to my co-author, Alexandra Zissu,
without whom this book would never have been possible. Lexy
was an absolute pleasure to partner with and showed her passion
and talent every step of the way. Seventh Generation's own
Science Man and a longtime friend, Martin Wolf, was essential
to ensuring the scientific, factual, and statistical accuracy of
this great endeavor.

My team at Melcher Media, who served as invaluable partners
from concept to editing and design, made the challenges of
producing this book an absolute pleasure. Special thanks to
Holly Rothman, Megan Worman, and Charlie Melcher. I'd also
like to thank the team at Clarkson Potter, especially Doris
Cooper and Angelin Borsics, who have supported this book
wholeheartedly.

My thinking about systems was shaped by some of my teach-
ers, most notably Carol Sanford, Gregor Barnum, Cheryl Heller,
Martin Murson, and Peter Senge.

Without the lessons, learning, and total support of the entire
Seventh Generation community, none of my work would be
possible. Special thanks goes to Lee Pelletier, who takes special
care of me every day.

While many organizations have supported and generated the
knowledge required to learn about our endlessly interconnected
world, none plays the role of being an ongoing teacher better
than Greenpeace.

This book is dedicated to my wife, teacher, and lifelong
partner, Sheila Hollender.

from Alexandra Zissu:

I would like to thank Olli Chanoff, Aili Chanoff Zissu, and
my wide-ranging, helpful, supportive, and multitasking family—
immediate and extended alike. Thanks also to Jeffrey Hollender
for entrusting me with this project, Holly Rothman, Charlie
Melcher, Martin Wolf, Megan Worman, Doris Cooper, Angelin
Borsics, Sheila Hollender, Lee Pelletier, Chrystie Heimert, and
Maureen Wolpert.

...

Melcher Media wishes to thank Kay Banning, Christopher Beha,
David E. Brown, Amélie Cherlin, Cheryl Della Pietra, Marilyn
Fu, Barbara Gogan, Diane Hodges, Coco Joly, Robin Kamen,
Julia Marks, Myles McDonnell, Lauren Nathan, Minju Pak,
Katherine Raymond, Lia Ronnen, Jessi Rymill, Julia Sourikoff,
Alex Tart, Scott Thares, Shoshana Thaler, Anna Thorngate, and
Rebecca Wiener.

CONTENTS

What Is a Conscious Home?

There comes a time in anyone's life when the current state of the earth becomes too obvious to ignore, and taking some steps to green and protect your own environment—your Planet Home—seems like a good idea. For many, becoming pregnant or looking into your child's eyes for the first time can trigger a deeper concern for global issues. And no wonder. Countless others have been motivated to action by climate change and, more recently, by images of oil gushing into the Gulf of Mexico. Whatever has inspired you to pick up this book and make some changes, first steps tend to be simple—switching to organic milk, buying toilet paper made from recycled fiber, packing lunch in reusable containers, swapping in energy-efficient light bulbs. These are popular adjustments because they're better for you and your family. But it's the rare person who sees that the organic milk is also better for the cows, for the people who raise them, and for our shared environment. This makes sense; human beings tend to be compartmentalized thinkers. We see the individual puzzle pieces rather than the whole picture. Indigenous and Eastern cultures based on spirituality are more likely to see the puzzle in its entirety; with spirituality comes an understanding of the interconnectedness of who we are and what we do. Still other cultures are forced to be aware of the bigger picture because of their limited space on the planet. America is so vast that many activities that are harmful to the environment—like removing mountaintops to mine coal or endlessly filling garbage dumps—take place where we don't see them. Out of sight, out of mind. When you don't see the interconnectedness of your daily decisions and actions in a holistic way, you also can't see their unintended consequences. There are plenty of resources available for people interested in "eco-friendly" living. And primarily, *Planet Home* provides a road map for anyone who wants to green and clean a home. But the following pages also go well beyond offering typical "go green" advice. This book is an attempt to inspire us all to open our minds, expand our collective consciousness, and think without compartmentalizing. It's an invitation to stop and examine how our individual choices—that milk, that light bulb, and even where you choose to bank—ripple out to affect our neighbors, our community, and the environment as a whole. Because when we're only told to lower our thermostats and stop there—one piece of the puzzle—we remain fundamentally confused about the whole of what matters and how to truly make a difference. *Planet Home* is a call to arms that will inspire you to ask better questions and move beyond just going green and toward connecting the green dots all around you, holistically and systematically. Visualizing just how connected we all are to each other and the earth when, say, you're wandering the aisles of the supermarket isn't obvious. But if you try to take the simple yet revolutionary notion that we're all connected as a point of departure, the systems behind everything from the water running out of our taps to the cotton grown for our sheets, clothing, and even feminine care products start to become clear. You'll see the entire puzzle, not just the pieces. The ability to see the total environmental impact of any one choice is paramount—the real takeaway of *Planet Home*—whether you're just beginning to consider going green or you're living off the grid and growing your own food. Being more aware of how your actions influence everything else will change how you behave. It will help you go greener faster than just doing a few green things, and with a less vague sense of why you're taking the steps you're taking. It will have a far-reaching impact. It will also enable you to recognize when systems break down or are incomplete—like when you place your pesticide-free organic produce on a cutting board cleaned with a conventional product containing pesticides.

Imagine a country full of people who understand the social and environmental implications of everything from their choice of toothpaste to the cleaning product residues they wash down their drains—people who want to make better choices for their families, their communities, and the earth. This consciousness could make a real overarching environmental impact at a time when it is sorely needed—making green the new normal. We can't turn back the clock, but we can all work together to ensure that our children, our children's children, and the planet we all share will be healthy enough to continue to sustain us. Human beings have unlimited potential when we put our minds to solving a problem. And there are many people working hard to do the right thing right now. This is your invitation to join them.

***

Use the following chapters as a jumping-off point. There are plenty of practical steps detailed; remember as you undertake any number of them that we're not alone in our little green bubbles. Keep in mind that going green shouldn't involve losing sight of the quality and richness of life. Pause for conscious rituals—like watching the sunset as a family—as often as possible. The emotional nourishment these moments offer is what we need to build happy and fulfilling lives. Living consciously—being aware, awake, and thoughtful—includes treading lightly on our shared home planet while embracing our right to happiness, which will enable us to better enjoy the happiness that a responsible and sustainable life so bountifully brings.

Jeffrey Hollender

The 7 Inter-Connected Principles of Conscious Living

We need revolutionary change in the world, and we need it now! You can begin by shifting your mind and reframing the way you look at the immediate challenges in your home. Conscious living extends beyond these challenges to how we think about ourselves as a society, and our responsibility to one another and the planet.

1. THINK HOLISTICALLY

Try to see the whole interconnected systems that live just behind everything that you do. Using ethanol as fuel may seem like a good idea, but look beneath the surface. Ethanol isn't just energy derived from corn; it's grown from genetically modified seeds, it requires the use of petroleum-derived sprays, and it drives up the price of corn—which then affects tortilla prices in Mexico, for example. It takes more energy to grow the corn used to make ethanol than the ethanol itself provides. Looking beyond the surface of the actions you take in your everyday life will better inform your choices.

2. LIVE BY THE PRECAUTIONARY PRINCIPLE

Whenever the potential of an activity, product, or chemical raises the threat of harm to human health or the environment, precautionary measures should be exercised. Precaution should be taken even if the absolute cause and effect relationships that might lead to harm have not fully been established scientifically. Thus, the maker of a product or chemical, or one who proposes an action or business endeavor, must prove the safety of such in advance of its exposure to people or the planet and bear the burden of proof for its safety. The Precautionary Principle shifts responsibility for the proof of safety to business and industry and ensures that people and the planet are not guinea pigs subject to uncertain experimentation.

Chemicals and consumer products today are "innocent until proven guilty." This makes human beings those guinea pigs in an uncontrolled experiment. There have been 80,000 to 100,000 new chemicals introduced since World War II, but the health effects of less than 5 percent of these are known. We don't yet understand the impact of having combinations of these chemicals in our bodies, or what daily low-dose exposure to them means for us down the road. If a chemical or a product is "guilty," i.e., harmful, we pay the price. It can show up as disease, cancer, or chronic illness. We need to change this process so that chemicals in a product must be proven safe by their manufacturer before they enter the market. It's difficult to connect the dots and pinpoint the impacts and implications of chemicals due to the sheer amount of them gushing into our society. If a bird in the Gulf is covered in oil, you know where that oil came from. But when a child gets cancer, you rarely know its source. Until there is regulatory change, common sense says that you should adopt as many of the changes suggested in these pages as you can and live by the Precautionary Principle, too.

3. ACQUIRE LESS STUFF

Prior to World War II, we were a culture of reuse, recycling, and restraint. But following the war, huge factories suddenly had nothing to make. Our government created a national strategy and built our whole economy around consumerism. We see now that this is irresponsible and unsustainable. The sequence of events that brings all this stuff to the stuff-buying masses is destructive. The materials contained in any old household product are global, rarely local. There's an elaborate system needed to extract, process, and transport the building blocks of stuff from where it was found (Saudi Arabia? Malaysia? Texas?) to where it can be manufactured. Manufacturing is another system. Then there are the systems of equipment needed to package, warehouse, and distribute stuff to consumers. There is also the system of waste: we have no place to keep all of the trash our consumerism creates. The products themselves—from manufacture to disposal—are polluting our earth and releasing untold chemicals into the air in our homes. There are better, less toxic versions of many products described in these pages, but ultimately we as a culture need to back away from the overabundance of stuff in our lives. How much do you really need compared to how much do you want? It's a question of quantity versus quality. We must simply buy less stuff, and what we do buy must be made to last, leaving the smallest possible footprint behind. All this stuff doesn't lead to happiness or fulfillment. True satisfaction comes from relationships and community, not cars or cell phones. Think about your relationships: would you rather have 25 superficial ones or three totally trusting, open, honest ones? Meaning comes from deep, quality relationships.

4. THINK LONG TERM, NOT SHORT TERM

In a fundamental sense, we have collectively pushed the long-term consequences of our decisions entirely out of our consciousness.

Other than the relationships we have with our families, most of the time we're unconscious of the lasting repercussions of our actions—of what we eat, what we buy, what we do. How many things can you name that you do out of concern for the next generation? For most people it is generally out of sight, out of mind. We must shift our perspective and take a longer-term point of view.

5. THINK "WE," NOT "ME"

When you're thinking only about yourself, it doesn't matter if you buy another T-shirt or you take another flight or you put pesticides on your lawn. In the "Me" world, none of these things matter. In the "We" world, they all do. When we all behave as if we were alone, the results are catastrophic. Can you go through the traffic light when it is turning red? Can you not take time to help someone who is lost and needs directions? What would happen if we lived in a world in which no one helped anyone else? For anything of great substance to happen positively, the power is in what We can do, not in what I can do. If we start to see how our everyday individual actions affect the people around us, if we consider ourselves members of the community and act accordingly, good things will come. Start by smiling.

6. DON'T CONFUSE LESS BAD WITH GOOD

We have totally confused less bad with good. We don't know what good is anymore. Ninety-nine percent of what we think of as good is actually just less bad. So what is good? It tends to show up in a few specific areas—in meaningful relationships, education, nature, biodynamic farming. It shows up in services, too, but it very rarely rears its head in products because of what it takes to make and get products to the market. In many cases, getting something to consumers will tilt the scale dramatically from good to bad, not even less bad. Think of honey. That's good, right? Well, where did it come from? Consider how it was collected, processed, packaged, and shipped, and by whom.

7. GET ACTIVE

There is only so much a holistically thinking individual can do to affect global change. Joining forces with groups working to influence both our government and big businesses to bring about systemwide change is a great thing to do. The right legislation will have wider impact than any one person's changes. Voting, calling, e-mailing, spreading the word, aligning yourself with the organizations working tirelessly to protect our shared earth and generally making noise all help.

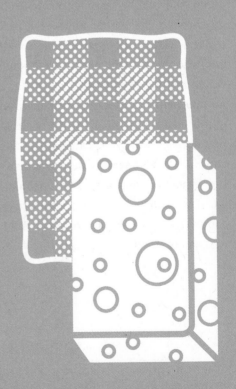

CLEANING PRODUCTS AND CHEMICALS
Your Essential Guide

It's ironic that most of the cleaners we rely on to keep our homes looking their best actually pollute them and the environment. They contain many unsafe chemicals that have been linked to everything from asthma to various cancers to ozone depletion. Normally a consumer could memorize which ingredients are bad and look for those chemicals on product labels in order to avoid them. But cleaning product formulas are considered trade secrets, and so, manufacturers aren't required to disclose their contents to consumers. If something is really dangerous, a product will have a general hazard warning but still no specific ingredients. It's up to the general public, then, to play cleaning product sleuth—some answers can be found online. The following pages contain the nitty-gritty on how chemicals in cleaning products do their job. A far safer, easier, and eco-friendlier route than becoming a citizen scientist is to purchase only natural cleaners. The companies that make these tend to list their ingredients voluntarily on their packaging. If they don't, don't buy them. Or take it a step further and make your own cleaners out of household staples you probably already have.

How to Read Labels

Cleaning product labels are a quick read, as they typically contain very little information. By reading one, you will discover the type of product it is, directions for use, safety information, and any storage and disposal guidelines. What you *won't* discover is a list of ingredients. These are usually undisclosed, government-protected trade secrets, unless they are disinfecting agents, pesticides, or listed as hazardous by the U.S. Consumer Product Safety Commission (CPSC)—then those specific ingredients must be disclosed. Until recently, regulation of the chemicals in cleaning products has essentially been neglected. For decades, manufacturers have been legally allowed to include untested and potentially harmful chemicals in household products without informing the consumer about them on the label. Recently, though, man-

ufacturers have started to pay more attention to growing legions of curious label readers. The launch of the Safer Chemicals, Healthy Families coalition to reform the Toxic Substances Control Act, and other public actions, like the Consumer Product Ingredient Communication Initiative, have helped, too. Although information on ingredients products contain is now becoming more available (whether on the label or—more commonly—on the manufacturer's website), the need for tighter regulation and broader transparency remains. It is still currently up to the consumer to seek out ingredient lists, read between the lines on the labels, and make a conscious, informed decision about what to buy and bring into the home. Here's how:

Label Literacy 101

1. **Look for warnings.** Avoid any product that has the words "danger," "poison," "toxic," "hazardous," or "flammable" printed on the label. They are dead giveaways that there are harmful chemicals inside. Be sure to check the front and back labels, including the fine print.

2. **Check the listed ingredients.** Avoid anything with no ingredients listed or that lists chemicals with known or probable chronic or acute toxicity (see the Ingredients Guide on page 334).

3. **Check to see if the product is fragranced.** Stay away from synthetic fragrances, which may contain hormone-disrupting phthalates (see page 341). Most products claiming to have the "fresh scent" of "morning air" contain synthetic fragrances. Fragranced products (including perfumes, air fresheners, cleaning products, and candles) can also release harmful volatile organic compounds (VOCs) into your home environment. Many VOCs from cleaning products, such as formaldehyde, are known to be hazardous air pollutants and can have short- and long-term health effects. Look for labels that read "VOC-free" or "free from dyes and fragrances." If you want a fragrance, seek out products that are scented naturally with essential oils.

4. **Think about what the performance claims are telling you.** These are the selling points clearly stated on the front label. Products claiming to "whiten" likely contain bleach, and products claiming to "brighten" usually contain optical brighteners. Use the Ingredients Guide to see what you're really getting with that "streak-free shine," and to learn why an ingredient is or is not hazardous.

5. **Do a sustainability check.** Choose products in packaging made with the highest PCR (post-consumer recycled) content and that can be recycled or reused. As for the products themselves, buy ones that are biodegradable or compostable and claim to be "petrochemical-free," "nontoxic," or "septic-safe."

6. **Go to seventhgeneration.com and download the Label Reading Guide.** It will help you better understand the ingredients in cleaning products and their risks.

Types of Cleaners

Cleaning products can be divided into two general types: all-purpose and specialty. All-purpose cleaners can be used on multiple surfaces, whereas specialty cleaners are designed for a single type of surface material, like wood, glass, or carpet.

Most cleaning products contain multiple ingredients, each serving a unique function to produce a desired result. These ingredients fall into the following categories:

* **Abrasives:** Mineral particles made from silica, feldspar, quartz, or calcite, commonly used to remove soil stains and provide smoothing, scrubbing, or polishing action. Abrasives are usually found in household cleaners and dishwashing products, as well as in personal cleansers.

* **Acids:** Chemical compounds used to dissolve calcium and metal salts or adjust the pH (acidity or alkalinity) of other ingredients (see page 20). Commonly used acids include phosphoric acid, hydrochloric acid, sulfuric acid, acetic acid (vinegar), lactic acid, and citric acid. Acids are typically found in household cleaners claiming to remove hard-water stains from your tub, tile, sink, or toilet bowl.

* **Alkalis:** Chemical compounds used to adjust the pH of other ingredients. Increased alkalinity improves the effectiveness of builders and surfactants to remove fatty and greasy stains. Some alkalis provide protection against corrosion or prevent soil that has been removed from

redepositing. Alkalis are commonly added to laundry detergents, personal cleansers, dishwashing products, and household cleaners.

* **Bleaches:** Chemicals used to remove stains, whiten fabrics, and disinfect surfaces. Chlorine and oxygen bleaches are present in many laundry, dishwashing, and household cleaners. Oxygen bleach (sodium percarbonate) is a safer and greener alternative to chlorine bleach (sodium hypochlorite).

* **Builders and chelating agents:** Additives in dishwashing and laundry products used to soften water (by removing calcium and magnesium ions) for more effective cleaning. Phosphate was once a widely used builder but was removed from laundry products in the 1990s and from automatic dishwasher detergents effective July 2010, because of its harmful effect on aquatic ecosystems. Washing soda or soda ash (sodium carbonate), sodium silicate, sodium citrate, and zeolite compounds are safer alternatives.

* **Disinfectants:** Antimicrobial agents that kill viruses, fungi, and bacteria. Some disinfectants are more harmful to humans than others. Natural disinfectants, like thymol, are a safer and greener alternative to conventional disinfectants like chlorine bleach and triclosan.

* **Enzymes:** Proteins made by living organisms used in both natural and conventional cleaning products to break down certain soils, such as grass, blood, fats, and starch, so that they can be removed by detergents. Proteins are classified by the type of soil they break down. Amylase enzymes remove starch soils; lipase enzymes remove fatty and oily soils; protease enzymes remove protein soils; and cellulose enzymes remove particulate soils and reduce the pilling and graying of cotton. Enzymes are eliminated as they perform their function; they are safe for humans and do not persist in the environment.

* **Fragrances:** Either synthetic chemicals or plant-derived essential oils that are added to cleaners to mask the smell of the product or what you are cleaning. Artificial fragrances are synthetic chemicals that often produce such air pollutants as benzenes, aldehydes, and hormone-disrupting phthalates. Natural essential oils are a safer and greener option.

* **Solvents:** Liquids used to dissolve other substances. Water is known as the universal solvent, but for cleaning purposes you often need more than just water; other chemical solvents are added to cleaners to enhance their performance. Solvents liquefy grease and oil and dissolve soils to help surfactants do their job. Solvents are also used to ensure the product remains stable and properly mixed over time, or as a thickener or thinner. In glass, dishwashing, and all-purpose cleaners, solvents are responsible for "fast-drying" and "streak-free" performance.

* **Surfactants:** Also known as "surface active agents." The active ingredient in any cleaning product responsible for soil removal. They speed up the cleaning process by loosening and removing soils from a surface. Many surfactants, such as linear alkyl benzene sulfonate (LAS), are derived from petroleum. Some surfactants, such as decyl glucoside, are naturally derived from coconut or palm kernel oil. Still others, like sodium lauryl sulfate (SLS) and sodium lauryl ether sulfate (SLES), can come from either natural or synthetic sources. The performance of

surfactants is reduced by water hardness, so they often require the presence of builders or chelating agents.

STORAGE AND SAFETY

✔ Safety Checks

☐ Read and follow all directions and safety instructions on the label.

☐ Never mix any conventional products together. Many contain chemical ingredients that, if combined, will produce harmful reactions.

☐ Keep the area you are cleaning—even if you are cleaning with a natural product—well ventilated to avoid inhaling noxious fumes or triggering allergies.

✔ Storage Checks

☐ Always be mindful of the effects of heat and humidity. Never store flammable products near a heat source or dry powders in areas exposed to high humidity.

☐ Never store ammonia and chlorine bleach in the same room, as the fumes can mix and yield a potentially lethal toxin.

☐ For homemade solutions, always label with their intended use, a list of their ingredients, and the date they were made.

☐ Keep all cleaning products out of reach of children and pets.

✔ Disposal Checks

☐ Read and follow all disposal guidelines on the label.

☐ Products that contain hazardous materials should not be disposed down the drain or in the trash. Contact your local hazardous waste or environmental agency to arrange proper disposal. Find the center nearest you at earth911.com.

The pH Scale

The pH scale is used to measure the acidity and alkalinity of a solution. It ranges from 0 (most acidic) to 14 (most alkaline/basic). Solutions considered neutral, as well as water, have a pH level of 7.0 on the scale.

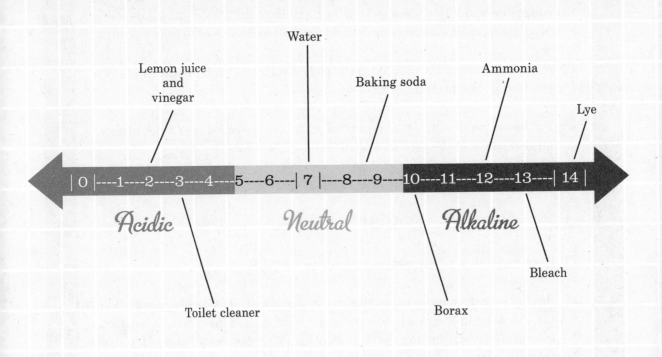

Water

Lemon juice
and
vinegar

Baking soda

Ammonia

Lye

| 0 |----1----2----3----4----| 5----6----| 7 |----8----9----10----11----12----13----| 14 |

Acidic

Neutral

Alkaline

Toilet cleaner

Borax

Bleach

pH is important because it affects the performance of the product. Different pH levels are desirable for different types of cleaners. Detergents are more effective when they're alkaline. Bathroom cleaners are more effective when they're acidic. Most cleaning products contain ingredients specifically added to adjust the pH to an optimal level.

It's important to know the pH of a cleaner for safety reasons. Products claiming to be "mild" or "gentle" on hands are often close to neutral pH (7.0) and can be handled without too much concern. Cleaning solutions with extremely high or low pH levels are corrosive and require rubber gloves, eye protection, and good ventilation when handling. Being mindful of how a solution's pH affects different surfaces, soil removal, and your personal safety is relevant when creating your own cleaning products at home, too. Cleaning products with a neutral pH will not harm you or the environment, but those with an extremely high or low pH can.

LOW PH = ACIDIC
breaks down tough stains, dissolves rust and mineral deposits

* Hard-water stain removers

* Toilet bowl cleaners

* Rust stain removers

HIGH PH = ALKALINE
removes fatty and oily stains

* Tub and tile cleaners

* Mold removers

* Oven cleaners

* All-purpose cleaners

* Laundry detergents

Health, Safety, and the Environment

CLEANING INGREDIENTS AND TOXICITY

Many ingredients in conventional cleaning products are known to be harmful to humans, animals, and the environment. In terms of human health, the National Institute for Occupational Safety & Health (NIOSH) views hazardous chemicals as having either short-term effects (acute toxicity) or long-term effects (chronic toxicity).

Acute toxicities include any skin, eye, or respiratory irritation; mild to strong allergic reactions; and even death after less than twenty-four hours of exposure. The CPSC requires that any product that is so highly toxic that it can cause death within 24 hours be labeled "DANGER: Poison." It's rare that a cleaning product is so toxic—more typically, they're stamped with a caution statement that warns of possible irritancy ("CAUTION: Irritant. Avoid contact with eyes or skin.") or toxicity ("CAUTION: Do not swallow"). This system of warning labels is not monitored by any third-party or government agencies. It's just up to manufacturers to determine on their own what level of warning to apply to their products.

Chronic toxicities appear after long-term or repeated exposure, resulting in cancer, neurological or autoimmune disorders, hormone and reproductive effects, tissue damage, or death. The Ingredients Guide on page 334 lists ingredients commonly found in conventional cleaning products and explains their potential dangers. Unfortunately, much of the time the manufacturers of these products don't list their ingredients.

Luckily, it's easy to avoid the human- and eco-unfriendly chemicals found in most conventional cleaning products by choosing nontoxic, environmentally preferable products at the store. Natural cleaning versions do tend to voluntarily list their ingredients. The following pages include some of the ingredients you might find listed on eco-friendly cleaners, plus safe and effective cleaning products you can make at home.

Safer Ingredients Used in Natural Cleaning Products

The following ingredients are generally considered safe for humans and the environment; however, it's important to be aware that no ingredient is 100 percent safe. Some may cause mild side effects such as skin and eye irritation.

Acetic acid (white distilled vinegar)

Function:
- Solvent, pH adjuster, masking fragrance, preservative, or disinfecting agent

Found in:
- Whitening detergents, oven and drain cleaners, bathroom cleaners, glass cleaners

Reason to Choose:
- Biodegradable

Alkyl polyglucoside (polyglucose, decyl glucoside, lauryl polyglucose, APG)

Function:
- Surfactant

Found in:
- Glass cleaners, dishwashing detergents, paint strippers, metal polishes

Reasons to Choose:
- Non-irritating
- Plant-derived
- Biodegradable

Citric acid

Function:
- Chelating agent, pH adjuster

Found in:
- Bathroom cleaners, dishwashing detergents, automatic dishwashing detergents, laundry detergents

Reasons to Choose:
- Nontoxic
- Safe for the environment
- Plant-derived

Glycerin

Function:
- Solvent, denaturant (a substance used to destroy the character of another substance), humectant (promotes moisture retention), or fragrance

Found in:
- Laundry detergents, dishwashing liquids

Reasons to Choose:
- Nontoxic
- Plant-derived (may also be animal-derived)
- Biodegradable

Lactic acid

Function:
- Exfoliant, pH adjuster, fragrance, disinfecting agent, or humectant

Found in:
- Toilet bowl cleaners, sink and shower cleaners

Reasons to Choose:
- Low toxicity
- Biodegradable
- Naturally derived

Di-(Palm Carboxyethyl) Hydroxyethyl Methylammonium Methyl Sulfates

Function:
- Fabric softener

Found in:
- Fabric softeners

Reason to Choose:
- Plant-derived
- Biodegradable

Sodium bicarbonate (baking soda)

Function:
- pH adjuster, abrasive, deodorant

Found in:
- Bleaches, deodorants, drain and oven cleaners

Reason to Choose:
- Nontoxic

Sodium carbonate (washing soda/soda ash)

Function:
- pH adjuster or water softener

Found in:
- Dishwashing detergents, laundry detergents, deodorizers, drain and oven cleaners

Reason to Choose:
- Nontoxic

Sodium lauryl sulfate (SLS)

Function:
- Surfactant

Found in:
- All-purpose cleaners, laundry detergents, dishwashing liquids, carpet cleaners

Reason to Choose:
- Biodegradable

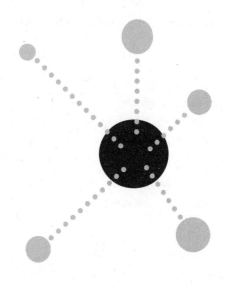

Safe and Effective Cleaning Products You Can Make At Home

* **Air freshener:** Put baking soda or vinegar with lemon slices in dishes around your home to absorb odors. Small bowls of coffee (whole beans or ground) or dried herbs will also do the trick. Household plants are also good at cleaning the air and can reduce smelly (and potentially harmful) VOCs in your home.

* **All-purpose cleaner:** Put 2 teaspoons washing soda, 2 teaspoons borax, $1/2$ teaspoon plant-based liquid soap, and 1 cup water in a spray bottle and shake well. Lemon juice or essential oils can also be added for fragrance. Washing soda may leave a harmless white residue on a surface if not wiped well.

* **Carpet stain remover:** Blot stain immediately, then cover with baking soda, borax, or cornstarch and let dry. Rinse with club soda, blot dry, and vacuum. For a stronger cleaner, mix equal parts salt, borax, and vinegar into a paste. Rub paste into carpet and leave for a few hours, then vacuum. For highly colored stains, such as wine or fruit juice, wet with hydrogen peroxide and blot dry.

* **Disinfectant spray:** Mix 1 part 3 percent hydrogen peroxide with 2 parts water in an opaque spray bottle. For moldy surfaces, spray mold with solution and let sit for one hour before wiping. For extra disinfecting, first spray with vinegar, then spray with disinfectant spray.

* **Drain cleaner:** For light cleaning, mix $1/2$ cup table salt with 4 liters boiling water and pour down the drain. For stronger cleaning, pour $1/2$ cup baking soda down the drain, followed by $1/2$ cup white vinegar to break down fatty acids. Wait 15 minutes, then pour boiling water down drain to clear residue.

* **Furniture polish:** Mix $1/4$ cup lemon juice with $1/2$ teaspoon olive oil in a glass jar. Dab solution onto a soft rag for use. Make only as much as needed; it doesn't keep.

* **Glass cleaner:** Make a 50-50 solution of white distilled vinegar and water.

* **Moth repellent:** Cedar chips, dried lemon peels, lavender, and rosemary are all-natural moth repellents. Wrap any of these (or a combination of a few) in cheesecloth and hang in closets or stash in drawers. The stronger the smell, the stronger the repellent. Use multiple sachets in large spaces and replace annually to maintain freshness.

* **Oven cleaner:** Sprinkle a good layer of baking soda over grease and grime in oven. Spray with water until damp, then re-wet occasionally. Allow to sit overnight. In the morning, grease and grime will wipe away easily.

* **Powdered laundry detergent:** Make a 50-50 solution of borax and washing soda. Use 2 tablespoons per full load.

* **Wood cleaner:** Mix $1/4$ cup lemon juice or $1/4$ cup white vinegar with $1/2$ teaspoon olive oil in a glass jar. Moisten sponge with mixture and wipe surface. Store cleaner in an airtight container.

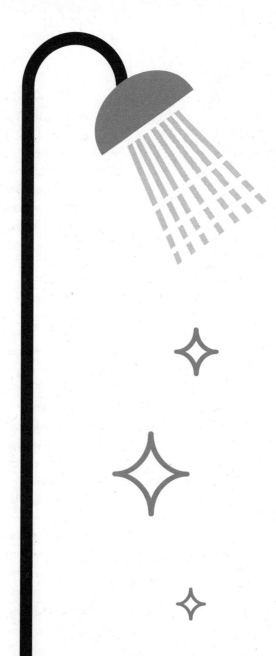

Household Ingredients for Safer Cleaning Products

Some cupboard staples that can also be used to care for your home

Active Ingredient	Description	Home Uses
Baking Soda (Sodium Bicarbonate)	A safe substance composed of multiple mineral-derived ingredients (similar to washing soda).	Deodorizer (skin and air) Nonabrasive scouring powder Polisher/smoother
Beeswax	A natural wax produced by honeybees. Has been used for centuries in candles, hair wax, soap, and body cream. Bonus: it's a renewable resource.	Floor and furniture wax/polish Soap ingredient
Borax	A mineral composed of sodium, boron (a metal element), oxygen, and water. It has detergent, fungicidal, insecticidal, preservative, and disinfectant properties. (Continual exposure to high quantities of borax may adversely affect male fertility.)	Laundry additive Deodorizer Nonabrasive scouring powder All-purpose cleaner Mold inhibitor Rust stain remover
Cornstarch	Starch that comes from the heart of corn kernels.	Carpet cleaner and deodorizer Stain remover (blood, grease)
Essential Oils	Plant-derived essential oils are versatile. Many have antiseptic qualities. Some are possibly irritating to skin, eyes, and lungs, but they do not pose serious or long-term health effects to most individuals and are not harmful to the environment. Essential oils that are particularly useful in DIY cleaners include eucalyptus oil, grapefruit seed extract, jojoba oil, lavender oil, neem tree oil, and thyme oil.	Air freshener Disinfectant Fragrance Insect repellent Wood polish
Hydrogen Peroxide	An oxidizing and bleaching agent made from oxygen and hydrogen. Commonly used in chlorine-free bleaches. When used in concentrations of 3 percent for cleaning, it's nontoxic but may be irritating to eyes and skin.	Whitener (bleaching agent) Disinfectant Stain remover (blood, ink) Antifungal (mold inhibitor)

Active Ingredient	Description	Home Uses
Lemon Juice	Has a pH of 2.0, making it a useful cleaning tool. Can be mixed with vinegar or baking soda to make solutions and pastes.	Grease cutter (for tables and glass) Stain remover (ink, perspiration) Rust remover Bleach alternative Deodorizer
Liquid Soap (Plant-Based)	Soap made from the oils of vegetables or plants as opposed to animal fat or petroleum. Often referred to as castile soap. It is nontoxic and biodegradable and comes from renewable resources.	Detergent
Natural Toothpaste	Typically made from a silica or baking soda base, natural toothpaste can clean surfaces as well as teeth.	Silver polish Removing water stains from wood furniture
Olive Oil	A versatile, ubiquitous, and moisturizing oil. Can be used in a variety of cleaners.	Wood polish Lubricant Paint remover (from skin and hair)
Sea Salt	A natural mineral composed of sodium and chloride harvested from the evaporation of seawater with little or no processing.	Deodorizer Scouring powder
Washing Soda Soda Ash (Sodium Carbonate)	A mineral-derived substance (similar to baking soda but with higher alkalinity). Helps adjust pH. Used as a water softener to remove water hardness. Slightly irritating to skin.	Grease and grime cutter Wax remover Deodorizer Stain remover (chocolate, lipstick, paint) *Do not use on wax floors, fiberglass, or aluminum*
White Distilled Vinegar	An acid derived from the fermentation of dilute alcoholic liquids. Vinegar kills most bacteria, molds, and germs. The smell of vinegar dissipates within a few hours of use.	Disinfectant Antifungal (mold inhibitor) Deodorizer Hard water deposit remover Greasy buildup remover Tarnish remover Stain remover Wood and glass cleaner

the
KITCHEN

The Conscious Ritual

The kitchen is arguably the heart of any home. It serves as restaurant, home office, art project and homework station, and living room. It's also a place where all of the systems involved in running a house collide, where the outside world interacts most with our personal lives. Pause to acknowledge how agriculture, energy, municipal water, and waste all come into play as we snack in the middle of the night, have important discussions over coffee, and clean up after Sunday pancake parties with the kids. Be grateful for the ease of a dishwasher or even turning on a stove. Switching on a burner is a simple act, but try to visualize all that is entailed in forming that flame. Chapter 3 describes how to make sure the ingredients in those pancakes—and all other food—are as conscious as can be. Take a moment to consider why such lovingly sourced food deserves to be cooked, stored, and washed up in an equally mindful and holistic fashion. Then make it happen.

The Conscious Components

A conscious kitchen is a space filled with energy-efficient appliances and cookware made from eco-friendly materials. It's well ventilated and always scrubbed with natural cleaners. It's prepared for any pests that might attempt to scuttle or squeak their way in, and any methods of dealing with them if they do arrive are as minimally toxic as possible. It's a place of reuse, repair, and recycling, as well as composting. Maintaining a conscious kitchen isn't more time intensive than taking care of a conventional one. Make a few simple changes now to set up a good conscious system. Then you can go back to what we all enjoy most about kitchens: eating.

Here's a handy checklist to help you remember the pieces that make up a conscious kitchen ➡️

☐ Open windows for ventilation

☐ Table set with reusable plates, flatware, and cups

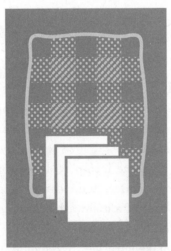

☐ Napkins, place mats, and tablecloths made of natural materials like cotton, linen, and hemp

☐ Energy-efficient appliances

☐ Safe, natural cleaning products

☐ Tried-and-true cooking materials like cast iron, stainless steel, and glass

☐ Glass food storage containers instead of plastic

☐ Sink free of dirty dishes to avoid pests

☐ Properly ventilated stove

☐ Garbage cans lined with recycled, fragrance-free bags

THE ISSUES

There's almost no issue in a kitchen that doesn't also pop up in other rooms of the house: ventilation, water safety and filtration, concerns about the manufacture and chemical contents of plastics, conventional cleaning product overload, and the need for integrated pest management. Still, in a kitchen, these issues weigh heavily because much of what's questionable is being ingested—a very direct route into the body. Additionally, issues of energy efficiency are more of a consideration in an appliance-filled room—specifically the energy used to heat and chill our food and wash our dishes. In a kitchen, we must also consider the reuse and recycling of packaging and the disposal of food scraps.

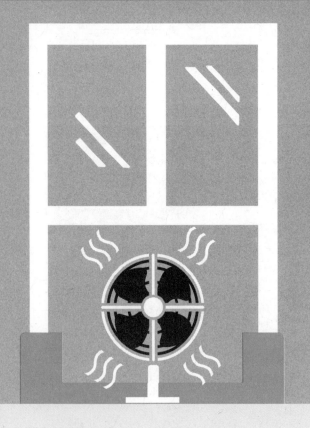

Ventilation

IMPROVING AIRFLOW

A kitchen often communicates with another area of the house by being entirely open to a dining or living area, or constructed with a half wall or a pass-through to these spaces. All of these scenarios make it easier for chemicals and various vapors in the kitchen to disperse throughout the home, including smoke with known carcinogenic properties, possible carbon monoxide emissions from a gas stove, VOCs (volatile organic compounds) from conventional cleaning products, gases from composite wood cabinets and other construction materials, pollution from self-cleaning ovens, and aerosols from spray cans of cooking oil or cleaning products. (Aerosols with propellants, it bears mentioning, pollute the air and waste terrible amounts of resources, especially as the cans are typically discarded. These products are best avoided.)

There are several ways to improve airflow in a kitchen:

* Use a stove vent. Ideally your range is vented outside, since hood units don't do much more than recirculate air.

* Open windows to create an air exchange. If you happen to burn something like plastic— a pot handle on the stove or a food storage lid that slips down and melts in a dishwasher—remove the ruined item from the kitchen so it isn't sitting there, releasing its contents into the air. Take it outside if you can. Then use fans to get the bad air out of the room.

* Don't use air fresheners; they are like adding insult to injury. Covering up odors with potentially toxic synthetic scents won't get rid of any underlying bad stench. It just pollutes the air further.

CLEAN HOOD FILTERS

Clean hood filters according to manufacturer instructions. Most can be washed with plain old soap and water. Getting the grease off filters means dust won't stick to them.

Renovations

Kitchens, along with bathrooms, are among the most renovated rooms in any home. Because renovations require so much energy, add to indoor air pollution, and create a lot of land-fill items (like old cabinets and appliances), avoid them if you can. If you'd like your kitchen to look better, try to make a few cosmetic changes instead of ripping the whole thing apart. Repaint or replace cabinet doors rather than pulling them out of the wall entirely. If you're embarking on a gut renovation, try to reuse as much of what is currently in your kitchen as you can. And all new construction materials used should be as green as possible—this includes countertops, glues, paints, and finishes, as well as appliances. Be careful even with natural materials—some granite used for countertops, for example, can contain and emit high levels of radon.

RENOVATION RESOURCES

There are a number of stores devoted to selling eco-friendly construction materials, and more appear to pop up weekly. Unfortunately, greenwashing (making false or misleading eco claims) abounds, and it can be difficult for consumers to find what is truly green. To help, here are some solid resources:

Eco Haus: *ecohaus.com*
Green Depot: *greendepot.com*
Greenguard Environmental Institute: *greenguard.org*
Healthy Building Network: *healthybuilding.net*
The Pharos Project: *pharosproject.net*
U.S. Green Building Council: *usgbc.org*

Cookware

There are many different surfaces and substances your food will come into contact with before you sit down to eat it: plastic wrap, knives, cutting boards, pans, spatulas, and plates. These may or may not leach some of their chemical components into your food. Some are better than others, and a few are downright unsafe, so it's prudent to always consider what exactly you're cooking in and on, what you're storing in, and what you're eating on. The best materials are durable, time tested, and multipurpose. Most of the metals used for pots, pans, coffeemakers, and even sink faucets are energy intensive and environmentally destructive to mine and manufacture. That's why it's important for these items, once created, to last a lifetime or to be recyclable when they're past their useful lives.

POTS, PANS, AND BAKING SHEETS

There are many materials for cooking or baking. The safest are cast iron, enamel-coated cast iron, stainless steel, and glass.

* **Cast iron** has been used for thousands of years. It is known to be safe, is extremely durable (families hand pots and pans down from generation to generation), and quite inexpensive. It can impart iron, a beneficial nutrient, into food as it cooks, and it can transfer from stovetop to oven. It is also energy efficient, retaining heat so well that cooking temperatures can be lowered. Cast-iron items require specific care: their surfaces need to be reseasoned from time to time (this involves baking the item for an hour

coated with fat, like vegetable oil, according to manufacturer's instructions), and they should only be cleaned with hot water and a stiff brush. One caveat: cooking acidic foods in cast iron that hasn't been properly cured might produce a metallic flavor.

* **Enamel-coated cast iron** is cast iron covered with a fused hard coating of glass particles. Glass is inert—as safe a cooking surface as any. Enamel-coated cast iron is multipurpose: there's almost nothing that can't be cooked in it. It will last a lifetime if treated well, helping to offset its cost, which is substantially more than uncoated cast iron.

* **Stainless steel** is lighter than cast iron—enamel coated or not—which makes it easier to work with. Stainless steel is a corrosion-resistant steel alloy. High-quality food- and medical-grade versions (designated in stores as 18/8 or 18/10) are the least likely to leach their components into cooking food. The various metals that go into one stainless-steel item (mainly iron, chromium, and nickel) give it a pretty hefty carbon footprint, but it is long lasting and can be recycled. Some pans have cores made of other metals, but completely stainless is best. While it's fine to cook tomato sauce in stainless steel, don't store it in there; the acids can cause the stainless steel to leach.

* **Glass** is nonreactive, mainly made from sand, and a very safe material for cooking and storing food. It's also inexpensive, reusable, and recyclable. Ovenproof glass dishes work well

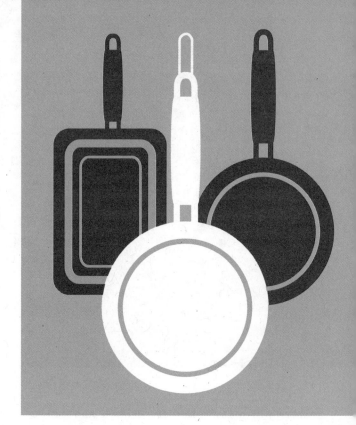

for baking cakes, cookies, pies, and breads, or even roasting vegetables. Keep in mind that most glass cannot work on a stovetop.

* **Aluminum** has been shunned over the years because of a supposed—and scientifically unsubstantiated—link to Alzheimer's disease. It's a fairly inexpensive but not hugely durable material. There are better options.

* **Copper** conducts heat well and is long lasting, but it's very expensive. It should be lined with stainless steel, as too much copper in our diets isn't healthy.

* **Ceramic** can be used for all kinds of baking and roasting projects, provided that it is lead-free. Always check this when

purchasing new, and don't use a painted ceramic dish you already own unless you know for sure it doesn't contain lead. For this reason, it's not a cooking material you should buy secondhand.

* **New "green" pots and pans** made using various materials and technologies are being marketed as replacements for toxic nonstick cookware (see below). Some are ceramic-based, which is preferable to those created with a recent technology. If you'd like to buy one, read the fine print to find out what's green about it, and check customer reviews online for honest assessments of how it fares in the kitchen. Anything new can have kinks.

* **Nonstick** cookware should be avoided. The chemical used in the manufacture of the polymer that makes nonstick pans so slick—perfluorooctanoic acid, or PFOA—is being phased out; the perfluorochemical has been linked to cancer (the EPA calls it "likely to be carcinogenic to humans"), and it is so widespread that it has been found in the blood of 98 percent of Americans. To make matters worse, it might be the most persistent man-made chemical ever created: it doesn't biodegrade at all, which means it's just accumulating in increasing amounts in the environment and in humans as it is manufactured or when it breaks down during use. In 2005, DuPont, one of the largest manufacturers of PFOA, settled with the EPA for $16.5 million for allegedly withholding information about the chemical's health risks. The EPA has also asked DuPont and seven other chemical companies to eliminate PFOA and similar chemicals from their products and plant emissions by 2015. Brand names that contain PFOA include Teflon and Silverstone. The jury is out on the safety of the chemicals being used to replace PFOA in various nonstick applications, including cookware and stain proofers for fabric. In the interim, consumers can say no to PFOA by refusing to buy nonstick items.

If you already have nonstick cookware at home, there are risks to be aware of. Scratched pans are unsafe to use and must be thrown away (they cannot be recycled). And nonstick cookware must never be heated on high or placed in the broiler: at elevated temperatures (500°F) it may release fumes that can sicken humans and even kill birds. If you still want to use an unscratched nonstick pan, treat it very carefully and according to manufacturer instructions so it won't become scratched.

Food Storage

Plastics are everywhere in the kitchen. And it seems that there are news reports daily on the hazards of hormone-disrupting chemicals found in plastics, which get into our food, beverages, and even baby formula (see page 42). Although there are plastics on the market that are generally considered safe to use with food, there is a growing body of evidence showing that plastics need to be treated gently, washed by hand, and never, ever placed in a microwave, where their chemicals leach into what's being heated, especially things with a high fat content, like meat and cheese. Plastics are ubiquitous because they're supposed to be easy, but none of that sounds easy. Plastics are also derived from a nonrenewable resource (petroleum), and not all kinds are recyclable. Even the ones that are recyclable often wind up overcrowding landfills or floating around in our waterways. Both the Atlantic and the Pacific oceans now have great garbage patches. Aquatic life is currently ingesting broken-down bits of these plastics, some of which contain those hormone-disrupting chemicals. Humans are then eating fish that have eaten these plastics. It's an ugly cycle.

It might be difficult (but not impossible) to avoid plastic packaging at the supermarket. When it comes to storing your leftovers at home, why not bypass plastics altogether—baggies, wrap, or containers—and use reliable, renewable, and reusable containers made of glass, stainless steel, and lead-free ceramic instead. This way you won't have to worry about what's migrating into your food or hope the plastic currently considered safe doesn't become tomorrow's must-avoid. Glass storage containers are widely available, or you can use what you already have in your kitchen: old jelly, peanut butter, or pickle jars. Glass can also go in the freezer—just make sure to leave enough room for liquid to expand. Recycle your old plastic containers if you can, or use them to store nonfood items (screws, coins, pencils). If they're made from a safe plastic (see the list on page 42), they can also be reused as bath toys. If you'd like a replacement for plastic wrap, try a reusable wrap, or opt for wax paper coated in non-genetically-modified (GM) soy wax instead of petroleum-derived wax.

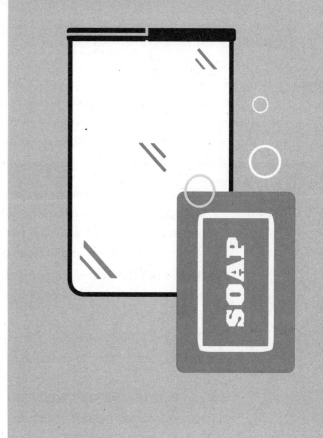

PLASTICS SAFETY

Of course, there are certain circumstances under which no plastic is safe to use. Heat, harsh detergents, and old age all promote the degradation of plastics and the leaching of compounds they contain. Here are some rules for using plastics safely in the kitchen:

* Never microwave food in plastic of any kind, including plastic wraps and so-called microwave-safe containers. Transfer microwaveable foods to a safe glass or ceramic alternative before heating. The term "microwave-safe" only means the plastic in question won't become visibly damaged when heated, not that it won't leach.

* Don't serve or store hot foods, acidic foods, or foods with a high fat or oil content in plastic containers of any kind, as these types of edibles are more likely to encourage leaching. Use glass, metal, or lead-free ceramics instead. A simple storage system can be created with any bowl and a similarly sized plate used as a lid.

* Avoid the temptation to save and reuse commercial food packaging and drink bottles, including plastic water bottles, which are not designed for repeated uses and become more prone to leaching with repeated cleanings.

The Leachin' Teach-in: A Guide to Safe Plastics

In recent years, plastic's image as a symbol of technological progress has been tarnished by reports suggesting that it may be less than safe, especially in the kitchen. At issue are the chemicals in plastics and whether or not these building blocks leach into our food. The answer to that question starts with understanding the different kinds of plastic available today. Here's a list by recycling code number:

1. **PET or PETE (polyethylene terephthalate)** is a common plastic used to package a variety of foods and drinks. PET has long been considered a safe, nonleaching plastic, even though some studies have found that it can release the toxic metallic mineral antimony over time, especially when subjected to heat.

2. **HDPE (high-density polyethylene)** is another common plastic used for milk and water jugs, dairy product tubs, and plastic bags. HDPE is not known to leach toxins.

3. **PVC (polyvinyl chloride)** is found in plastic wrap, especially commercial varieties used to package deli meats and similar items. These plastics use hazardous compounds called phthalates to maintain their pliability. Phthalates have been found to easily leach out of PVC products. PVC can also release a material called di-(2-ethylhexyl) adipate (DEHA) when in contact with fatty foods. The use of #3 plastics is not recommended.

4. **LDPE (low-density polyethylene)** is used for bread and frozen-food bags, squeezable bottles, other types of packaging, and reusable containers. It is not known to leach toxins.

5. **PP (polypropylene)** is found in bottles, food tubs, and reusable containers. It is not known to leach toxins.

6. **PS (polystyrene)** is often found in foam food containers. It can leach a number of chemicals into foods and is not recommended in the kitchen.

7. **OTHER** is a catchall category that includes everything else. One common #7 plastic is polycarbonate, a shatter-resistant material used in things like baby bottles and reusable water bottles. Polycarbonates readily leach a toxic compound called bisphenol-A (BPA) into food and drink. But new corn-based polylactic acid (PLA) plastics, which are generally recognized as safe, are also labeled #7. Be sure to look for bottles that say they are BPA-free.

To sum up: types 2, 4, and 5 are generally safe to use. Types 3 and 6 should be avoided. And type 7 is safe if marked "BPA-free."

* When reusable plastic containers made from #4 and #5 plastic become heavily worn or scratched, retire and recycle them.

* Always wash plastic containers by hand with warm water and mild dish liquid. Keep them out of the dishwasher.

* Avoid putting cling wraps in direct contact with food. Instead, use unbleached wax paper or a glass container for food storage.

* Plastic sandwich and food-storage bags are typically made from polyethylene, which is considered nontoxic. However, there is little to no data available that verifies the safety of washing and reusing such bags. Since this practice could potentially make them prone to leaching, it's difficult to recommend it. Instead, use wax paper bags or reusable solutions like the Snack-Taxi, the Wrap-n-Mat, or the alternatives at reuseit.com.

* Practice caution and use only glass bottles for infant feedings.

* When it comes to buying cling wrap and reusable food containers, purchase only those that tell you exactly what type of plastic they're made of and whether they are PVC-free.

Beware of BPA

The hormone-disrupting chemical bisphenol-A can be found in other places besides plastic #7. It's also in can linings. So avoid canned food to reduce your exposure to BPA. There are plenty of alternatives: dried beans, frozen corn and peas, and glass jars of tomatoes and olives. Shop for organic versions to avoid pesticide-heavy and genetically modified crops. There are a few companies, including Eden Organic and VitalChoice, that claim to use BPA-free cans. Look for these.

Question Alternative Plastics

Corn- and sugar-based plastics sound like a great idea. But they're largely made from genetically modified plants (primarily corn) and are very energy intensive to produce due to the large amount of fertilizer used. Additionally, most municipalities don't recycle them yet. Some of the biggest beverage companies are now experimenting with making the switch to using PET bottles made with some plant-derived material, which are still fully recyclable. Coca-Cola is using a version called PlantBottle, which contains up to 30 percent sugarcane juice or molasses. These bottles are slowly being rolled out in places like Denmark and Canada, as well as in the United States.

Setting the Table

UTENSILS

Carefully consider all the other objects in your kitchen. Knives, spoons, spatulas, tongs, cookie cutters, rolling pins, and garlic presses all come in plastic-free versions. Avoid gadgets you don't need, even if they tempt you. These will likely become dust-attracting clutter and will eventually be garbage. Instead, spend money on durable basics that will last a lifetime. And take care of the kitchen gear you have to lengthen its useful life. Sharpen your knives; don't put them in the dishwasher; and store them in a drawer or on a magnetic strip instead of in an impossible-to-clean knife block.

CUTTING BOARDS

Choose wood cutting boards over plastic ones, and have one board designated specifically for meat to avoid cross-contamination. These should be hard wood, never particleboard, and preferably local or Forest Stewardship Council–certified. (FSC is an independent nonprofit dedicated to responsible forest management. For more on its criteria and what its certification entails, check out fsc.org.) Wood has natural antibacterial properties, and unlike with plastic, small cuts in its surface often close up, leaving nowhere for bacteria to live. Look for wood that is bare; you don't want sealants coming off on the food you're chopping. Care for your wood cutting boards well: wash them by hand (never soak them or put them in the dishwasher) and dry thoroughly. Rubbing coarse salt into a wood board can smooth out some of the cracks made by knives and draw out impurities. If a board starts to look too dry, treat it with food-grade tung or linseed oil. Most oil sold for this purpose is petroleum-derived mineral, so be sure to read the ingredient list.

PLATES

Paper or other disposable plates have no place at a conscious table. The safest plates are made from glass. Ceramic can be harmless, but if you have older china or are considering buying antique china, test it with a home swab kit to make sure it's lead-free prior to using it to serve food.

GLASSES

Drink out of glass. Glasses can safely be purchased secondhand, and some manufacturers are now making recycled glassware. Reuse glass jelly jars instead of relying on plastic for kids or when drinking in the yard. Avoid leaded crystal; it might be pretty, but the lead in it is very easily disturbed and released.

FLATWARE

If you have silver, use it—don't save it for special dinners. It's a good, safe option. Stainless steel silverware is also a fine choice.

KIDS' WARE

Parents tend to trot out plastic cups and plates for kids so their own glass and china won't be broken, but plastic isn't a good choice, especially for growing bodies. Stainless steel, enamel-coated metal, and even shatterproof glass are preferable. Antique silver baby spoons or cocktail-sized stainless steel utensils—easily found at kitchen-supply stores—are better than plastic for small mouths.

LINENS

Napkins, place mats, and tablecloths should be made of natural, reusable materials: cotton, linen, hemp. Avoid using paper. Tablecloths that are plastic, backed with plastic, or treated with a stainproofing chemical should also be avoided. If buying new, look for organic cotton versions. Even better, buy secondhand.

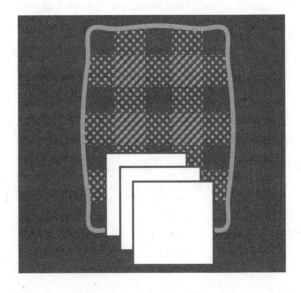

Tarnish Be Gone

One whiff of traditional silver polish and you know it cannot be safe. Here are two safer and highly effective ways to shine silver:

1. Scrub with natural toothpaste.

2. Place what you want shined in an old aluminum pan, if you have one, or in a glass or stainless steel bowl lined with aluminum foil. Fill the pan with warm water and add 2 tablespoons of table salt. Allow your silver to soak for two to three minutes. An electrochemical reaction will occur, pulling the tarnish off the silver, fume-free.

Appliances

REPAIR BEFORE REPLACING

There are many ways to save energy in a kitchen, even without buying new, energy-efficient appliances. Get a reasonable lifetime of use out of what you already own. There is a lot of energy and material invested in making any appliance. So for starters, always try to repair something rather than replace it. That said, if you're buying new, choose wisely, relying on Energy Star (energystar.gov), the voluntary joint government program of the EPA and the U.S. Department of Energy that rates energy efficiency, as well as on Consumer Reports (consumerreports.org). Whether you're putting an old appliance out on the curb, or the installers of its replacement are carting it away, ask to make sure that your old appliances will truly be recycled. Not all are.

REFRIGERATORS

Because fridges are on 24/7, they use the most energy in any kitchen. Replacing something more than ten years old can drastically reduce energy use—some new models use up to 40 percent less energy. That said, if everyone suddenly put decade-old fridges on the street in front of their home, we'd certainly have (even more of) a landfill situation. If you're buying a new fridge, ask to ensure that your old one is really being recycled—that the foam, refrigerants, and oils, as well as scrap metal, will be recovered. The plastic can also be recycled but isn't often.

Energy Boost

* Clean the condenser coils (usually located at the back of the unit) regularly—just unplug, then wash with warm, soapy water or vacuum with an attachment.

* Help it work less. If it's next to the oven or a very sunny window and you have the room, relocate it. Don't overstuff your fridge, and never put hot food in it.

* Reset the thermostat a few degrees warmer. Fridges between 35°F and 38°F; freezers between 0°F and 5°F.

* Check the door seal. If there is cold air coming out, or if you place a piece of paper in the door, shut it, and the paper doesn't stay put, head to the hardware store for a new seal.

* If your model has an energy-saver mode, use it. Do keep the freezer full; it's more energy efficient this way. If you don't have enough food in there, freeze water in empty milk jugs.

* Turn off any energy-consuming extras you might not be using (ice maker, automatic defrost).

* Place a box of zeolite, a type of clay, in the fridge to absorb moisture. This is a trick used by the food-service industry. The less moisture in your fridge, the less work it has to do to cool the air inside.

STOVES

Currently, the Energy Star program doesn't rate stoves, so consumers must rely on the operating-cost tags when shopping. The three main stove choices are induction, gas, and electric. Induction uses electromagnetic energy, requiring less traditional energy than the other two choices. It also releases less air pollution into the home when operating. Unfortunately, induction is expensive, and not all cookware works on it. By comparison, gas is a nonrenewable resource, though quite energy efficient. If buying new, don't buy a stove with a pilot light, which can add to air pollution. Chefs prefer gas to electric, but there are indoor air-quality benefits to electric over gas, since you're not combusting anything. Of course, it takes three to four times more total energy to deliver electric energy than to obtain it by combustion at home. This means more pollution outside your house from the electric power plant. Keep in mind that solid electric tops use more energy than the coil variety. Match your pot size to the coil size for the most efficient cooking.

Energy Boost

* Perform a maintenance check to make sure all the parts of your stove are in working order. Unclog flame-burner holes and fix anything else that's broken.

* Place reusable reflector drip pans under burners to save energy and keep them clean. Instead of being absorbed by the stove, the heat will be reflected back to the bottom of the pot.

OVENS

Self-cleaning ovens and convection ovens have more insulation than conventional ones, so they tend to be most efficient.

Energy Boost

* Calibrate your oven so it's true to temperature (see your owner's manual for instructions), and check the oven door's seal the same way you check your fridge's seal (see page 49). It should be tight, not loose.

* Don't bother preheating an oven, and keep it shut when in use. Opening the door to check on what's cooking wastes heat.

* Only use the oven for cooking large amounts of food. Don't use something so big to toast a single slice of bread.

* Use a sheet pan to catch drips so you won't have to clean the oven often. Don't self-clean often; it uses extremely high temperatures (a lot of energy) and produces fumes (as it burns off drips and splatters from the bottom and walls of the oven). Using the self-cleaning feature after cooking capitalizes on the residual heat.

HOODS

Hoods do come with Energy Star ratings, so look for these.

WHERE'S YOUR ELECTRICITY FROM?

If your electric company offers customers greener power sources, like wind, choose them. They can cost more money than traditional power, but the environmental savings far outweigh the extra cash. Work to make your home more energy efficient across the board to make up the difference.

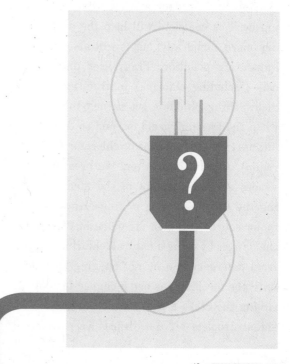

DISHWASHERS

Running a dishwasher filled with scraped—not rinsed—dishes using eco-friendly detergent free of chlorine and phosphates is preferable to washing by hand, especially if the machine has a good Energy Star rating and you don't use the energy-draining heated dry option. Only run the dishwasher when it is totally full (although be sure you're not blocking the water or aeration methods with any dishes, or they won't get clean). Face everything inward. Enzymes in detergent are there to eat off scum. If you have over-rinsed your dishes, they will have nothing to work on and will therefore dull the surfaces. Get to know your dishwasher: Does it have a heater or a fan? Does it have a grinder? Operate accordingly. Don't put everything under the sun in a dishwasher. Opening the door a crack after the washing cycle is complete will help the dishes air-dry more completely, but it will also increase indoor air pollution. Fragrances and chemicals (including chlorine) in traditional auto-dishwashing products get turned into vapors when the machine heats up, and so do the pollutants (possibly chlorine or chloroform, maybe radon) in municipal water. We breathe these vapors as they vent out of the machine during the washing cycle, making dishwashers a major source of indoor air pollution. Minimize the danger by using a natural (chlorine bleach–free) detergent and by not opening that door until the machine has had a chance to cool off. Giving the racks a shake will help get the residual droplets off the dishes. Keep in mind that your municipal water supply will likely provide your machine with chlorine anyway. A whole house water filter will reduce some of the worst vapors, as will keeping your kitchen well-ventilated. If your dishes aren't getting as clean as you'd like them, try using less detergent if you have soft water and adding a natural rinse aid if you have hard water. This keeps minerals in the water from redepositing on your dishes. You can buy a natural version, or simply use white vinegar. If you're in the market for a new dishwasher, consider stainless steel interiors, which retain heat and reduce noise. They also don't off-gas (i.e., release fumes from the plastic) when heated to very high temperatures.

GOOD NEWS ABOUT PHOSPHATES

Companies have agreed to voluntarily remove phosphates from auto-dishwashing detergents effective July 1, 2010, because they cause algae to grow in lakes and streams, causing some of them to fill in, disturbing aquatic life. Keep in mind you may still find products with phosphates on the shelf for up to a year or so after this date.

 Kitchen Systems

Organic Potatoes Cooked the Wrong Way

The energy it takes to cook an item can add to its overall carbon footprint. If you've gone out of your way to walk to the farmers' market, shop around for the least-pesticide-sprayed items there, and walk all the way back home, cook accordingly so you won't undo all of your good work. Boiling anything with the top off—but especially something that takes a long time to cook, like potatoes—is a waste of energy. Think about your cooking method before you rush to get dinner on the table for a hungry brood, or just yourself. Put the top on! You'll save time, too. To save even more energy and time, use a pressure cooker.

Small Appliances

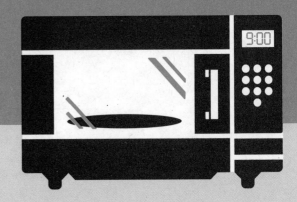

MICROWAVES

If energy were your only concern in a kitchen, you'd microwave most meals, as it uses very little. However, there are other concerns in any kitchen, like flavor, and microwaved meals, for the most part, don't taste great. So most of us rely on microwaves solely to reheat and defrost, or to reduce cooking time. There has been much speculation about the safety of microwaves; they have been questioned and re-questioned. If a microwave is properly maintained and the door and seal aren't damaged in any way, the scientific community considers them safe. If you're not comfortable standing very close to something emitting microwaves, take a few steps back. Radiation decreases with distance. Or don't use a microwave. They're hardly necessary. As for what microwaves do to nutrient levels, the science varies. But unless you're exclusively eating microwaved meals, this shouldn't be an issue. Vary your cooking methods and you'll get all of your nutrients in. Never put plastic in your microwave. The additives in any kind of plastic will leach into your food. The term "microwave-safe" isn't third-party certified. What a manufacturer considers microwave-safe may not be what you would consider safe. Use glass instead.

PRESSURE COOKERS

Another way to drastically reduce cooking time in an unequivocally safe and flavorful fashion is to use a stainless steel pressure cooker. It makes fast work of long-cooking rice and enormous root vegetables, and it can turn out a beef stew in 30 minutes. You'll save hours of stove time. Double boilers and steamers can also help save time and energy.

THE OTHER APPLIANCES

As for the rest of the small appliances in the kitchen:

* Use what you already have. If something breaks, try to repair it. If it cannot be fixed, try to recycle it.

* When shopping for something new, consider all the materials. Nonstick coatings lurk in the oddest places: the interiors of toaster ovens, slow cookers, panini presses. As it gets quite hot in all of these, there's potential for PFOA to be released. Avoid!

* For blenders and mixers, glass or stainless steel bowls and pitchers are preferable to plastic.

* See what you can get secondhand. Old toasters and cast-iron waffle irons are true finds.

* Always consider if there is a nonelectric version of the machine you want. Manual press coffeemakers, hand-crank grinders, and citrus reamers use no energy at all, other than elbow grease (a highly renewable resource).

UNPLUG. LITERALLY.

Appliances use energy even when turned off. Pull plugs out of the wall to stop energy draw. Alternatively, plug them all into a power strip and turn the strip off when not in use, as well as overnight.

Floors and Lighting

KITCHEN FLOORS

Bare floors with cotton rag rugs that can be machine-laundered are your best bet in any kitchen, especially one that experiences high traffic.

Some kitchens may have asbestos vinyl tiles. If you suspect yours does, read about how to identify them online and compare images to your own floors. These were particularly popular from the 1920s to the 1960s. If asbestos tiles are cracked, they need to be dealt with. Removing them can release more asbestos into the air and should only be done by a trained professional. If they're intact and in good condition, they're not considered hazardous, but they need to be treated carefully. For more on asbestos in the home, check out the EPA's website: epa.gov.

Wall-to-wall carpeting traps moisture and dust, so if you have it, consider pulling it out and replacing it with real wood, ceramic, cork, or natural linoleum instead. If you're putting in a new wood floor, in the kitchen or anywhere else, pay attention to what you're finishing it with. There are eco-friendly, low-VOC products on the market (see page 345). Vinyl floors should never be used; they release phthalates into the air and are environmentally destructive during manufacture and disposal by incineration.

LIGHTING

Many old kitchens have fluorescent lighting. If this lighting was made and installed before the EPA banned toxic polychlorinated biphenyls (PCBs) in 1979, they may still be in your fixtures. If the ballasts burn, they can release PCBs into the air. Remove fluorescent lighting fixtures if you think they might be from before 1979. Call your municipality's hazardous waste center for advice on how to dispose of the fixtures. Replace with a new non-PCB ballast (you can do this yourself if you're handy, and they're only about $10) or buy a whole new energy-saving fluorescent or LED fixture.

Cleaning Your Kitchen

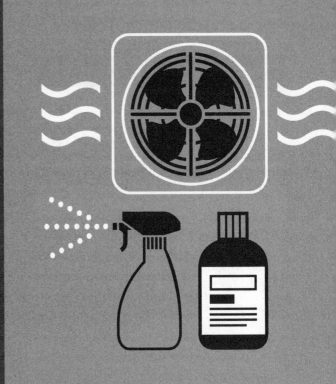

DISINFECTING

Although fear of food-borne bacteria like salmonella and E. coli makes us all keen to disinfect kitchens, soap and water remove a large percentage of the microorganisms that exist. If there's a flu or other illness in the household, if you know the cat has been walking on the counter after a visit to the litter box, or if you just cannot shake the idea that the space needs to be disinfected, a cleaner containing antimicrobial hydrogen peroxide will do the trick, as will homemade concoctions containing lemon, vinegar, or some essential oils. For a stronger natural cleaner that has been tested and proven to kill 99.99 percent of all types of germs, try a spray or wipe containing thymol,

an EPA-registered botanical disinfectant. It's made from thyme.

The most important surface to clean in any kitchen is actually your own two hands. Wash them before handling food, after handling food, after cleaning cookware and dishes, and always before eating. Bacteria and other microorganisms exist throughout our environment—in our homes and out in the world. It's all part of a bigger cycle of life that can't be, and shouldn't be, disrupted by disinfecting. There are going to be microorganisms in your kitchen and throughout the home. Disinfect them and they won't stay disinfected for long. It's when you ingest these germs, fecal matter, or even salmonella that microorganisms can cause intestinal distress. Washing your hands with warm water and soap will keep them from being transferred from your kitchen to your food and into your system.

ANTI "ANTIBACTERIAL"

All hand soap is not created equal. Avoid soaps that contain unnecessary and dangerous antibacterial chemicals, including triclosan, which, according to the American Medical Association, may encourage bacterial resistance to antibiotics. Unlike cleaning products, hand soaps do have ingredient lists on the bottles for consumers to read. Read them.

Triclosan is known to produce toxic chlorinated substances that aren't biodegradable. In fact, studies, including one by a U.S. FDA advisory committee, have found that household use of antibacterial hand soaps provides no benefits over plain soap and water. None. The purer the hand soap—no synthetic ingredients, no antibacterial—and the fewer ingredients, the better; the questionable always lurks in the additives.

Hand Gels

Washing your hands is always preferable to sanitizing them all of the time with a gel. The alcohol in most hand gels used to be petroleum derived. These days it is mainly made from genetically modified corn. If you'd like a bottle of something to stash in your purse for when a sink and a bar of soap aren't an option—like after a subway ride or to clean a child's hands in the playground before lunch—read ingredients. Make sure the product doesn't contain an antibacterial like triclosan or a synthetic fragrance. CleanWell makes a thyme-based hand spray.

What You Need to Clean Your Kitchen

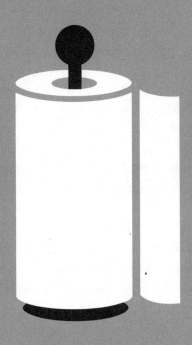

What's best for your hands is good for everything else in the kitchen, too. There's pretty much nothing in the kitchen that cannot be cleaned with a natural liquid dish soap and water. Natural soaps are made from the oils of vegetables or plants and are often referred to as castile soaps. They are nontoxic, biodegradable, antibacterial-free, and not synthetically fragranced. As with any product, read the label. Even natural castile soap could have synthetic additives. Choose ones that don't.

You might also want:

1. An all-purpose kitchen cleaner containing hydrogen peroxide

2. A thyme-based disinfectant

3. Vinegar, lemon, and baking soda to use in various DIY products

4. Natural, chlorine-free dishwashing powder or gel

5. Tools (dishrags, a sponge, a stiff brush, a broom, and a mop)

TOOLS

Hands are the best tools for cleaning a kitchen. Here are a few other items that can help:

* **Kitchen towels or rags:** Challenge yourself to limit or give up paper towels. Keep ample clean cloth towels and rags in a drawer and use them for everything. Designate one spot—the fridge handle, for example—for hand towels so you won't attempt to dry hands with something that just cleaned a spill. Launder your cloths frequently. Cotton is preferable to microfiber, which is made of plastic.

* **Sponges:** Because sponges rarely dry out, they can be a breeding ground for bacteria. You can avoid sponges altogether and only use kitchen towels. Or you can carefully wring sponges out between uses and allow them to dry completely to minimize the likelihood of germs growing. A smelly sponge suggests colonization. If that sponge contacts food surfaces, you could be transferring germs to food. Sponges can be sterilized in a pot of boiling water, the microwave, the washing machine, or even the dishwasher—a few minutes or a cycle is all it takes. When they start to fall apart, downgrade their status from surface sponges to floor sponges. When shopping for new sponges, read the small print on any package. Some contain antibacterials (i.e., pesticides), mainly to resist odors—don't buy these if you have a choice. If the directions tell you not to use with bleach, this is likely because it would react with the antibacterial agent they contain. If available, undyed sponges are preferable to brightly colored ones.

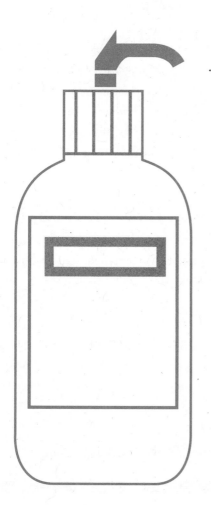

DO YOU KNOW WHERE YOUR CLEANING PRODUCTS ARE?

If you have young kids—or even wily pets—put a lock on the cabinet under the kitchen sink. Or move the products to a less accessible place. If you take something out to clean, always put it back where you found it. Be especially vigilant if you own conventional cleaning products. But even natural products weren't designed to be eaten by children or the family dog.

Basic Cleaning Timeline

DAILY

Dishes

* Try not to leave dirty dishes hanging around in the sink. This attracts pests, plus it takes more energy to remove caked-on food than it does to wash dishes shortly after use.

* Run the dishwasher only when full and use a natural detergent. Powdered products tend to work better than gels, and they don't involve the high environmental costs of shipping water. Natural dishwasher tablets are best since they are highly concentrated and ensure you don't overuse.

* Don't mix metals in the dishwasher. Sterling silver, aluminum, and stainless steel cleaned all at the same time can have a battery-like effect and will tarnish the sterling. You can get it off, but it will take considerable elbow grease.

* Items that can't go in the dishwasher—wood, good knives, pots, pans, gold- or platinum-rimmed china, and most plastics—should be hand washed with warm, soapy water and dried well.

* If you have a hard-to-remove mess, make sure you're using the right material for the job. Steel wool is too harsh for most materials—a stiff brush or a nylon scrubber is preferable. If you've burned food on a pot and can't get it off, try boiling water with a spoonful or two of baking soda. If it doesn't come off right away, leave it to soak overnight and then scrape it off in the morning. Don't soak wood or cast iron.

Surfaces

* Wipe surfaces with soapy water or a natural kitchen spray before and after food preparation. Cutting food on boards rather than directly on countertops will save some cleanup time.
  Be sure to wipe down spots where hands linger (cabinet, fridge, teapot handles, oven door, microwave oven handle, coffee machine on/off switch, stove and sink knobs). Hands tend to be germier than anything else in the kitchen.

Stove Top

* Wipe your stove top once it's cool enough to do so. By not allowing spills and splashes to accumulate, you'll be less likely to reach for a harsh conventional cleaner. While you're at it, pass your rag over the backsplash and walls surrounding the stove. Tomato sauce travels, and it's best to get it off your walls before it stains.

Floors

* Sweep up crumbs or spot-clean with soap and water if you've spilled something.

WEEKLY

Fridge

* Once every week or two, go beyond wiping the handle and face of the fridge. Pull everything out and—working quickly so that nothing has a chance to spoil—wipe down the interior surfaces with warm, soapy water.

* Take the vegetable bin out and wash it in warm, soapy water. This also gives you a chance to take stock of what vegetables or fruit need to be eaten quickly before they spoil, and to compost or toss anything that might have gone slimy. Plan meals accordingly.

* Sometimes in the summer, when the kitchen is hot but the fridge is cold, there may be black mold spots or bacterial growth from condensation trapped in the door seal. Wipe that clean.

* If you have odors in your fridge, an open box of baking soda can help. Better yet, eliminate the source.

Garbage Pails

* When you take out the garbage, check to be sure nothing has leaked into the pail. If it has, use a natural kitchen cleaner, or just soap and water on a rag, to wipe it out. Dry well before replacing the garbage bag.

Floors

* Depending on the size of your kitchen, you may choose to spot-clean your floor by just spraying and wiping every week or so. Or you may prefer to mop it. Either way, use warm, soapy water or a natural cleaner.

Stove

* Wipe carefully around the stove as well as the vent or hood filter. Oil from cooking settles on nearby surfaces and becomes grimy when dust clings to it. Soap, water, and elbow grease is all it takes. If it's really greasy, vinegar, lemon, or some dish liquid can cut through it.

More Tasks

MONTHLY

The Drain

* Never pour grease down the drain. Pour it into a nonrecyclable plastic or metal item, allow it to harden, and then put it in the garbage. And turn to "Adopt a Clog-Prevention Regimen" on page 206, for details on good drain maintenance.

Laundry

* Pot holders, rag rugs, and curtains could stand a wash from time to time.

Oven

* If the oven smells of food whenever you turn it on, get out a box of baking soda and sprinkle some on the bottom. Spray water to wet the baking soda. Wipe as you go, or let it sit overnight. In the morning, wipe out the baking soda and rinse. This is both effective and nontoxic. Conventional oven cleaners, on the other hand, contain highly toxic lye. Self-cleaning ovens don't require the use of a caustic cleaner. They use extremely high heat to essentially incinerate everything off the interior surfaces. This can emit an unpleasant odor and fumes—usually a mix of soot and some ammonia compounds from proteins. Baking soda paste is far preferable.

Cabinets

* Wet-dust where you store your glassware and plates, as well as where you keep your dried goods. If you're using a natural cleaner, spray it on the cloth rather than into the cabinet.

Other Interiors

* Wash the inside of toasters and microwaves with warm, soapy water when you start to see some buildup.

Kitchen Systems

Chlorine-Free Chicken Meets Chlorine Residue

One of the many hot-button topics when it comes to chicken—conventional vs. local/pastured vs. free range organic (local or not)—is how the birds are disinfected post-slaughter. Conventional chickens in the United States tend to be disinfected in chlorine baths, a procedure that has long been banned by the European Union. It's also banned by USDA organic rules. There are other ways of decontaminating poultry: ozone baths, eco-water baths, or air chilling. If you've sought out and spent good money on a chlorine-free chicken, be careful where you put it. Cutting it on a counter or board that has been cleaned with chlorine or any other disinfectants and retains its residue undermines your choice. Think it through. If you clean with conventional cleaners in a kitchen, you're applying them to your meals, adding toxic chemicals you were trying to avoid by buying organic or low-sprayed local food. Shift your mind-set to consider your kitchen in a holistic, systemic fashion. Don't compartmentalize the food from counter cleaners or even pots and pans. If you don't want your chicken to be contaminated with chlorine, don't contaminate your kitchen—or any room in your home—with it, either.

INTEGRATED PEST MANAGEMENT

If you don't want pesticides on your organic apple, then you certainly don't want them in your kitchen. And yet so many of us turn to conventional exterminators when it comes to roaches, mice, water bugs, ants, and other uninvited guests. A conscious kitchen should be protected by IPM (integrated pest management), a system that attempts to address pests before they arrive. Prevention is the key to avoiding indoor pesticide applications down the road. Start by sealing up all the holes in your walls with low-VOC caulk and steel wool. Keep your kitchen clean and devoid of crumbs. If an infestation arises, there are a number of nontoxic or less toxic pest-deterring methods to try at beyondpesticides.org. If you're battling something you cannot handle or contain, look for an exterminator who practices IPM. A good place to search for one is greenshieldcertified.org.

BAG THIS

Avoid garbage bags that have been treated with antimicrobial chemicals or deodorizing synthetic scent. Either reuse plastic shopping bags you might have picked up at the store or seek out fragrance-free ones that contain recycled plastic.

Materials Matter

While most things can safely be cleaned with soap and water, check with manufacturer instructions for the best solutions for your materials. What's good for stainless steel might not be great for a butcher block or bamboo floors. Granite and marble, for example, don't react well to acid. If you can't find a natural cleaner made specifically for the surface you want to clean, check out the DIY cleaners on page 26. If what you're looking for isn't there, check out the encyclopedic *Better Basics for the Home*, by Annie Berthold-Bond.

FOOD

The Conscious Ritual

While sitting at a table with family members or friends sharing food, perhaps you say some version of grace, be it religious or secular or spiritual, or maybe you do this only once a year, on Thanksgiving. Try bringing the sense of appreciation that the holiday embodies into your daily life. You can even do this mentally while prepping food. When pulling leeks, or a steak, or berries out of the fridge, take a minute to remind yourself of how these items made their way to you. Acknowledge the farmers, the animals, the land involved. Thank Mother Earth for the bounty she endlessly provides us. Take pleasure from the flavor, of course, but also the colors, the nutrients, the smells. Embrace the routines, sounds, and acts of cooking and eating. If you're eating with others, take joy in their reactions to what you've prepared. If alone, revel in how silence allows you to truly experience your meal.

The Conscious Components

Eating consciously means really thinking about and being aware of the origins and implications of what you eat. Our modern agriculture system is largely industrialized, and for the most part, factory-farmed food isn't conscious food. Local, organic, and sustainably grown produce in season, on the other hand, is. To find the good stuff, you have to learn which places are most likely to carry it, as well as the right questions to ask when shopping. This is extremely worthwhile, as what we eat can have a tremendous impact, both positive and negative, on our health and the planet. And choosing to eat items that were grown in a conscious—i.e., eco-friendly and sustainable—fashion can also have a large impact on our communal surroundings.

Here's a handy checklist to help you remember the pieces that make up a conscious diet ⟶

☐ Organic, local bulk grains

☐ Artisanal cheeses and butter

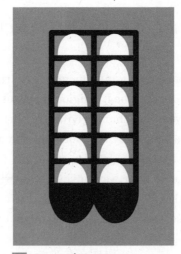

☐ Pastured eggs

☐ Wild, sustainably caught seafood

☐ Window box for growing herbs

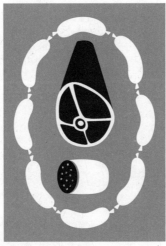

☐ Local grass-fed meat

☐ Local, lightly pasteurized, grass-fed milk in glass bottles

☐ Reusable cloth shopping bags instead of plastic or paper

☐ Glass bottles and glass or ceramic drinking cups instead of plastic

☐ Fair Trade coffee, tea, and sugar

THE ISSUES

Eating consciously means more than just buying organic. It involves buying and consuming food produced in a sustainable manner. Sustainability is a concept that looks at both social and environmental effects. Ask yourself the following questions:

* How do you want your food raised or grown: organic or otherwise?

* Where do you want it raised or grown?

* How do you want the people raising it or growing it to be treated?

For those of us just starting to move toward conscious food, filling a fridge and cabinets with the answers to those questions can feel overwhelming. Start with implementing simple changes that make sense to you. It doesn't have to be all or nothing.

What Kind of Food to Buy

ORGANIC VS. LOCAL

The organic versus local debate is a question of choice, and there is no wrong decision. While it may be true that certain foods produced in faraway places can have singular benefits over some locally produced foods (if you're British, for example, eating New Zealand lamb is said to generate fewer CO_2 emissions even including the transportation impact for a number of reasons), from a conscious and holistic point of view, local is better.

Ask yourself:

* Are you mainly concerned with buying food that is free of chemical pesticides? Then you're going to want to buy USDA-certified organic, preferably from domestic farms, which tend to be better regulated than foreign ones.

* Are you interested in keeping small local farms in business? And would you be okay with the farms following the tenets of Integrated Pest Management (see page 66) and spraying the smallest possible amount of the least harmful chemical if they're about to, say, lose an entire orchard to blight, making them ineligible for organic certification? Then you're going to want to shop mostly local.

Most conscious shoppers and eaters find it difficult to eat only organic or eat only local and therefore do a mix of the two, with some conventional items thrown in from time to time. If you can find organic *and* local, all the better.

UNDERSTANDING ORGANIC CERTIFICATION

There are a few other things to keep in mind when considering organic foods. First is what this term covers. The "USDA organic" seal means the food is grown according to government standards defined and regulated by the U.S. Department of Agriculture. In order to earn this certified organic stamp of approval, produce must be:

* third-party certified

* not genetically modified or irradiated

* grown without synthetic pesticides or fertilizers. This is important because not enough is known about the health effects of the small but consistent doses of pesticides we all eat

daily, or what happens when they build up inside our bodies over time. Some of the insecticides and herbicides used most widely in the United States are actually banned in the European Union because they're groundwater contaminants and known endocrine disruptors. Some have even been linked to increased incidences of cancers.

Poultry, eggs, meat, and dairy receive organic certification if they are:

* free of certain chemicals, antibiotics, and hormones.

* from farms where animals had a more reasonable lifestyle than those raised in conventional confinement operations. (Still, this doesn't necessarily mean the animals were wandering around outside, on pasture.)

As of press time, there is no such thing as USDA-certified organic seafood; there are some issues that make fish nearly impossible to regulate. For starters, wild seafood—just like water—cannot be certified. It's very hard to standardize and certify anything wild. There are farmers attempting to breed and farm-raise fish according to organic principles, but their claims, true or not, are currently unregulated by the government. The Marine Stewardship Council's certified sustainably managed seafood program is as close as you can get. MSC (msc.org) is a reputable third-party certifier that works with Whole Foods, among others.

SUSTAINABLE AND LOCAL

Terms like "sustainable" or "local" aren't certified, but they can be very meaningful if you know your farmers or shop at markets where you have the opportunity to ask questions. Sustainable means farming that doesn't harm the environment and does support farming communities. It's an approach that considers the whole system—from the health of the earth to the health of the laborers. Generally speaking, a local farm is one within about 150 miles (give or take) from where you live. Local farms tend to be smaller-scale farms, and smaller-scale farms tend to not use the worst chemical pesticides, fertilizers, hormones, and the like. Ask what your local farmer uses.

For more information on specific pesticides used on big crops and small vegetable patches both here in the United States and abroad, go to the Pesticide Action Network of North America website, panna.org. They also run an eater-friendly website, whatsonmyfood.org.

ORGANIC RESOURCES

Organic Consumers Association: *organicconsumers.org*

The USDA's National Organic Program: *ams.usda.gov/nop*

Food Miles and Carbon Footprints

Locavores—people who eat local food—say that food grown close to you has a lower carbon footprint than food grown far away. This simple and straightforward claim is oddly contentious. Dissenters like to point out that efficiencies of scale, climate, and shipping can give things grown far away—even continents away—a lower carbon footprint than those grown locally and driven to a farmers' market. But it's almost impossible to quantify the importance of having local farms. Or that we're ten times more likely to have a conversation at a farmers' market, where local items are sold, than at a supermarket, where nonlocal ones are. If your take on conscious eating involves being a member of a community, this dialogue might be an important dimension of choosing local.

One way to lower the carbon footprint of any food—local or nonlocal—is to eat less of the worst offenders like conventionally raised meat and crops that traditionally require the most spraying. Things like nitrogen fertilizer require natural gas to make and can turn into greenhouse gases when spread on fields. Some supermarket chains (Britain's Tesco, for example) and countries (such as Sweden) are starting to require carbon labeling to make it easier for consumers to find the most conscious options. The United States isn't quite there yet, but never say never. Another way to drastically lower the carbon footprint of your diet is to walk, bike, or take public transportation to and from the store or the market.

WHAT TO BUY WHEN YOU CAN'T FIND ORGANIC OR LOCAL

Sometimes buying local or organic isn't an option. Maybe what you want to eat doesn't grow near you, or it's not in season in your area, or maybe your neighborhood stores don't carry local products. Perhaps you find the cost of organic prohibitive. Whatever the reason, if you're going to buy conventional produce, keep in mind that some fruits and vegetables are more contaminated than others. The Environmental Working Group (ewg.org), a nonprofit consumer watchdog, has researched and ranked pesticide contamination for almost 50 of the most popular fruits and vegetables to help shoppers navigate this very issue. The full results are at foodnews.org and are updated yearly, so check back with the site. Here are the basics:

Dirty Dozen: Produce You Should Always Buy Organic:

* celery, peaches, strawberries, apples, blueberries (domestic), nectarines, bell peppers, spinach, cherries, kale, potatoes, grapes (imported)

Clean Fifteen: Produce That Is Lowest in Pesticide Residue:

* onions, avocado, sweet corn, pineapples, mango, sweet peas, asparagus, kiwi fruit, cabbage, eggplant, cantaloupe, watermelon, grapefuit, sweet potatoes, honeydew

The EWG says consumers can lower their pesticide exposure by a whopping 80 percent by avoiding the Dirty Dozen and eating the Clean Fifteen. Stick these lists in your wallet so you'll always have them with you when shopping.

RINSE, DON'T WASH

Washing produce with a store-bought product brings up two issues. First, what's in the bottle may be worse than what's on your apple. And two, washing gives a false sense of security. The pesticides are not only on the produce, they're *in* it. Rinsing and peeling are still a good idea, but it won't remove all residues, and peeling will also remove nutrients.

Food Systems

The Real Expense of Food

Many people complain about the price of organic food. An organic apple costs considerably more than its conventional counterpart at a supermarket. But here's what is expensive about conventional apples: the ecological toll of the chemical sprays used to grow them plus the health toll of those sprays both on the orchard workers and the people who ingest their residue. And if you knew that the farmer down the road—who maybe has known your family for generations—was struggling and needed to charge a bit more to stay afloat and to compete with the larger corporations that are able to charge less per pound, wouldn't you be willing to pay a little more? That relatively small price difference will provide us, our families, the farmers, and the earth with a huge bonus along with a sweet, healthful snack. Larger farms sell produce more cheaply by externalizing their costs onto society and the environment. They don't pay the cost of polluting the water with pesticides, or for the soil erosion they cause, or the impact of petroleum-based fertilizers—we do! The price difference can be made up by limiting packaged foods—they add up—shopping wisely, and buying a farm share (see page 78).

Bring Your Bags

Shopping with reusable bags is a great way to minimize the amount of plastic you use. Take it a step beyond the big canvas bags and bring some smaller reusable produce bags to the market with you. These mesh or (organic) cotton sacks are easily purchased online and mean you'll never reach for a plastic baggie to hold your lettuce, broccoli head, or even bulk items like nuts or grains again.

* If you have access to farmers' markets, frequent them—often.

* Buy a share in a local farm via a system called Community Supported Agriculture (CSA). This is a wonderful way of getting local, often organic, vegetables and sometimes fruit in growing season. And your investment in the farm means the farmer has an insurance policy of sorts. If the weather takes a turn for the worse, CSA farmers don't have to worry that they won't be able to make ends meet; their members share in lean as well as bountiful times. For people who would like to garden but are unable to, CSA farms provide a direct connection to one parcel of land and its microclimate. Find a list of local CSAs at localharvest.org/csa.

* If you're able to plant a garden, start digging now, even if it's just a window box of herbs. Make sure to plant in containers that are safe for food. Reusing random items—bathtubs, tires, unmarked plastic containers—to grow vegetables or herbs may seem like a good green idea, but these aren't prudent for edible plants as they can contain lead and other toxins. Don't forget to use organic soil and organic seeds or plants. Gardenerssupply.com is a great resource for everything you'll need.

* Some farm stands stock a mix of foods, but not all of it is necessarily local. If you see cherries at your farm stand months before the fruit is

growing regionally, ask where they're from and if they're sprayed.

* Specialty-food stores, natural-food markets, and some supermarkets sell conscious food. If a piece of fruit has a sticker on it, knowing how to read it can also help you determine its origin. Look for a Country of Origin Label (COOL) or a Price Look Up (PLU) code. Organic produce begins with the number 9 and has five digits. Conventional produce begins with the number 4 and has four digits. Natural-food markets and chains like Whole Foods tend to have more conscious food than supermarkets, but reading labels, ingredient lists, and signs is a good idea no matter where you're shopping. Just because a store is considered a haven of conscious food doesn't mean everything on its shelves is good to eat. Organic cookies are still cookies! They may not be good for you, and the palm oil in them might not be sustainably grown.

* If you get all of your food at a supermarket—and most Americans do—keep an eye out for USDA organic, preferably domestic, and any local items the market may stock. If you would like your store to stock more of both, speak up. Customer requests can influence supply. Recently even retailers like Wal-Mart have started to bring local produce into their stores in larger and larger quantities at competitive prices.

RESOURCES FOR FINDING CONSCIOUS FOOD

There are, thankfully, many websites dedicated to connecting shoppers with conscious foods. Try these to locate farmers' markets and Community Supported Agriculture farms near you:

Community Supported Agriculture Center: *csacenter.org*

Local Harvest: *localharvest.org*

Slow Food USA: *slowfoodusa.org*

Sustainable Table: *sustainabletable.org*

The USDA National Agricultural Library: *nal.usda.gov/afsic/csa*

The USDA's site for Farmers' Markets and Local Food Marketing: *ams.usda.gov/farmersmarkets*

Animals

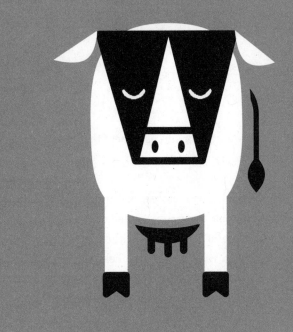

POULTRY, BEEF, PORK, LAMB, AND MORE

FACTORY-FARMED MEAT VS. CONSCIOUS MEAT

The omnivore's most conscious option is meat from pastured animals that ate what they're supposed to eat. Though you can read about this in any children's book, most adults don't remember that steer, cows, and sheep eat grass; pigs forage; and chickens peck at grubs and worms. Unfortunately, this isn't the modern way of raising animals, especially to feed masses of people. So animals tend to get crammed in pens, or caged instead of pastured, and are raised as quickly and inexpensively as possible. This is not only inhumane, it has drastic environmental repercussions.

Not all penned animals are equal. Pigs rotated from uncrowded outdoor pen to uncrowded outdoor pen may just be a farmer's way of keeping them from wandering off. That's perfectly conscious. But factory-farmed pigs kept indoors in confinement their entire lives—who have all of the fat bred out of them to produce the leanest meat and therefore would freeze if they were allowed outside, and whose tails are cut off to avoid being bitten by their fellow inmates— that's not conscious.

Most pastured animals today are fed supplementary grains. Depending on where in the country they're being raised, this may be unsprayed corn from the very farms they're roaming around on. That's conscious. So is 100 percent grass-fed. But industrially raised animals tend to be given feed containing some mix of genetically modified soy or corn, antibiotics, bird feces, pesticide residues, arsenic, and hormones (depending on the animal. Hormones aren't allowed to be administered to any animals in Europe, or to poultry or pork in the United States, but our government does permit them for ruminants, e.g., cows/steer and lamb). This grim mix is cheap for the producers, keeps disease down in overcrowded situations, and promotes growth. The quicker the animals grow, the sooner they can be slaughtered. It's a time-is-money thing. Clearly, it's not conscious. The antibiotics in the feed may prevent widespread illness on factory farms, but they also create drug-resistant strains that affect all of us. These are of particular concern if you work with meat; poultry factory workers are 32 times more likely to be infected with antibiotic-resistant E. coli than the rest of the population, according to a 2007 Johns Hopkins University study. Keep in mind that by eating animals, we eat what they eat, as it is concentrated in their flesh. If we were given the option, conventional feed isn't something we'd choose to offer our families for dinner.

Besides the health and humanity issues, the environmental ramifications of farming animals for food, especially on an industrial scale, are alarming. Raising livestock and transporting its meat is energy- and water-intensive and pollutes the air and waterways. The bigger the animals, the heavier the footprint. Conventional beef is often likened to gas-guzzling Hummers.

Pastured animals do tread lighter than those conventionally raised. They don't eat food from sprayed crops, and they generally require less medical intervention and antibiotics. If they're well maintained and rotate pastures, they can actually help combat such overgrazing issues as soil erosion, and their waste can fertilize pastures instead of becoming a feedlot hazard. This contributes to rebuilding our soils, which in turn captures CO_2 out of the atmosphere and slows the progression of global climate change. Grass-fed meat also tends to be sold locally, not transported far and wide. This small-farm, local product is preferable to USDA organic. Both are better options than conventional meat.

Thankfully, access to this product is on the rise. You can find great meat by asking around at farmers' markets and specialty butcher shops. Or buy directly from a farm, or possibly through a pastured meat and poultry CSA. If you already belong to a vegetable or fruit CSA, your farmers can often connect you to meat. Natural-food stores and even chain supermarkets and butcher shops should stock better alternatives, too. Keep in mind that pastured meat may taste a little different and require different cooking times and methods than its conventional counterpart. When shopping, ask for cooking tips.

How to Read Labels

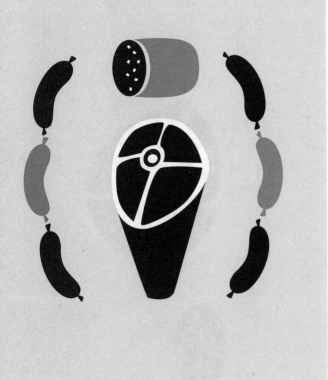

To navigate any store, it's important to read labels. One plastic-enshrouded package of chicken might contain many labels and claims, so it's crucial to know which ones are meaningful and which ones mean very little. Keep in mind that many of these claims aren't ever verified, nor do they legally have to be. And while it would stand to reason that an animal dubbed "natural" might mean it also roamed on pasture, these claims rarely overlap. Usually, they're mutually exclusive marketing gimmicks. We would all be wise not to infer anything when it comes to our meat. For in-depth help deciphering everything from "free range" to "natural" to "fresh," check out sustainabletable.org and greenerchoices.org/eco-labels. Here are the basics:

CERTIFICATIONS

* USDA Organic: These government-regulated standards must be third-party certified. Animals must have some access to air, sunlight, and the outdoors. Their feed must be certified organic and cannot contain animal by-products, hormones, antibiotics, or genetically modified ingredients. (ams.usda.gov/nop)

* Animal-Welfare Approved: This non-profit annually audits the family farms using its logo and only grants use—at no charge—to those complying with progressive and humane animal-welfare standards spanning birth to death. Animals must be on pasture. (animalwelfareapproved.org)

* Certified Humane Raised and Handled: This is another nonprofit with an animal-welfare labeling and certification program. It doesn't allow antibiotics in feed, but, unlike USDA organic, it does permit their use to treat sick animals. (CertifiedHumane.org)

CLAIMS

* Free Range: Shoppers really like this claim, but it doesn't mean much. The USDA has only defined it for poultry, not what they lay, but it can be found on egg cartons. It sounds like chicks are roaming open fields but actually only means they have access to the outdoors and may not even make use of it.

* Grass-fed: This means that animals are raised on pasture, but it's a voluntary and unregulated claim. It implies that ruminants ate only grass, but most grass-fed animals in this country tend to have a diet supplemented with grain. If you want 100 percent grass-fed, ask questions when shopping. In certain climates, fresh (not frozen) grass-fed meat is available only during warmer months, when animals have access to grass.

* Natural: The USDA allows products to be labeled "natural" if they contain no artificial ingredients or added colors and are minimally processed.

* No Antibiotics Administered: This isn't a very well-regulated claim, as the USDA permits the use of antibiotics. Sometimes the industry will self-regulate, tipping the government off if someone is using this claim falsely. If and when this happens, a producer won't be allowed to use the claim and will get fined.

* No Hormones Administered: Ruminants (cows, sheep, goats) are the only animals in the United States allowed to be given growth-promoting hormones. This claim is redundant on poultry and pork, and not very well regulated on ruminants.

Dairy and Eggs

Organic milk is usually the first edible organic product a consumer will buy. With good reason: it comes from animals that weren't given antibiotics or rBGH (recombinant bovine growth hormone). But there's more to consider when it comes to milk than the organic stamp.

* Where is your cow? Is it local or does it live across the country from you?

* What is it eating? Cows should be eating only grass/pasture, or as much of it as possible. If you prefer a local milk that isn't certified organic, you'll want to ask questions about hormone and antibiotic use and make sure that any feed, including corn or soy, isn't genetically modified.

* Was the milk ultrapasteurized, low pasteurized, or not pasteurized at all (i.e., raw)? Pasteurization means heating milk to certain temperatures for a set amount of time to kill bacteria. Most milk, including organic, tends to be ultrapasteurized these days, as this extends shelf life. Unfortunately, it also strips milk of some nutrients. Raw is said to be the most nutritious option, but, depending on where it is from and how it is handled, it might contain harmful bacteria, which is why it is illegal in most states.

* The best bet seems to be a local, preferably organic milk—from a cow with a (mainly) grass diet—that has been lightly pasteurized. If you can find it in reusable glass bottles instead of cardboard cartons or plastic, even better.

* If conventional is all that's available to you, some producers do not use hormones or antibiotics. Choose their products.

* To find the best milks near where you live, including goat's and sheep's milk, visit eatwild.com and cornucopia.org/dairysurvey. If you don't have access to local organic milk near you, look for the Organic Valley brand in your store. Since 1988, Organic Valley's milk and other dairy products come exclusively from a cooperative of family farm owners.

OTHER DAIRY PRODUCTS

Milk also makes an appearance in yogurt, ice cream, butter, and cheese. Look for versions of these made from your favorite milk. Plain yogurt is your best bet to avoid added sugars. Always read ingredient lists for yogurt and ice cream—they should be short and understandable. Though cheese and butter are widely available at supermarkets, try buying these at farmers' markets and cheese stores, where you're more likely to run into the most conscious varieties. Talk to the people at market stalls and behind cheese counters to find out what sort of milk their offerings are made from. At farmers' markets, you may even find yourself chatting with the cheese makers themselves. Then taste and sample until you find what you like.

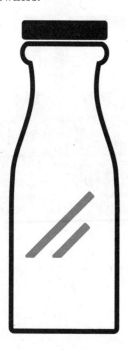

EGGS

The best eggs come from pastured poultry. Look for them where you buy your chicken. The proof is in the yolk: a pastured diet including worms and grubs makes yolks a deep orange or yellow. If the yolk is too pale, shop elsewhere. If you don't have access to pastured eggs, try the organic versions your supermarket is likely to carry. If they don't sell any, ask the management to stock local and organic eggs. And if you have the choice, buy eggs in paperboard cartons rather than Styrofoam or plastic. Whatever carton you get, bring it to the farmers' market the next time you go; most farmers will gladly take empty cartons off your hands and reuse them.

Seafood

Eating fish and other sea creatures presents a unique health issue: fish is considered a heart-healthy protein, but the systematic pollution of our waterways has led to mercury- and PCB-contaminated fish. Specifically, pollution has led to methylmercury, which is created when a mercury atom bonds with a hydrocarbon. It is a very persistent pollutant that comes from the burning of fossil fuels, specifically coal. It can cause birth defects, developmental delays and disorders, cognitive impairment, motor difficulties, and brain and nervous system dysfunction. It's bioaccumulative, meaning once it gets inside an organism, including human beings, it tends to stay put and accumulate as additional amounts are encountered. PCBs (polychlorinated biphenyls) are a family of chemicals deemed "probably carcinogenic" by the EPA. The United States stopped manufacturing them in 1977, but they persist in our environment, and therefore our food. They were used most commonly as cooling fluids in electrical equipment because they're nonflammable.

When we eat fish, these toxins enter our bodies. Concentrations are highest in large predator fish (e.g., shark, king mackerel, swordfish, tuna, and tilefish). It goes like this: little fish eat a little bit of contaminants; bigger fish eat a bunch of little fish; in turn they are eaten by the biggest fish. At each meal, the contaminants add up until they have traveled all the way up the food chain to saturate the animals at the top: us. Beyond mercury and PCBs, seafood swimming in toxic waters presents other issues. Hormone-disrupting chemicals from plastic garbage, excreted by-products of birth control pills, and industrial chemicals that contain endocrine disruptors—including detergents and pesticides—have feminized wild male fish so much that they produce eggs.

So even though seafood is considered a good-for-you food, it's no longer safe to eat in any routine fashion, especially if you're pregnant or a growing child. There is still safe seafood to be eaten, but it takes time and education to find. And even then, it should be eaten only in moderation. Regarding environmental issues, wild seafood and farmed seafood present separate concerns.

Talking About Tuna

What's more American than a tuna fish sandwich? Think before you bite. Tuna is consistently quite contaminated. While canned tuna tends to come from smaller tuna than tuna steaks and is therefore less contaminated, most cans are lined with the hormone-disrupting chemical BPA. This might be a food you're willing to give up. If not, look for tuna packed in glass or in cans lined with something other than BPA.

WILD SEAFOOD

Only wild seafood that is currently not over-fished should be eaten, and it must be caught in an eco-friendly fashion. Hook-and-line and trolls are okay, but trawls can disturb the ocean floor. Some fish are caught by using dynamite or cyanide to blast or stun them out of reefs. These should clearly be avoided.

FARMED SEAFOOD

For farmed seafood, the environmental concerns are linked with health concerns. Most aquaculture is given feed similar to what conventionally farmed animals eat—that is, filled with drugs and additives. Ironically, this feed often contains ground-up wild fish, which not only further depletes the oceans but also means that farmed fish have high concentrations of PCBs. About 80 percent of the farmed seafood in America comes from abroad, mainly from Asia and Central America. Choose something else, as it's often raised in sewage-like pits and chemically treated. There are some farmed specimens raised in open net pens in the ocean, where they can escape and harm wild stock by breeding with them.

FINDING CONSCIOUS SEAFOOD

Some people who learn about the issues with seafood deem them too overwhelming to consider and stop eating it altogether. But there are ways of finding better options. In the absence of organic standards (see page 83), consumers can turn to a number of trustworthy marine institute fish buyers' guides. Many of these can be downloaded to a smartphone or printed from websites as "wallet guides." One innovative program—FishPhone from the Blue Ocean Institute—allows consumers to text for instant information. The next time you're standing at the fish counter and don't know what barramundi is or can't remember which salmon is okay, text 30644 with the word "fish" and the species you want to know about (e.g., "fish salmon"). Moments later you'll hear back that "U.S. farmed" barramundi gets a "green" rating for "very few environmental concerns," while farmed salmon gets a "red" for "significant environmental concerns" plus a health advisory for containing "PCBs." Regarding wild salmon, FishPhone gives U.S. West Coast salmon a "yellow" rating for "some environmental concerns," while Alaskan salmon, if Marine Stewardship Council (MSC)-certified, gets a "green" rating for "very few environmental concerns."

SOLID SEAFOOD SITES

Monterey Bay Aquarium's Seafood Watch Program: *montereybayaquarium.org/cr/ seafoodwatch.aspx*

The National Resources Defense Council Sustainable Seafood Guide: *nrdc.org/oceans/ seafoodguide*

Seafood Choices Alliance: *seafoodchoices.com*

Cooking In and Eating Out

The best and easiest way to eat consciously is to cook at home. Seek inspiration from wherever you can get it: cookbooks, magazines, food television. If you travel or have to eat out often for work, eating consciously is inevitably more difficult. Some people find it is easier to attempt at restaurants by ordering only vegetarian dishes. Others avoid meat but do eat fish. Doing a little research to find restaurants that serve local and organic foods and suggesting to colleagues that you meet there is a good practice. That way you can maintain your conscious commitment no matter where you are.

Beverages

The most conscious thing to fill your glass or reusable bottle with is plain old tap water. For information on whether you should filter before you sip and why you should avoid bottled water, turn to pages 312–313; for the best reusable bottles, see the Resources on page 342. Beyond water, beverages can have various environmental and health repercussions and should be chosen carefully, especially as we drink them daily. Their impact can add up.

BOTTLED DRINKS

Sodas and various energy drinks loaded with sugars and possibly genetically modified corn syrup aren't conscious drinks. A single liter of soda takes on average 250 liters of water to produce when you factor in the water needed to grow the ingredients, to say nothing of the health impact of the sugary content. You may still choose to drink them, but be aware of what they contain, who manufactures them, and what happens to their containers once you recycle them. Fruit juice can be a better option, especially if you're home-juicing local fruit in season. If you're buying juice, make sure to read the label before you purchase, which will tell you how much sugar, additives, and juice the product actually contains. And keep in mind that something like orange juice is energy intensive to produce, due to the use of toxic crop sprays and the high environmental costs of transportation. If you live near a grove, that's one thing, but if you don't, look for a more regional product. Or drink it in moderation.

COFFEE AND TEA

Coffee and tea can and should be bought in organic versions. They also come Fair Trade–certified, which indicates, on the most basic level, that the workers growing your beans and leaves were treated right and paid a fair wage. For more information on this program, go to transfairusa .org. Fair Trade certification also takes into account environmental sustainability, as does Rainforest Alliance Certified (rainforest-alliance.org). Most coffee is grown in the shade in rain forests, but it's easier and cheaper to grow it in the sun, so some companies cut down trees to let light in, destroying bird habitats in the process. If you see the words "Bird Friendly" on a bag of beans, it indicates the coffee was shade grown. Although coffee is not a local product for most coffee drinkers, locavores who don't want to give up their espressos can at least buy beans from a local roaster. If you drink decaf, look for versions that have the caffeine removed through water—not chemical solvent—processing. If you drink flavored tea or coffee, choose organic versions to avoid artificial flavoring.

BEER, WINE, AND LIQUOR

When it comes time to relax, do so without pesticide residues. Many breweries—small and local as well as big and national—currently make organic brews. Pop open a bottle (these are preferable to BPA-lined cans) and kick back. If you're a wine drinker, you likely already know that there have been great strides made in the natural wine community, and organic wine, which was once considered undrinkable, is now something to seek out. Grape options abound: choose from biodynamic (a sustainable, third-party-certifiable method of farming based on historical practices), certified organic, organically grown, or sustainably grown. Small certification entities and labels seeking to call attention to truly sustainable wines seem to be popping up daily (to wit: salmonsafe .org, liveinc.org, sipthegoodlife.org). Some are greener and purer than others, but all of these options are more desirable than highly sprayed conventional grapes concentrated in one bottle. If you prefer cocktails, there's no hard alcohol that doesn't come in a certified organic or local variety at this point. And you can mix it greener, too, with organic tonic, local juices, and homemade seltzer.

Packaged Foods

It's a good idea to avoid or drastically reduce the amount of packaged foods in your diet. There's a distinction to be made between packaged food, which might contain only a handful of ingredients and can be a healthy option, and processed packaged food, which has mile-long ingredient lists, many of them filled with unpronounceable, questionable names. This is true even for certified organic processed packaged foods.

If you're in the market for a one-ingredient boxed or bagged food like rice or quinoa, opt for organic versions, preferably local. When it comes to several-ingredient items, including bread, read labels carefully. You want to get the most minimally processed item. Even an artisanal jam from the farmers' market could have several sugars in it of varying origins.

SUGAR

Speaking of sugar, always look for Fair Trade and organic versions. And don't think that because something is brown it is healthier. Most brown sugar in the United States has been processed to white (to kill bacteria, similar to pasteurization for milk) and then has molasses added back in to make it varying shades of dark. Depending on where you live, local and less processed sweeteners can include maple syrup and honey, preferably raw.

CORN SYRUP

High-fructose corn syrup does technically come from corn, but it is so processed it's hardly corn any longer. It's also ubiquitous, found in just about every processed food item there is at the supermarket, and has been linked over and over again to America's obesity epidemic. It tends to come from genetically modified, synthetically fertilized, heavily sprayed corn and is best avoided. If you're mainly eating whole (as in unprocessed) foods and drinking water instead of canned beverages, you're less likely to encounter it.

PACKAGING

Pay attention to the packaging of packaged foods. To cut down on extraneous packaging, buy in bulk—this works for grains, dried beans, nuts, cereal, spices, and more. Bring cotton produce sacks and other reusable containers with you to the store so you won't have to take a plastic bag for your bulk items. If you know there are certain plastics that your municipality recycles, keep these in mind as you shop for packaged goods that don't come in bulk. Get yogurt in plastic #5 instead of plastic #6 if your town only takes #5. If you shop with recycling in mind, you'll wind up with less trash and more recyclables.

FOOD RESOURCES

BOOKS

The Conscious Kitchen
by Alexandra Zissu

The Omnivore's Dilemma;
In Defense of Food; and *Food Rules*
by Michael Pollan

This Organic Life
by Joan Dye Gussow

What to Eat and *Food Politics*
by Marion Nestle

MOVIES

The Cove; Food, Inc.; King Corn;
The Price of Sugar

Who Owns Whom?

Over the past decade, many natural and organic food brands have been purchased by multinational food companies. While not necessarily bad, these larger businesses are unlikely to hold to the same values as the smaller company you've come to know and love. Coca-Cola owns Odwalla; Kraft owns Balance Bar; Groupe Danone owns Stonyfield Farm—and that's just the tip of the iceberg. Get to know who owns your food products. To get a more complete picture of who owns whom, visit organicconsumers.org and type in "who owns who."

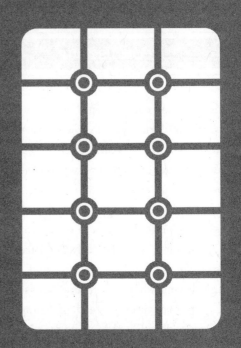

the
BEDROOM

The Conscious Ritual

We all need time to unwind, to rest our bodies, to just *be*—asleep or awake. Relaxation can happen anywhere, although the bedroom is ostensibly set up for it. Pause to consider the spaces in your bedroom that are the most calming, that make you feel the most serene. Maybe it's the view: deep forest, expansive water, or even just a strand of ivy snaking up an urban fire escape. Notice how it changes each season, or with the light at different times of the day. Take pleasure in the little things: shadows on the wall, the slope of the ceiling, a piece of art that draws you in. Focusing on these small details might be just what you need to withdraw from the demands of daily life. Consider implementing simple rules to encourage comfort in the bedroom, like barring the use of computers or television, at least after a certain hour.

The Conscious Components

Remembering that you are part of a larger ecosystem can stop right here. This doesn't mean the bedroom exists in isolation. Of course it doesn't. The air is still shared, and everything in a bedroom, from sheets to clothing, is clearly part of an agricultural and manufacturing system. But this is a place to leave those thoughts behind as much as you can. The bedroom should be personal, private, restorative. A buffer from stress and a place for dreams. In order to achieve this, you have to make this space sacred. All bedroom items should be conducive to calmness.

Here's a handy checklist to help you remember the pieces that make up a conscious bedroom ⟶

☐ Open windows for ventilation

☐ Curtains made of natural, washable fabrics like organic cotton, canvas, linen, or hemp

☐ Bare floor or rugs made of natural fibers like wool, hemp, or cotton

☐ 100 percent organic cotton sheets

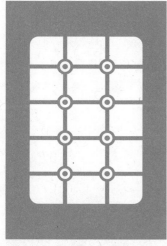

☐ Safe mattress made of organic materials

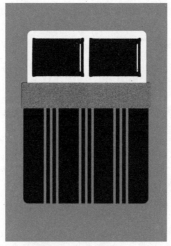

☐ Hardwood or metal headboard and bed frame

☐ Antique wood furniture instead of upholstered, padded, or particleboard pieces

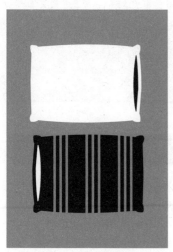

☐ Pillows made of organic cotton or wool, natural latex, or buckwheat

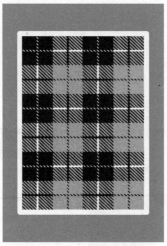

☐ Blankets made of natural materials like wool, organic cotton, linen, and hemp; never dry-cleaned

☐ Air filter to lessen allergens and purify air

THE ISSUES

Because we while away so many hours in bedrooms, often with the door and windows shut, the main concerns here are what's in the air and what's in the dust. Everything from the paint on the walls to the nonskid mat under the rug has the potential to add to the mix of chemicals we're breathing and to the dust bunnies under the bed. It's common sense to choose the purest bedroom furnishings you can find, but keep in mind that it's impossible to completely rid the space of toxins. Something like flame-retardant dust from an old mattress can linger in a room long after prior inhabitants (and their beds) move out or you upgrade mattresses (although the dust will diminish when you remove the source of exposure). Wet dusting and vacuuming frequently with a machine equipped with a HEPA (high-efficiency particulate air) filter are a must.

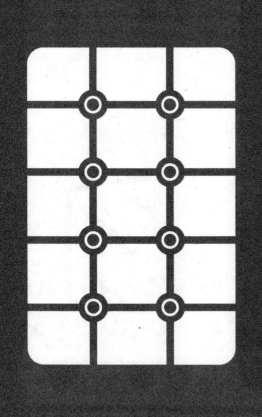

The Bed

MATTRESSES

Mattresses are the No. 1 concern in a bedroom because most contain foam. Most foams are polyurethane, a petroleum-based, nonrenewable, and highly flammable resource that requires more flame retardants than other mattress materials. By law, all mattresses in the United States must contain some sort of flame retardant so they meet cigarette-ignition resistance as well as address open-flame heat sources. While federal flammability laws have prevented many deaths and injuries resulting from mattress fires, some of the chemicals used to meet the requirements are harmful to our health and the environment. The worst are brominated flame retardants (BFRs) called polybrominated diphenyl ethers (PBDEs). Some versions of these are banned in the E.U. and are slowly being phased out Stateside. This is good news, because they are not only potentially carcinogenic but are also reproductive toxicants and endocrine disruptors. They escape from mattresses and then basically piggyback on the dust particles in our homes. Due to their widespread use in everything from mattresses to electronics to upholstered furniture, PBDEs can be found in the blood of just about every American, as well as in breast milk, at levels higher than those found in citizens of other countries.

Considering their ubiquity, it makes sense to reduce exposure to PBDEs in mattresses, especially if you're of reproductive age, pregnant, a kid, or have small kids sleeping with you. Pound for pound, children are exposed to higher levels of these chemicals than adult bodies are, and at vulnerable moments of development.

Find out what your current mattress is made of and what flame retardants it contains. It won't be enough to read the Do Not Remove tag on it; call the manufacturer and ask about the flame retardants, materials, stain guards, and mold inhibitors used.

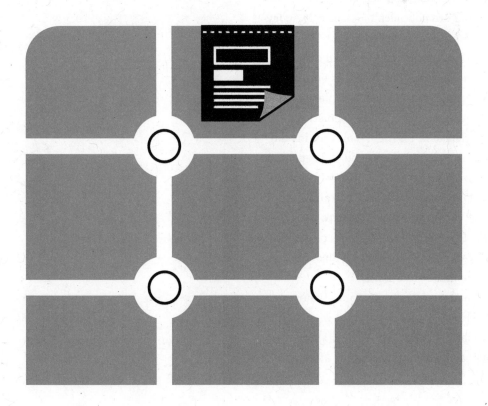

MAINTAINING YOUR MATTRESS

Once you know what you're dealing with, encase the mattress to reduce the dust coming out of it. If you're chemically sensitive or have allergies and are trying to reduce contact with dust mites, you may already have a mattress case. The most effective versions are plastic, which are impermeable. Never use vinyl/PVC, which contains phthalates—not something you want to be breathing all night long. Look instead for something made of a safer plastic, like #4. If you choose to avoid plastic altogether, cotton cases—preferably organic—can act as a similar barrier, though these are permeable, no matter how tightly woven they are. Sheets lessen direct contact and the transfer of dust onto skin, but are not much of a block. Memory foam mattresses are saturated with flame retardants to meet flammability standards, so if you have one, look into replacing it entirely. If you prefer to encase the foam, use plastic only.

To protect your mattress from moisture, use wool pads instead of plastic. Wool contains lanolin, which repels moisture, and it keeps you warm in winter and cool in summer. If you prefer plastic, opt for polyethylene. Again, do not use vinyl/PVC. Avoid other synthetic mattress pads, like foam egg-crate toppers or similar puffy polyester pads; these may also contain questionable flame retardants.

To even out wear and tear, rotate your mattress a few times a year. Be careful when doing this, especially if pregnant. Wear a small dust filter mask and vacuum thoroughly afterward.

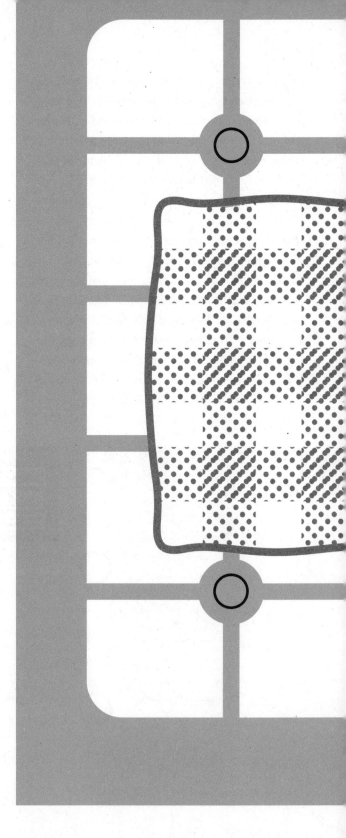

BUYING A NEW MATTRESS

When considering a new mattress, keep in mind that they off-gas most when you first bring them home. If you can, leave them in a garage, basement, or sheltered, clean, and dry outdoor space for a week prior to use. After that, they release their fumes at a fairly steady rate. As they get older, the dust released can increase again as the interior foam begins to deteriorate and crumble. To avoid this, replace your mattress every ten years, give or take. Mattresses aren't easily recycled—municipalities don't offer the option, and it's the rare organization that accepts used mattresses as donations. They're iffy secondhand—bedbugs are a growing problem, and moisture trapped within the mattresses from sweat and other bodily fluids over the years can pose a health issue. Many tossed mattresses are incinerated, releasing PBDEs and other toxic fumes into the air. If you can't bear that idea, encase your old mattress and move it to where it will get the least amount of use, like a guest bedroom.

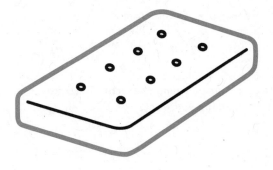

CHOOSING A MATTRESS

Shopping for a new mattress can be a Wild West experience. There is no question, given the issues, that buying a mattress made with organic or at least more-natural materials is the best option for you and the environment. That said, natural doesn't always equal pure: conventional cotton is one of the most heavily sprayed and polluting crops in the world. While there are plenty of organic options on the market, there is no government agency or even mattress trade group to establish the guidelines or monitor claims for this. Greenwashing abounds—some so-called organic mattresses made of natural latex, cotton, or wool may still contain vinyl, BFRs, pesticide residues, optical brighteners, formaldehyde, phthalates, and more.

Unfortunately, this means it is largely up to consumers to research and find the greenest possible mattress in their budget range (some of the purest versions are prohibitively expensive). In the absence of standards, groups like the Greenguard Environmental Institute can be helpful. They test products and have certified a few mattress brands for low emissions. You can also look for third-party certifiers for organic cotton, wool, natural latex rubber, and sustainable wood.

Mattress Shopping Guide

No matter what kind of mattress you're considering, always ask a salesperson and the manufacturer what is being used to meet federal flammability requirements. Give yourself time to review the responses you receive and read any literature provided. Purchasing a mattress in a hurry can lead to a poor choice you'll be stuck with for a decade. There are issues that arise with most flame retardants. Something like boric acid may not be 100 percent great, but it is preferable to the semimetal antimony, which is preferable to BFRs. If you would like to avoid chemical flame retardants altogether, mattresses made without them are available—wool is naturally flame retardant—though some states require a doctor's prescription to order one.

Here are some guidelines to keep in mind while shopping for a greener mattress:

1. If you like a springy surface to sleep on, choose natural latex over synthetic foam.

2. If you prefer coil springs, make sure the layers of batting inside are organic cotton and wool, not foam.

3. Futons can be a good option for people seeking out a green mattress on a budget. Some are made with organic cotton, and most are constructed with a core to keep them from becoming too flat and hard over time. Look for one with a wool core instead of a traditional foam one. Ask questions about any material touted as eco-friendly. Soy foam, for example, might contain only a small percentage of (genetically modified) soy. The rest might be regular foam.

4. Do not buy anything treated with a waterproofing or stain-guarding chemical. These may contain perfluorochemicals (PFCs), which are not something you want to be sleeping on or want anywhere in your home.

HEADBOARDS AND FRAMES

Your bed should be similarly pure: Opt for hardwood or metal frames—new or antique—with no particleboard or composite woods, as they are made with glues and other chemicals that emit dangerous fumes like formaldehyde. Formaldehyde is a carcinogen—known in Europe, suspected in the United States—that has also been linked to allergies and asthma. If you're going to use a composite wood, plywood outgases less than particleboard or fiberboard. Choose formaldehyde-free plywood or plywood made with phenol-formaldehyde (PF) resin. Plywood can still emit formaldehyde, though, when urea-formaldehyde (UF) is used as the adhesive. Avoid upholstered headboards or footboards, which are havens for dust mites and might contain foam.

BOX SPRINGS

Don't neglect what lies below your mattress. Traditional box springs present the same issues as mattresses. Look for the simplest one you can find: hard, sustainable wood covered in untreated cotton, preferably organic. Hardwood platforms are another good, cost-effective option. Do not place mattresses directly on the floor; air needs to circulate around them.

The Conscious Boudoir

Flame retardants aren't sexy. Neither, particularly, is a home filled with noisy children. If you have young kids or other distractions, it can be hard to remember that the bedroom is also a space for intimacy, not just sleep. Consider what might be getting in the way—if not a tot snoozing between you and your partner, maybe it's a big snoring dog—and try to restore intimacy to your bedroom. Here are a few thoughts:

* Many plastic sex toys are made of PVC and contain dangerous phthalates. Greener options are available, made of natural rubber, undyed silicone, shatterproof glass, and FSC-certified wood. Vibrators come solar powered. And props can be given a second life at RecycleMySexToy.com.

* Some conventional lubricants are made of nonrenewable petrochemicals containing potentially carcinogenic and endocrine-disrupting preservatives (parabens) and synthetic hormone-disrupting scents. *Not* arousing. Far preferable are water-based versions containing natural and even some organic ingredients.

* What's eco-friendlier than population control? But not all birth control options are created equal. Condoms are crucial for STD protection, but they and their wrappers clutter landfills (never flush condoms, always toss). Some brands attempt to be greener, using natural latex over petroleum-derived polyurethane. There are condoms made specifically for vegans (they don't have a milk protein found in some latex) and for people concerned with Fair Trade (the organically grown rubber is fairly traded). Avoid lambskin, which is biodegradable but doesn't prevent STDs. Reusable devices, like an IUD or a diaphragm, are a green option, though they also don't protect against STDs. When using birth control hormones, in IUD, pill, or implant form, keep in mind that trace amounts can get into waterways, mess with aquatic life, and slip through municipal treatment systems to wind up in tap water.

* Always choose organic aphrodisiacs: organic grapes not sprayed with earth- and people-polluting pesticides; Fair Trade organic chocolate; local strawberries (when in season); ocean-friendly oysters. The Environmental Defense Fund says U.S. oysters farmed on suspension systems are eco-preferable to dredge-harvested wild oysters, as dredging can damage bottom habitats. Wild oysters can also contain elevated levels of PCBs. Worrying about wild contaminants isn't conducive to wild sex.

Bedding

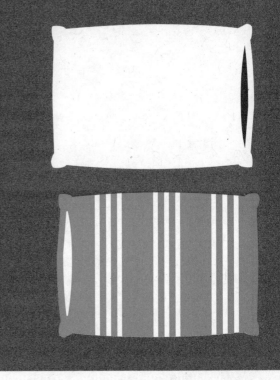

PILLOWS

Pillows, like mattresses, are often made of foam and sometimes contain flame retardants. As Annie Leonard says in *The Story of Stuff* (storyofstuff.org), "We take our pillows, we douse them in a neurotoxin (BFRs), then we bring them home and put our heads on them for eight hours to sleep." As troubling as this is, a conscious consumer can avoid this fate. Call the manufacturer to find out what is in your pillow. Pillows are a lot less expensive to replace than mattresses, so if you don't like what you hear, shop for something with natural fibers: organic cotton, natural latex, organic wool, and even buckwheat. Always ask what flame retardant or chemical treatment has been used on the pillow before purchasing. Consider using an organic cotton pillow protector to make it last longer.

SHEETS

The greenest sheets are the ones you already have. But if buying new, choose 100 percent organic cotton, either undyed or dyed in an eco-friendlier fashion. Choosing organic is mainly about making a positive environmental impact; the exposure to toxins from contact with the cotton itself while sleeping is minimal. Dyes, on the other hand, can come off on skin and are environmentally harsh. If you see something called "green" cotton, don't mistake it for organic. It's conventional cotton that hasn't been bleached with chlorine or treated with formaldehyde, a carcinogen. Bamboo is an eco-friendly material, but not when it is made into a fabric. Bamboo sheets are basically rayon and not a great choice. If you're going to use conventional sheets, natural fibers are best.

Do not purchase anything with a permanent press finish, which is treated with formaldehyde, a VOC that you will inhale as you sleep.

BLANKETS

Blankets should be as pure as sheets. Organic cotton, linen, hemp, and wool are good choices. Electric blankets surround us with potentially hazardous electromagnetic fields as we sleep (see page 111). If you have one and would like to use it, do so only to warm the bed before you climb in. Turn it off when sleeping. A hot water bottle is a tried-and-true option for continual warmth.

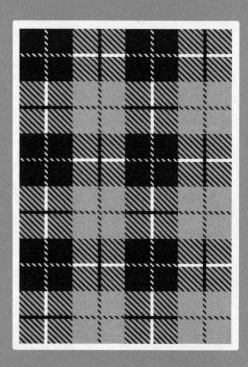

Ventilation and Air Quality

Open the windows frequently to get the air moving in your bedroom, even in the winter. Chemical companies rate their products based on how many parts per million get released into the air. Even if a substance is known to be harmful, as long as it falls under that specific part per million, it's considered "nontoxic." But if many of these different chemicals at their correct parts per million accumulate in an unventilated bedroom, where we're spending a third of our lives, what does that mean for our health, not to mention the environment? It's quite a chemical cloud to be dozing in.

If you have allergies or other reasons to be concerned about the air in your room—like living near a highway or in a smog-filled city—you might want to consider an air purifier. Some people feel the jury is still out on their efficacy, but there is no harm in using one with a HEPA filter, which removes particulates, including dust. Avoid ozone generators in the bedroom; they are not shown to control air pollution. Make sure whatever you're using is appropriately sized for the room you're filtering, and close the door when it's on. This way it won't be working to purify a bigger space than it's meant for. Change the filter often, following the manufacturer's directions. Do this outside if possible, so whatever dust is displaced won't go back into your home.

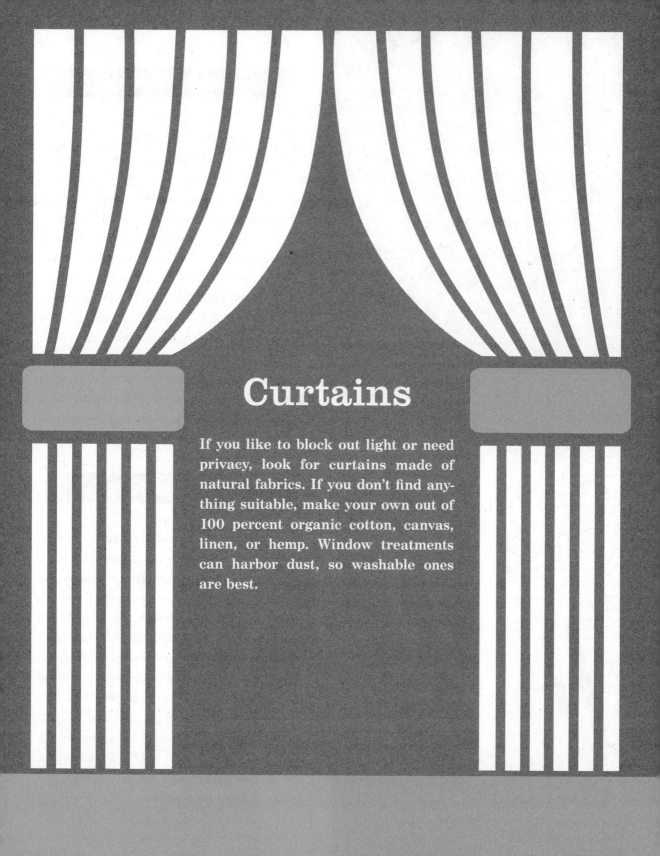

Curtains

If you like to block out light or need privacy, look for curtains made of natural fabrics. If you don't find anything suitable, make your own out of 100 percent organic cotton, canvas, linen, or hemp. Window treatments can harbor dust, so washable ones are best.

Setting Up a Bedroom

ANTIQUE FURNITURE

Hand-me-down furniture is the most conscious option. Fill a bedroom with pieces that have history and maybe even happy memories attached to them: a dresser you discovered at an antique store, or maybe a chest from a grandparent. Lead, a neurotoxin, can be a concern with painted older furniture, so if you have a side table or dresser with crumbling old paint, test it with a home kit. Avoid upholstered furniture or padded items with cushions, as these can contain flame-retardant-filled foam. If you have an old chaise or chair with a ripped cover and exposed foam, either reupholster it using greener materials, place an intact barrier cover on it, or, if the foam is crumbling, replace the foam or the item entirely.

NEW FURNITURE

Much new furniture is made of composite woods like particleboard and medium-density fiberboard, which are temptingly inexpensive but best not brought into the bedroom; these can off-gas formaldeyde. Though the vapors from new furniture containing formaldehyde glue diminish over time, they remain in high concentrations in smaller and improperly ventilated rooms. If you have reason to suspect the fumes in your home are too high, there are inexpensive kits available that have been used by the Sierra Club to test levels in FEMA trailers. For less serious levels, there are also houseplants known to act as air filters (see page 276). If you have a piece of composite wood furniture you love and don't want to part with, move it to a room in the house where you spend less time. You can also seal in the emissions.

Other materials to leave at the store: non-FSC-certified woods and pieces that aren't reusable or recyclable. Always consider durability when furniture shopping. You want whatever you buy to last as long as possible. Vote with your dollars by buying from companies and artisans who make it easy for consumers to know what they're doing—good or bad. A place like Ikea might not have the most durable furniture and is filled with composite wood items, but it's fairly simple to find out what materials are being used and what standards are being followed. Ikea says they follow strict German standards for formaldehyde off-gassing levels and that they don't use BFRs or antimony on mattresses, textiles, or upholstered materials.

ATTENTION TO DETAILS

Paints, caulks, and finishes should be as nontoxic as available. Unfortunately, as with mattresses, this is an arena where greenwashing rears its ugly head. There is little certification in place to ensure that a nontoxic product truly is. Ask questions to ensure you're buying something safe for use in a bedroom. Everything used should be no- or low-VOC. The Pharos Project (pharosproject.net) is a useful tool for locating and evaluating green building materials.

BUZZ KILL

Electric alarm clocks emit an electromagnetic field. While the scientific community isn't collectively convinced by the body of evidence suggesting the electromagnetic fields (EMFs) generated by electronics can be harmful to health, it feels like a solid precautionary step to minimize exposure by moving these devices farther away from our heads and bodies. Relocate them elsewhere.

Lights On

Choose lights that draw the least amount of electricity; this means the least amount of coal burned. Incandescent lights require the most. They're banned in Europe and will be phased out Stateside in 2012, and gone from the marketplace by 2014. Compact fluorescents (CFLs) are a better option. They're inexpensive, widely available, and can last for years (though not all do). According to the Department of Energy, if every household in the United States replaced just one incandescent bulb with a CFL, we would save enough energy to light more than three million homes for a year and create the carbon-savings equivalent of taking 800,000 cars off the road. The downside? They contain a small amount of mercury. So don't use a CFL in a lamp likely to tip over. Handle them carefully and dispose of them at a local hazardous-waste collection site or a big-box store like Home Depot or Ikea that collects them. LEDs are the longest-lasting (some claim they'll last for 25,000 to 50,000 hours) and most energy-efficient option and don't contain mercury. They can be expensive, and some people don't love the light they give off, but they're perfectly fine for reading lamps, and improvements are being made constantly.

Air Systems

Keep Candles and Perfume Out of the Bedroom

Wearing perfume and lighting candles in a room where you're actively working to improve air quality are very contradictory acts. Most synthetic perfumes contain hormone-disrupting phthalates and can be lung irritants. Conventional candles made from petroleum emit plumes of soot and phthalate-containing scents. Their wicks can contain metals like zinc, tin, and even lead. If you really like fragrance, non-petroleum-based candles, like unscented beeswax or essential-oil-scented non-GM soy wax versions with cloth wicks, are far preferable to their conventional counterparts. But you're still burning something and polluting the air.

Beneath Your Feet

FLOORS

The preferred bedroom floor is real (not composite) bare wood: it's easy to clean and doesn't provide a haven for chemical residue or dust mites, like rugs do. If you're putting in a new floor, look for responsibly harvested hardwood, bamboo, or even cork. Finishes should be as nontoxic as available.

RUGS

If you want a rug, choose a natural fiber like wool, hemp, or cotton over synthetic. Your best bet is something that does not have backing and can be thrown in the washing machine, like a rag rug made from organic cotton or reused fabric scraps. If a rug has a backing, check to see that it isn't PVC and that it was woven—not glued—on. Adhesives can contain formaldehyde. Skid pads for rugs should also not be PVC; look for natural rubber versions. Avoid deep-pile rugs, which are black holes for

dust and very hard to clean. When the time comes to clean a carpet that cannot be put in the washing machine, rent a steam cleaner and use it with no detergent.

CARPETS

Wall-to-wall carpeting is not ideal, as it is usually synthetic, installed using questionable glues, and comes treated with a toxic stain guard. If you have it, vacuum often. Steam cleaning can result in mold and so isn't ideal for wall-to-wall carpets. If you do steam clean, be careful the carpet doesn't get overly wet.

If you'd like to install some new wall-to-wall, greener versions are increasingly available in the marketplace, including modular tiles that don't require glue and can be recycled.

In the Closet

Hand-me-downs, vintage, and what you already own are the most conscious garment options. But inevitably you'll want to buy something new. As with food, it's a good idea to buy local or at least domestic. It's critical for our economy not to lose all of our U.S. manufacturing base, and factories are easier to verify Stateside. Think about the materials before you shop. The eco-friendliest fabrics are reused, recycled, or certified organic. Always look for items that will not need to be dry-cleaned. Keep an eye out for durable, classic pieces that will last season to season, no matter what the trends are.

WHO ARE YOU WEARING?

Learn about what you're looking to buy and who made it. Vote with your dollars by seeking items from a company attempting transparency and sustainability. Patagonia, for example, thinks systemically about its business. You can even recycle its long underwear.

DRY-CLEANING

If you dry-clean your clothes, traces of dry-cleaning fluid are coming out of your closet—not something you want to be breathing all night long. The EPA says perchloroethylene (aka perc), the most common dry-cleaning chemical, causes cancer in lab animals. Dry-cleaning waste is in our air and water. Very few items labeled "dry-clean only" truly need it, but for the items that do, locate a professional cleaner that utilizes less-toxic methods like CO_2 or wet cleaning (check out nodryclean.com). Silk, rayon, and wool, while often labeled "dry-clean only," can actually be washed by hand if you know the proper techniques to avoid shrinking or ruining the texture of your garments. If there are no alternative cleaners near you, always remove clothes cleaned with perc from their plastic bags and let them air outside for several hours so the chemical can evaporate a bit before getting stored in your closet. Even better: Consider keeping items cleaned in perc in a non-bedroom closet.

MOTHBALLS

The vapors of mothballs (which usually contain paradichlorobenzene or sometimes naphthalene) are carcinogenic and can irritate the nervous system. If a child swallows one it can be fatal. Safer moth-repelling substances include cedar and dried lavender. Some people say dry-cleaning can kill moths (including eggs and larvae), but so can hot water washing. Storing things off-season in airtight containers—such as cedar chests—will keep moths out. Freezing sweaters for a few days can also kill off anything living in them.

Clothing Systems

Dry-cleaning, Mothballs, and Blankets Don't Mix

At the end of a long day, you slide between your organic cotton sheets, lovingly placed on top of your organic mattress. The weather is getting colder, so you climb back out and retrieve your favorite wool blanket. Since the last time you used it, you had it dry-cleaned and then stored it with mothballs. You yank it out of the plastic, bring it back to bed, and snuggle underneath it, inhaling its toxic mix of fumes for the next eight hours and for many nights to come. You can already tell what's wrong with this scenario. Blankets should only be machine-washed with nontoxic detergents or wet- or CO_2-cleaned, then stored with natural pest deterrents. Covering your organic haven with perc residue doesn't make sense.

Walk This Way

In order to keep outdoor pollutants outside, shoes should be taken off near where you enter the house. Outdoor shoes track in a vast majority of the dust and chemicals found in household rugs and on floors (this includes allergens, pesticides, and lead, plus other carcinogens and endocrine disruptors). If you happen to have some oldies but goodies stashed in your bedroom closet, repair them before buying anything new. If buying new, durable and local is best. Eco-friendly materials include canvas, wool, hemp, and recycled rubber. Many people choose to wear leather. Beyond animal welfare concerns, the process of tanning and dyeing hides is environmentally destructive. If you wear leather, there are a number of designers now repurposing old leather coats into accessories like belts, bags, and wallets. Well worth a look.

Cleaning

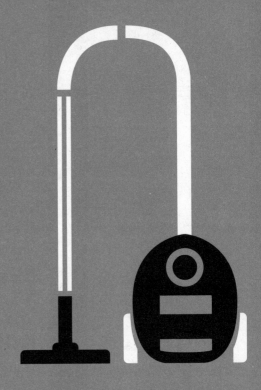

Vacuum weekly with a vacuum cleaner that has a HEPA filter. Don't forget to vacuum upholstered furniture and curtains. Vacuum your mattress when you change the sheets—weekly if you're allergic to dust mites. Change the filter often, according to the manufacturer's instructions. Do this outside, or at least out of your bedroom, so as not to reintroduce dust into the space.

DUSTING

The Silent Spring Institute identified 66 endocrine-disrupting compounds in household dust tests. And the Environmental Working Group refers to dust as "simply another way for the toxic chemicals in your house to reach your body." To remove these and keep them from reaching your body, dust often. Do not use a dry cloth, which will just scatter the dust. Use a wet one. You might want to wear a dust mask, especially if you're allergic or sensitive to dust.

POLISHING WOOD

Most conventional wood polishes come in aerosol cans. They work like this: the wax is suspended in a solvent, you spray it, the solvent evaporates, and the polish is left behind. The packaging, the propellants, and the ingredients should all be avoided. Instead, use a natural, non-aerosolized wax or oil with a list of ingredients you understand. You can also make your own polish by mixing $1/4$ cup lemon juice or $1/4$ cup white vinegar with $1/2$ teaspoon olive oil in a glass jar. Dab the solution onto a soft rag for use.

BEDDING

Wash sheets and mattress pads once a week. If you have asthma or allergies, you may want to do this in hot water to kill dust mites. If not, cold water is environmentally preferable and will suffice.

BLANKETS AND RUGS

Wash from time to time. Do not dry-clean. If these don't fit in your washing machine, take them to a laundromat and wash them in a large-capacity machine. Cotton and even down and feathers can be machine-washed and -dried. Most wool can be machine-washed and air-dried—just do it carefully.

PILLOWS

Over time, half a pillow's weight can be comprised of dust mites and other particles, so it's a good idea to wash it. Most can go in the washing machine. Down and feathers do best washed two at a time on the delicate cycle with a little natural detergent. Dry them in the dryer. Put wool pillows out in the sun a few times a year—the sun kills dust mites. Wash pillow protectors every few months.

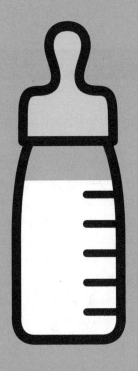

the
NURSERY and
KIDS' ROOMS

The Conscious Ritual

At some point during the day or night, children will sleep. The waiting can occasionally feel torturous. And when the moment at long last arrives, the universal human urge is to gawk lovingly at the still, living, breathing lump that has taken over our lives. This pause before running off to clean the dinner dishes, or check e-mail, or get on a conference call is not to be missed. Celebrate the beauty of the sleeping child. No matter how old or young the child is, be thankful. Once you've had your fill, try not to trip on the clutter as you sneak out.

The Conscious Components

A conscious nursery is a safe and nurturing space, a place of newness and hope. It's also a stimulating environment that grows as a child grows. Babies spend many hours daily—as much as nine-tenths of the day—in the nursery, being changed, feeding, waiting for sleep, sleeping.

When prepping a room for our children, we pay careful attention to conventional baby-proofing concerns, like blocking electrical outlets; making sure blind pulls aren't accessible to small, grabby hands; installing carbon monoxide and smoke detectors; searching for and removing choking and suffocating hazards; and taking SIDS precautions. An avalanche of stuff comes from baby showers: "must-haves" that family and friends claim they could never have parented without, such as baby head positioners, bathtub thermometers, piles of toys, scented lotions, and monitoring machines.

But 99 percent of this stuff simply isn't necessary, won't last long, will become trash, and, even worse, could harm your baby as he or she develops. Love, food, clothing, a place to sleep, and some sort of diaper are all a baby needs.

Here's a handy checklist to help you remember the pieces that make up a conscious nursery/kids' room ⟶

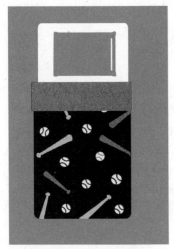

☐ Bedding made of natural materials like organic cotton or cotton flannel and wool

☐ Stuffed animals made of organic materials

☐ Art supplies made with natural materials and pigments, not synthetic ones

☐ Wooden toys instead of plastic

☐ Hardwood crib with organic mattress

☐ Hardwood furniture instead of particleboard or composite wood

☐ Secondhand clothing or new clothing made of organic cotton

☐ Natural, unfragranced lotions, soaps, and other products

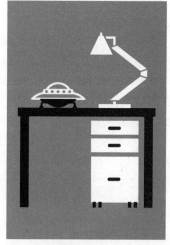
☐ Organic cotton diapers with wool covers, or eco-friendlier disposables

THE ISSUES

Air quality, humidity, and cleaning-product ingredients are concerns in any room. But whole-house issues in a kid's room are not quite the same as even your own bedroom, because children's undeveloped and growing systems are far more sensitive to toxic exposures than adults'. Pound for pound, children ingest and inhale exponentially more than their parents do. They also crawl and play on the floor, and put their toys and dusty hands in their mouths. So things that are a little questionable elsewhere in the home are must-fixes in a nursery or child's room. The focus in this chapter is mainly on the smallest, most vulnerable children, but even teenagers are still developing and should be sleeping in a safe(r) space. What follows is a good, comprehensive road map for a child of any age.

The Air We Breathe

BREATHING SAFELY

We breathe 20 to 40 pounds of air a day, much more than the amount of food we eat. And yet, air is the element of the nursery most often taken for granted; because it's invisible, it's easier to focus on tangible things like stuffed animals and night-lights. But it's all linked: air quality is being compromised when playing with off-gassing toys, sleeping on off-gassing mattresses, and using fragrance-filled creams.

RENOVATIONS AND PAINT

The first thing to do to ensure pure air is to not renovate. Renovation releases a who-knows-what's-in-it cocktail of dust into the room. If you must renovate, use only the greenest possible materials, and try to move out of your home during the process. If you're just freshening up a room with a coat of paint, test first to make sure that what lies underneath—especially around windows and door frames, which get the most friction and wear and tear—isn't lead paint. If it is, take the necessary steps to either remove it or seal it in. Before painting, clear the room of its items; fabrics absorb and

retain chemicals emitted from paint. And select a no-VOC product. Certain VOCs emitted from paint contribute to greenhouse gases, smog formation, and ozone depletion. Some VOCs will also react with ozone to form secondary pollutants, including formaldehyde. Most paints have a high-VOC content, and exposure to these has been associated with asthma, "sick-building syndrome," and respiratory and lung infections. Choosing no- or low-VOC is comparable to buying organic food in order to avoid ingesting pesticides. But even no-VOC paint contains chemicals, so give the room time to air out before moving any small people in. If you're going to use wallpaper instead of or in addition to paint, make sure that the product itself isn't vinyl and that the adhesive is safe for a nursery. Follow the same guidelines as you would for paint, and look for a no- or low-VOC product.

FURNITURE AND RUGS

When choosing cribs and furniture, follow the advice on pages 136–137. And when considering buying a rug, read the suggestions on pages 146–147. Keep in mind that even if you have avoided composite wood furniture containing formaldehyde glue and removed all rugs, you're not left with completely pure air. There may be things you can't control—wall-to-wall carpeting your landlord put in, a truck idling outside your window, a neighbor who smokes—that send bad air into the baby's room. So minimizing exposure to the items you *can* control is important.

AIR QUALITY

Unfortunately, there is no simple way to monitor the air quality in a bedroom. But you can open your windows frequently to get an air exchange, including in winter, and especially after a long sleep when the air is stale. Even in urban environments, the outdoor air is purer than the indoor air. You can filter the air if you have reason to suspect it needs it, or if your child has allergies (see "Clearing the Air"). Don't forget to change the filters according to manufacturer instructions, clean air conditioner filters regularly, and wash window screens every spring. If your kid has allergies and there's a family pet, banish Rover from your child's room, especially overnight.

HUMIDITY

If you have a very dry room or a kid with itchy, dry skin (which is no fun at bedtime), you may want to humidify. If you use a humidifier, clean it frequently to prevent mold growth. Use vinegar or peroxide, not chlorine, because its residue will mist into the air you breathe. Some humidifiers contain a nanosilver technology that prevents mold and bacteria growth in the water tank, eliminating the need for cleaning products. Unfortunately, nanosilver is harmful to aquatic life if and when it gets into waterways via a landfill. Do not overhumidify: a too-moist environment can produce mold. If a room is particularly damp, you may want to add a dehumidifier to inhibit mold

from growing and dust mites from thriving. These microscopic pests (500 can live in one gram of dust) eat dead human skin and trigger allergies and asthma. Bedroom humidity should be kept below 50 percent (you can use a digital hygrometer to measure this).

Clearing the Air

Source control and improving ventilation go a long way to purifying air. There are basically two types of air pollutants in a bedroom: gas and particulate. Gas is mainly VOCs from things like fragrance, paint, flexible plastics, and furniture. Particulates include dust, soot, pet dander, smoke, pollen, and mold, and can trigger asthma and allergies. HEPA air purifiers are your best choice to help with particulates. Avoid ozone filters; ozone is a lung irritant even at low levels. Always choose a filter that matches the space you need it to purify. Running it in the room with the door shut will increase its efficacy. For more information, visit epa.gov/iaq.

Smells From Neighbors

It's a strange moment when you get a whiff of smoke or a jolt of perfume in your child's bedroom. Maybe it's from his or her clothing? Or the fragrance ads in a magazine? If you live in a multi-unit building and you're sharing common air ducts, a more likely explanation is that it's coming from a neighbor. If the smell is really strong, you can try to appeal to your neighbors, then, if there's no response, to your landlord or management company. Or try to solve the problem. Seal up any visible cracks. If cigarette smoke is coming from a common shaft, set up a fan to blow it back. And don't let anyone smoke inside your home, near your child, or outside near an open window.

Food

For babies, breast is best. Yes, there are many women who cannot breast-feed—adoptive moms, breast cancer survivors, and mothers who don't want to. But for those who can, there's just no doubt in any of the scientific literature that breast milk is the healthiest option for any baby. Even the American Academy of Pediatrics suggests nursing for a full year and beyond. The rub here is that all breast milk, thanks to the environmental contaminants that swirl around us constantly, is now polluted. It can contain PBDEs, PCBs, traces of rocket fuel, dry-cleaning fluids, conventional cleaning-product chemicals, and other contaminants. Even so, breast-feeding is still the best and safest choice, as it bolsters a baby's immune system. It is medicine generated by a mother specifically for her baby—an amazing thing.

BOTTLE-FEEDING

If you're pumping your breast milk to bottle-feed, or if you're using formula, the safest bottles you can use are shatterproof glass—it's as inert a material as you'll find. If you're concerned about shatterproof glass breaking (it can, infrequently), slip the bottles into a silicone sleeve or a drop guard. Stainless steel baby bottles are also a good, safe, shatterproof option. If you insist on using plastic, keep in mind that there is currently no one regulating the claim "BPA-free" on any product. For information on the hormone-disrupting chemical bisphenol-A, see page 44. Safer plastics that can be used repeatedly and should be BPA-free include #2, #4, and #5 (see page 42). Avoid polycarbonate plastic (#7), which contains BPA. Choose a plastic that can be recycled in your municipality, if possible. Bottle nipples should be made of clear silicone (latex can cause allergic reactions and, according to the Environmental Working Group, can contain impurities linked to cancer). Discard them when they become thin, discolored, or ripped. Care for your bottles well and replace them when they start to show signs of wear and tear. Never heat a bottle in a microwave. Instead, place it in a bowl of warm water.

SCRUB WELL

Between uses, bottles should be washed in hot water and mild, natural dish soap, then rinsed well. Glass and stainless steel bottles can be washed in the dishwasher, with phosphate- and chlorine-free detergent.

PACIFIERS

Pacifiers should be entirely silicone. Avoid ones with hard plastic unless you can easily find out what the plastic is (this isn't always obvious). There are also one-piece natural rubber pacifiers on the market. This rubber isn't synthetic; it's harvested from rubber trees.

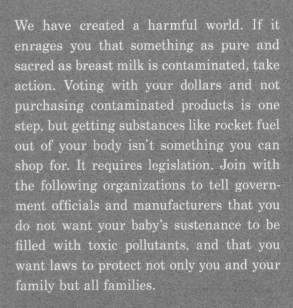

Take Action

We have created a harmful world. If it enrages you that something as pure and sacred as breast milk is contaminated, take action. Voting with your dollars and not purchasing contaminated products is one step, but getting substances like rocket fuel out of your body isn't something you can shop for. It requires legislation. Join with the following organizations to tell government officials and manufacturers that you do not want your baby's sustenance to be filled with toxic pollutants, and that you want laws to protect not only you and your family but all families.

* Center for Health, Environment and Justice: *chej.org*

* Environmental Working Group: *ewg.org*

* Healthy Child Healthy World: *healthychild.org*

* Making Our Milk Safe (MOMS): *safemilk.org*

* Natural Resources Defense Council: *nrdc.org*

* Safer Chemicals, Healthy Families: *saferchemicals.org*

Pump It Up

Some women use a hand pump; others prefer pricier electronic versions. It's eco-friendly to purchase one secondhand, take one as a hand-me-down, or pass one on after using, but it isn't advisable, according to the FDA (and most pump manufacturers). Home pumps are considered "single-user" items. Although pump parts can be cleaned, milk or blood (from cracked nipples) can potentially back up into the mechanism, and both could harbor bacteria. A better option is to rent a hospital-grade pump—which has barriers that prevent any buildup in the mechanism—and buy your own PVC- and BPA-free parts.

FORMULA

If you're formula-feeding, powdered is safer than liquid. Cans of liquid have liners that may contain the hormone-disrupting chemical BPA. And always choose organic. Mix the powder with filtered tap water. Tap water may contain fluoride, and even the American Dental Association doesn't suggest using fluoridated water for baby formula. Some filters, like reverse osmosis ones, remove more fluoride than others (see page 317).

SOLID FOOD

When your baby starts eating solids, use fresh, preferably local, organic food, rather than jarred or canned food. Making it yourself can be time consuming, but don't underestimate the benefits. First foods are about nutrients and health, sure, but they're just as much about setting up a relationship with food and awakening little taste buds. Why feed them something you yourself wouldn't want to eat? Studies show that kids fed a wide variety of food early on—spices, green stuff, and all—are less likely to be picky eaters. Why not take babies food shopping? Involve them in the kitchen: show them the colors; let them play with things like carrot fronds. The easiest way of feeding babies fresh real food daily is to take a food mill and grind what you're eating. Check with your pediatrician regarding food allergies before, say, sharing a peanut sauce. Grinding your food is the beginning of the family meal. Your children will be cooking, adding to the conversation, and even clearing and wiping the table in no time (make sure they do that with a nontoxic cleaner). Some families find that prepping purees and freezing mini portions in ice trays saves time. If you do this, look for trays made of stainless steel or plastic ones that are clearly marked (#2, #4, and #5 are currently considered the safest). For more on plastics, see page 42.

BREAST-FEEDING RESOURCES

Even though it's natural, nursing isn't always easy. Get help if you need it. For information on lactation consultants, safe nipple creams, what medications you can take while nursing, and more, turn to these sites and books:

American Academy of Pediatrics: *aap.org/breastfeeding*

International Lactation Consultant Association: *ilca.org*

Kelly Mom Breastfeeding & Parenting: *kellymom.com*

La Leche League International: *llli.org*

Newman Breastfeeding Clinic and Institute: *drjacknewman.com*

Medications and Mothers' Milk, by Dr. Thomas W. Hale (and his website: *neonatal.ttuhsc.edu/lact*)

The Nursing Mother's Companion, by Kathleen Huggins

Sleep

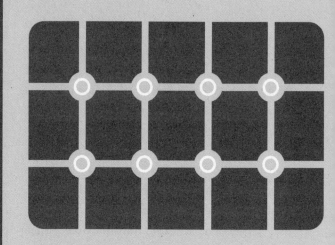

MATTRESSES

As discussed in Chapter 4, conventional mattresses are veritable clouds of questionable chemicals. Babies and children sleep more than adults—sometimes up to 18 hours a day—and are especially susceptible to toxic exposures. They should not be sleeping on conventional mattresses; even small doses of possibly carcinogenic PBDE flame retardants can affect developing bodies. Animal studies have shown PBDEs can harm brain, reproductive, immune, and nervous systems, as well as affect learning, memory, and behavior. They have also been linked to thyroid hormone disruption. Organic crib mattresses aren't always cheap, but some are only about $100 more than their conventional counterparts. If your budget is tight, cut back on items like toys or anything extraneous to make up the difference. If you can't afford a new organic mattress, or don't want to replace the crib mattress you already have, encase it (see page 100) to minimize exposure to chemical dust. One caveat: if you have a mattress from older siblings you want to reuse, it's preferable to replace it; not only might it contain toxic flame retardants, it may also be encased in vinyl to waterproof it. Vinyl, which contains hormone-disrupting phthalates, has been banned since 2009 in products for children under three years of age, as well as in toys produced for children under 12 years of age. For the safest waterproofing, avoid plastic altogether and opt for a wool "puddle pad." Lanolin in wool is naturally water resistant. Wool is also durable: a flat pad (i.e., not fitted) can grow with the child, transitioning to a single bed when the time comes. Sleeping on wool is also more comfortable and regulates body temperature better than plastic.

Sleep Systems

What's Lurking in That Lovie?

You go through the trouble and expense of creating a natural nursery. You lower your organic-cotton-swaddled bundle into a Greenguard-certified crib made of FSC-certified wood, outfitted with an organic crib mattress, a wool puddle pad, and an organic crib sheet. An air purifier whirs softly in the background. You change its filter religiously. Before you tiptoe out of the room, you drop a teddy bear, a present from a sweet neighbor, next to your baby in the hopes that it will become a favorite toy your child will reach for when she wakes up, instead of calling for you.

Hang on!

Do you know what's in the stuffed animal? Is it synthetic or natural material? Stuffed dolls, like mattresses, can contain flame retardants, and many of them are filled with plastic pellets of unknown origin. Some of them even smell strongly of off-gassing chemicals. You are the one introducing the lovie, not your two-month-old, so make sure whatever animal or baby blanket you place in the crib is as natural and untreated as the rest of the bedding. Also keep in mind that the safest crib is one with no stuffed toys (or pillows, quilts, blankets, or bumper pads); these can be suffocating hazards.

CRIBS

Cribs only get used for a few years, so it's tempting to accept a hand-me-down or buy one secondhand. But new safety features are added frequently, and older cribs often get recalled for a whole host of issues, including defective drop sides, slats, and hardware. If you're going the used route, make sure whatever you set up conforms to the latest Juvenile Products Manufacturers Association standards (jpma.org), that it hasn't been recalled by the U.S. Consumer Product Safety Commission (cpsc.gov), and try to find out as much as you can about its wood and finish.

If buying new, get the purest version you can afford. Beware of greenwashing; there are people claiming to sell "green" cribs that are actually finished with some nasty chemicals and are constructed with formaldehyde-filled composite woods. When buying a crib, look for:

* Hardwood, preferably local and made locally, with minimal or no composite wood, or for cribs with medium-density fiberboard with no formaldehyde added.

* Stains, paints, and finishes that don't include hazardous air pollutants. Water-based versions are best.

* An unfinished crib that you can finish yourself so you know what's being used—try beeswax. You can attempt to make your own or you can buy it. Read product labels, as not all store-bought beeswax is VOC-free, and

some even has "danger," "flammable," or "poison" warnings on it. Seal all composite wood parts with a product proven to reduce formaldehyde emissions, such as AFM Safecoat Safe Seal (AFMSafeCoat.com).

* Look for the few furniture brands that have received third-party certifications for their cribs from Forest Stewardship Council or Greenguard.

BEDDING AND PAJAMAS

Hand-me-down crib sheets are a solid option if they're made from natural fibers. If you're buying new, look for organic cotton or organic cotton flannel. They should fit tightly around the crib mattress. Blankets and pillows aren't recommended for young babies; they can obstruct breathing if one gets tangled in them. Until they get older, use sleep sacks—blanketlike bags with zip or snap fronts and armholes that babies can wear. These come in many materials, including organic cotton. Make sure any sleep sacks or pajamas don't contain flame retardants for the same reasons you want to avoid these chemicals in mattresses. Most fleece items do have these materials and are labeled "flame resistant" (read the fine print). Two alternatives to flame-retardant pajamas are ones made of fitted cotton (when the material is snug fitting, the flame-resistance requirement changes) or wool (which is naturally flame resistant). When children get old enough to sleep with pillows and blankets, use (organic) cotton and wool. Wool is a nursery and bedroom powerhouse: it's waterproof, resists mildew, and is a dust-mite deterrent. Hand-me-down blankets are great, provided they haven't been soaked in mothball fumes or dry-cleaning solution. Resist the pull of bamboo; as mentioned, it is an eco-friendly material, but not when made into a fabric.

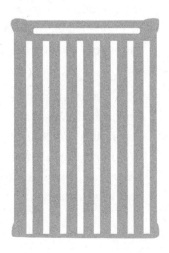

Materials Breakdown

Organic Cotton: Organic here means the same as with any other USDA-certified organic agricultural product: grown without chemical fertilizers or pesticides. Cotton is one of the largest and most heavily sprayed crops grown. Look for the USDA seal.

Organic Wool: USDA-certified organic wool comes from sheep raised without the use of synthetic hormones and on organic feed that wasn't grown with pesticides. You might also run into other wools that sound organic but might not be certified—like "pure grow wool" or "eco wool." Check out the manufacturer's website to see what the company philosophy is before purchasing. It may be from a growers' collective adhering to organic growing practices and following strict processing guidelines (cleaned and created without animal cruelty, bleaches, formaldehydes, or dyes) and well worth supporting, especially if the claims are backed up by third-party certification.

Natural Latex or Natural Rubber: This isn't plastic, but rather made from plants and rubber trees. It's naturally dust-mite resistant and antimicrobial. Most latex allergies have to do with the synthetic version, but natural latex allergies do occur. This material is usually "washed" to remove any allergens in it. The washing can involve any number of processes. If you're interested in purchasing something made of it, ask how it was washed.

CURTAINS

Some families hang blackout curtains to create a dark, womblike environment they believe to be conducive to sleep. Pay attention to materials. Some blackout curtains stink beyond belief—they're not considered children's products and are therefore often backed with light-blocking PVC. Better PVC- and plastic-free alternatives are available (see page 344 of the Resources). Seek them out. Or make your own, if you're crafty.

NIGHT-LIGHTS

Night-lights can chase away fears of darkness. There aren't CFLs small enough to fit in most night-lights, but there are plenty of LED versions. Choose these, and don't forget to turn them off during the day.

Diapers

There are a few ways to diaper a child, and all have varying degrees of safety and environmental impact. How you do it is ultimately a personal choice. If you're looking to narrow the field as you make your choice, how about knocking conventional disposables off your list? They're cheap and widely available, but they may emit VOCs and hormone-disrupting fragrance, and their manufacture involves chlorine. This leaves parents with one green choice—elimination control, meaning going mostly diaper-free from the get-go—and two semi-green choices—cloth or "eco" disposable. The NRDC says these two choices are six of one and a half dozen of the other.

CLOTH

Most environmentalists say cloth, hands down, is greener than eco-friendlier disposables. But not all cloth is created equal. If you're willing to use organic cotton diapers with wool (not plastic) covers, if the energy in your home is from a sustainable source, and if you plan on washing diapers in eco-detergent and line-drying them, then, yes, this is clearly greener than disposables. But if you're using a cloth diaper service that washes conventionally grown cotton diapers in copious amounts of very hot water and conventional detergent and bleach, then machine-dries them and drives them to you, *and* you use plastic diaper covers—you start getting into a gray area. Washing conventional cloth diapers at home means you have control over the detergent. But if you live in an area prone to drought, the water usage might be a deal breaker. And some day-care centers don't allow cloth diapers. Cloth can be cheaper in the long run, though the start-up costs are high.

ECO-DISPOSABLES

The other choice is so-called eco-friendly disposable diapers. A few companies make these, including Seventh Generation. Our wood pulp comes from certified sustainably managed forests, isn't processed with chlorine, and the diapers are fragrance- and latex-free. They fit well, and they're absorbent. We're always working to improve their sustainability, but all disposable diapers rely on man-made materials to deliver the high-level performance that parents expect of modern diapers. These materials are mostly petroleum-derived and are not renewable, which adversely affects the environmental footprint. And although they may not need to be washed, they're not reusable and they do sit in landfills. Don't wrap a diaper in a plastic bag before discarding—you're already throwing away enough plastic. And don't forget to empty waste into the toilet before trashing; human waste isn't allowed in a landfill.

The bottom line: we have two nonsustainable systems. If you have kids who sleep through the night, you might use cloth during the day and a more absorbent disposable at night to avoid having to wake them up and change them or laundering wet sheets daily. It's up to you.

WIPES

If you'd like to use packaged wipes, chlorine-free is best. Always read the ingredients before touching them to your baby's skin. It's remarkable how many unsafe chemicals are used in baby wipes. For infants, reusable cloths with a little water work just fine. Damp toilet paper or organic cotton balls do the trick, too.

Lotions, Potions, Soap, and More

Babies have beautiful skin. They do not need cosmetics. If a baby has a rash or a dry spot, you may want to put something on it. But until that moment, there is no need to put any lotion, cream, or ointment on a baby preventatively. If and when you're looking for something to dab on a spot, start with a little breast milk or some organic olive oil. One or both usually suffice. If you're going to use a store-bought product, make sure it is as pure as you can find. Baby skin is thinner than adult skin and can more easily absorb the chemicals these contain. Just because a product is formulated for babies or has been used for decades doesn't mean it is necessarily safe or devoid of petrochemical derivatives, artificial fragrances, mineral oils, formaldehyde, talc, alcohols, parabens, hard-to-pronounce things

Other People's Perfume

In the early weeks after baby is born, you might notice that the steady flow of well-wishers brings with it one unexpected consequence: your infant smells like them, long after they go home. While there isn't much you can do about one-time visitors (besides washing the baby and his or her blanket), you can delicately ask the constants in your life—nannies, grandparents, babysitters—to lay off the fragrance. Explain that babies have thin skin, small lungs, and vulnerable developing systems and that perfume and aftershave is too harsh to have around them day in and day out. If they're not convinced, cite your pediatrician for the household scent ban.

Sun

Sunshine is an excellent source of vitamin D, but we all know it's not great to get too much sun, especially for young skin. Babies under six months aren't supposed to wear sunscreen, and parents must work to keep them shaded. Once they're on the move, hats and clothing with SPF-rated fabric help. (Not all protective clothing is the real deal—look for brands that have been specifically recommended by dermatology and skin cancer groups.) When using sunscreen, look for nanoparticle-free mineral versions, which sit on top of the skin to do their job, rather than chemical ones that get absorbed into the skin (see page 222). One widely used sunscreen chemical, oxybenzone, has been linked to allergies, hormone disruption, and cell damage. This is a situation where what's good for the kids is good for parents, too.

like quaternium-15 or ethanolamines, and other unsavory substances. In 2009 Johnson & Johnson, maker of the iconic baby shampoo, was made to answer some tough questions by concerned parents after such known carcinogens as formaldehyde and 1,4-dioxane were detected in their infant products by the Campaign for Safe Cosmetics (safecosmetics.org). Choose only the safest USDA-certified organic or third-party-certified natural baby products you can locate via goodguide.com and cosmeticsdatabase.org. Keep in mind that a few truly safe third-party-certified natural-product manufacturers list their very natural fragrances in ingredient lists as "fragrance,"

which means they get low scores in the Environmental Working Group–run database. "Fragrance" usually signifies a phthalate-containing synthetic.

When it comes to what products to use, less is more. Bar soap works as shampoo. Just because grandparents say they used baby powder for you and you're fine doesn't mean you should shake it on your infant. Fine powder can be a lung irritant. If you must, use (organic) cornstarch instead.

Other Furniture

BEDS, DRESSERS, AND DESKS

Choosing hardwood items over composite wood is a must to keep the level of formaldehyde in the air at a minimum. If you insist on having particleboard or pressed composite woods in the nursery, seal them to reduce levels. Pay attention to the finishes of bed frames, dressers, desks, and other pieces: if they're painted antiques, test them for lead, a dangerous neurotoxin that has no place in a child's everyday space.

CHANGING TABLES

Changing tables are great items to snag secondhand—you won't use them for more than a couple of years. Changing table pads, if secondhand, could be PVC-coated. Use a wool pad or a newer, non-PVC plastic version instead. You may not even need a piece of furniture solely dedicated to changing—babies can be changed on beds, floors, or anywhere, really.

ROCKERS

Glider rockers tend to be upholstered, so pay attention to whether the cushions are foam, and query the manufacturers about what flame retardants they contain. Encase the padding accordingly. If any upholstered item has exposed foam, especially if it is crumbling, get rid of it.

TOY BINS

Plastic is a tempting material to use in a kid's room, especially as bins for toys. Natural materials—wood, canvas, and even some metals—are preferable. If you have plastic, make sure you know what kind it is. Some, like vinyl, are not safe, especially in a child's room. If buying new, seek out plastic with recycled content.

Gear

There are a number of items you might wind up with over the years, from nursing pillows to strollers to car seats to rain boots of all shapes and sizes to sports equipment. All of these can be made of some fairly questionable materials, though not all are. Avoid anything with foam or flexible plastic, especially if they're hand-me-downs. Always check secondhand items on the U.S. Consumer Product Safety Commission's website (cpsc.gov) to make sure they haven't been recalled. If you're purchasing new, choose natural fabrics whenever you can find them: organic cotton over foam-filled baby carriers or synthetic slings. Look for strollers made with some recycled materials and PVC-free rain covers. Methodically minimizing exposure where you can is important, as there are some items, like car seats, that are an absolute necessity even if they're filled with brominated flame retardants. Any car seat is better than no car seat, but don't allow your child to nap in one when at home.

FLOORS

Your child's floor is best left bare. Padded play mats are tempting to break the falls of kids learning to walk, but they're almost always made of synthetic rubber that off-gasses into the room's air. Cotton rag rugs that can be thrown into the washing machine are ideal for kids' rooms. Wool rugs without backing are also a good, washable option. Choose natural latex skid pads rather than PVC or other plastic versions. If you have wall-to-wall carpeting in some rooms in your home, set the children up in a room that doesn't have it. Do not install new synthetic wall-to-wall carpeting with a glue adhesive. Avoid all rugs and carpets that are treated with stain repellents, mildew treatments, or other chemicals. Ask questions when you're shopping. Deep pile rugs—even pure-grow wool ones—aren't something you want in a kid's room, as they're dust-mite and pet-dander motels. And no matter what is on the floor, vacuum often with a machine containing a HEPA filter.

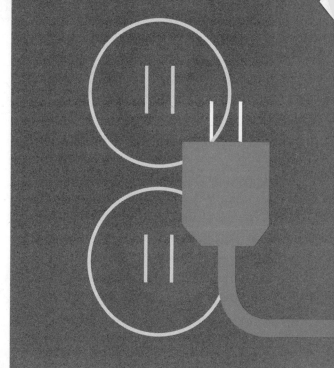

ELECTRONICS

Babies are surrounded by monitors, white-noise machines, infant soothers, electric mobiles, even movement sensor mats that lie flat between crib mattresses and sheets for parents concerned about SIDS. We should also be concerned about all of this electricity around growing systems. As discussed in the Bedroom chapter, since the scientific community isn't in agreement on whether electromagnetic fields can be harmful to health, moving these devices away from small heads and bodies—especially sleeping ones—seems like a safe measure to take.

CLOTHES, SHOES, AND COATS

Kids grow at a remarkable rate, which is why parents have long been interested in hand-me-downs and shopping at secondhand clothing stores, regardless of their environmental devotion. It saves money and is common sense to reuse something that might fit your child for only a few months. If you're buying new, seek out natural fibers and organic cotton. One widely quoted statistic is that it takes one-third of a pound of chemical pesticides to produce one conventional cotton T-shirt. Between spills, paint mishaps, the playground, and soccer practice, consider how many T-shirts your child might wear in even one day. Buying secondhand clothing or garments made of organic cotton means opting out of a system that furthers the destruction of the environment and harms the health of cotton field workers.

CLOTHING SWAP!

You may already be swapping items with your closest friends, but why not expand your options. Organize a clothing (and book and toy) swap in your community via a school, a parenting group, or the local playground. You can even charge a nominal entrance fee and give the proceeds to a local charity. Any leftovers at the end of the day can be donated to a group that collects gear for homeless families.

TOY SAFETY

It's infuriating and incongruous that toys are by and large unsafe. Many of them are manufactured with materials that, if found in a landfill, would be considered toxic waste. Thankfully, much attention has at long last been paid to toy safety over the past few years. Recall after recall of lead-tainted items from large mainstream toy companies—most of which have been manufactured in China—plus growing parent concern about environmental health has resulted in stricter regulations and new certification requirements. In 2009 certain phthalates—those hormone-disrupting chemicals linked to developmental disorders, cancer, and organ damage that are used to make PVC soft and flexible—were banned from toys for kids under a certain age. Despite this, some toys containing PVC remain on the market, and it's certainly present in old toys. Organizations like healthystuff.org continue to test and find unacceptable levels of hazardous chemicals beyond PVC (lead, cadmium, chlorine, arsenic, bromine, and mercury) in new toys. The writing is on the wall, and it appears that more restrictions will follow suit. Meanwhile, any toys purchased should be safe and free of these chemicals. This is a tall order and involves some guesswork as to what might be lurking in any given toy.

WOODEN TOYS

When children are very young and not yet asking for toys their friends have, parents would do well to stock a nursery with unpainted wooden toys, preferably from local and sustainably harvested trees.

TEETHING TOYS

Things like frozen celery or a stale bagel (when supervised) are far preferable to plastic teethers.

HAND-ME-DOWN TOYS

We all want to reuse by giving, lending, and receiving gently used kiddie gear, but hand-me-down toys are a mixed bag—some may have been recalled or contain recently banned or restricted chemicals. Check out the materials of any toy that has been handed down to your child. Avoid soft, flexible plastic or any plastic that is visibly deteriorating. If you suspect a toy might contain lead, test it with a home kit. When it comes to lead, no amount is okay.

NEW TOYS

When buying new, do research before leaving the house. If you're in a big toy store with an eager child, you will inevitably wind up with something that you wouldn't purchase if you had the time to make a thoughtful decision. Some good general rules of thumb are:

* Avoid plastic. If you'd like to have plastic toys, seek out ones made from polyethylene or polypropylene, both of which are nonchlorinated and not softened with phthalates.

* Avoid toys made in China and look for toys manufactured in Western Europe. The European Union has strong consumer-protection regulations. Toys made in the United States, especially local ones where you can speak with the people making them, are also good choices.

* Try to shop in small or boutique toy stores or their online counterparts. While there are no guarantees, smaller merchants tend to offer alternatives to the mass-market offerings that can be made of risky materials.

* Do not buy costume jewelry, which regularly tests positive for high levels of lead and cadmium, another toxic heavy metal that

has been showing up as a lead replacement. Make your own necklaces of wood beads and dried pasta instead. Or let kids play (carefully) with your real jewelry.

* Toys containing tiny magnets are unsafe. If two or more of these magnets are ingested, they can attract each other inside the body and twist organs.

* Avoid children's makeup, temporary tattoos, and nail polish, even when labeled nontoxic. This is not a regulated claim. And they rarely are—just smell their VOCs when you open the packaging and you'll know.

* When it comes to shopping for older children interested in electronics, consult Greenpeace's Guide to Greener Electronics (greenpeace.org) before purchasing.

TOY RESOURCES

GoodGuide: *goodguide.com*
Greenpeace: *greenpeace.org*
Healthy Stuff: *healthystuff.org*
U.S. PIRG: *uspirg.org*

While toy regulations are getting more organized, art supplies remain chemical-filled, largely unregulated, and very confusing for consumers. Many of them are labeled nontoxic, but this means next to nothing. Others say they conform to an ASTM (American Society for Testing and Materials) standard. This means that the ingredients were reviewed by a "qualified individual" who deemed the risk of harm to be sufficiently low. This person may or may not be a toxicologist and might even be on staff at the manufacturer, making this a weak and not very meaningful claim. Chemicals of concern when it comes to art supplies include those used to soften paints, solvents in markers, and heavy metals used in pigments. Other guidelines:

* Modeling clays tend to have very high levels of phthalates. Make your own play dough instead out of flour, water, oil, salt, and cream of tartar. It's simple, and recipes abound online. For color, use the water you boiled beets in or blueberry juice instead of a synthetic dye. There are USDA-certified organic natural food-grade dyes, which are also easy to find online.

* In the absence of meaningful third-party certification, look for supplies made with natural pigments and materials (i.e., opt for beeswax and soy wax rather than petroleum-derived paraffin wax).

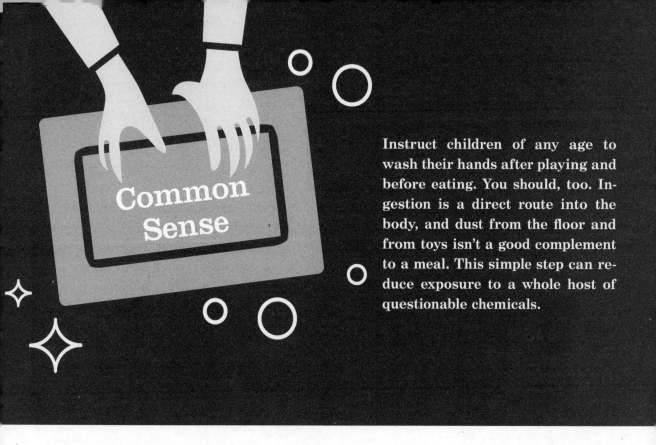

Common Sense

Instruct children of any age to wash their hands after playing and before eating. You should, too. Ingestion is a direct route into the body, and dust from the floor and from toys isn't a good complement to a meal. This simple step can reduce exposure to a whole host of questionable chemicals.

* Simpler is better (think crayons and pencils rather than markers).

* Avoid fragranced products.

* Carefully watch young children who might be tempted to put things like markers in their mouths.

* Always wash hands after making an art project, especially if paint and ink have gotten on the skin.

* If something smells strong and emits fumes—like permanent ink, rubber cement, and many paints—don't let your children use it.

Responsibility

One way to set up the concept of general responsibility at home is by getting kids involved with chores at an early age. A child can spray vinegar and water and clean a glass table, or clear their plates, or help fold the laundry. Try not to give chores that lack purpose or feel disciplinary. If you're asking children to weed the garden, help them connect to the value and importance of what they're doing in the scheme of things (e.g., they're helping the plants flourish so there will be food, and without the use of chemicals that would linger on the vegetables and harm the earth). Children are great recyclers and often enjoy helping compost, especially with worms. Another great teachable area is allowance. Say a kid gets $15: suggest he or she saves $5, spends $5, and gives $5 away. This simple device builds an invaluable consciousness about money and starts a conversation about what it means to give to others.

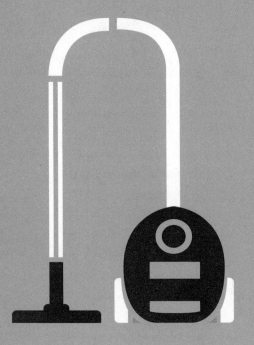

Cleaning

VACUUM

Do this at least once a week with a vacuum cleaner containing a HEPA filter. In addition to the rugs and floors, vacuum mattresses, pillows, curtains, and under the beds.

DUST

Use a wet rag to dust weekly, paying attention to bookshelves, toy bins, windowsills, and corners where dust tends to collect.

BEDDING

Wash sheets weekly in a mild, eco-friendly detergent. While hot water kills dust mites, use it only when necessary—for example, if your children are prone to asthma and allergies—as heating up water generates lots of CO_2. Mattress pads and pillow protectors should

be laundered frequently, especially if your kids have allergies. Blankets and pillows can be shaken outdoors—just make sure you're upwind. Machine-wash blankets according to manufacturer instructions every few months or when you know you need to. Pillows should be cleaned at least once a year.

LAUNDERING CLOTHES

Fragrance-free detergent is best for young skin. Hand-me-down clothes may smell of fragranced detergents. Washing them in eco-detergent and line-drying them in the sun should help air them out. Washing any new garment before letting your baby wear it is prudent to remove manufacturing residues.

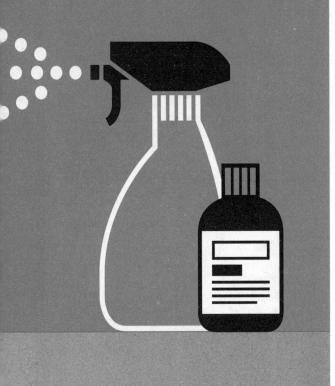

RUGS

Throw cotton rag rugs in the washing machine with eco-detergent when and if they look like they need it, or at least as often as you clean your blankets.

DEEPER CLEANING

Conventional cleaning products have no place in a kid's room. Choose a greener, safer, milder version to wipe all surfaces once a week. If the whole family comes down with a flu, or your kids bring home every germ under the sun

Let the Sunshine In

Sunshine kills dust mites. If you have access to outdoor space, drag wool blankets, pillows, and even the crib mattress outside to give them sunshine and air once in a while. Line-dry clothing, cloth diapers, and everything in between. (See pages 264–265 for more on line-drying.)

from school, you can disinfect with a hydrogen-peroxide-based cleaner (don't forget the doorknobs) or with a thyme-based EPA-registered disinfectant, which kills 99.9 percent of germs.

TOYS

Playthings can and should be cleaned in a soap-and-water solution from time to time. This works for wood, too—just don't let it soak, and dry well after washing. Usually that and a little elbow grease is all that is needed. If you know you need a deeper cleaning, use vinegar or a hydrogen-peroxide-based cleaner.

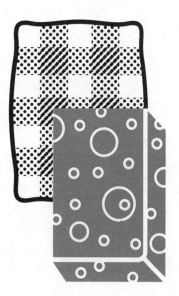

the
FAMILY ROOMS
Living Room, Dining Room, Media Room, and Den

The Conscious Ritual

The living room, dining room, media room, and den are places that draw the family together. Family life gets busy, so it's important to create rituals that ensure you all pause from the bustle to be a unit, whether it's taking a moment to watch the sunset every night, gathering around the dinner table for a family meal, or making popcorn for family movie night. Many times the mundane, when shared, can be wonderful.

The Conscious Components

A conscious family room is an open, welcoming space where people can connect and interact. It's an environment most of us think to hazard-proof and baby-proof—tucking TV wires out of tripping range, covering electrical sockets, and placing skid-proof mats under rugs. Some of us may even have tested old paint, especially around windows and doorjambs, for its lead content. But most of us haven't taken the time to further protect the air we're all breathing as we break bread together or gather to watch television or sit by the fire on a snowy night. Likewise, we probably haven't thought about protecting the family pet's health as well as our own (just think of the effects when our toddlers stroke the kitten after it's had a flea bath). Whether you're playing ping-pong or working out to a DVD as your kids play cards, your family space should be as free of harmful chemicals as possible.

Here's a handy checklist to help you remember the pieces that make up a conscious family room ⟶

☐ Hardwood antique or used furniture whenever possible

☐ Bare hardwood floors or floors covered in machine-washable natural fiber rugs

☐ Walls painted with no- or low-VOC paints

☐ Open windows for ventilation

☐ Rooms cleaned with natural products

☐ New furniture made of hardwood or eco-friendly upholstered pieces

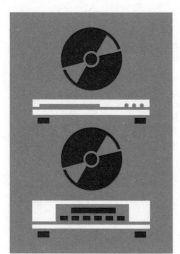

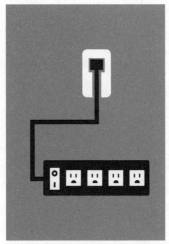

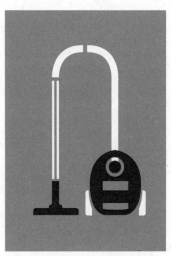

☐ Electronics like TVs, DVD and CD players, and computers chosen for their durability, recyclability, and efficiency

☐ Electronics plugged into a power strip that can be turned off when they are not in use

☐ Vacuum with a HEPA filter

THE ISSUES

The family rooms are a green-home litmus test. Think of all that is colliding in this space. One family room can include a kitchen, living room, media room, home office, utility room, and even a bedroom, if you live in a studio apartment or have a pull-out couch where guests regularly sleep. So every conscious concern that arises elsewhere in a house plays a role here, too. This is a great chance to test your eco-fluency and implement all you have learned so far. If you and your family spend most of your time daily in a shared room, changes you put into effect here will make a significant difference for both your personal health and the environment. Here's a quick reminder of advice given for other rooms, which you should also consider in a family room:

* Avoid renovations. But if you're sprucing up, paints, shellacs, and any floor resurfacing materials should be no- or low-VOC.

* Avoid buying new furniture. Hardwood antique furniture, including heirlooms, is lovely in a living room (provided it doesn't contain lead paint).

* Bare floors are best. If you'd like to cover the floors, do so with machine-washable natural-fiber rag rugs that aren't backed with glues or PVC plastic.

* Crumbling foam on upholstered items should be replaced, and any new foam-filled chairs, sofas, pillows, and cushions should be devoid of the worst chemical flame retardants.

* Precautions should be taken when using a fireplace, cooking, or burning candles; they all contribute to air pollution. Pay close attention to the materials you're burning and always ventilate well.

* The space should be vacuumed frequently with a machine containing a HEPA filter, wet-dusted often, and cleaned only with eco- and human-friendly products.

* Electronics (televisions, video game consoles, CD players, kitchen appliances, and home office equipment) should be chosen for their durability, recyclability, and energy efficiency.

* A few things that are unique to the family room include exercise gear as well as pets. Even if you have the workout gear stashed away in the basement and the animal wanders the house, eventually all things and beings in any home make their way to the shared family spaces. Both present potential hazards worth considering.

Air Quality

DUST

Modern, energy-efficient houses tend to lack fresh air. They're sealed tight to keep hot or cold air in, depending on the season. At the same time, we're filling these sealed homes with a whole host of fumes, from cleaning products, and the chemicals in furniture and fabrics, to those from weatherproofing, caulks, paints, and stains. The resulting mix we're breathing isn't completely safe.

Family rooms tend to house a fair amount of upholstered furniture, which likely contains foam to make it soft and comfortable. The foam is probably saturated with flame retardants, which release into the air as dust particles. These rooms also tend to house electronics, which, because they can heat up to high temperatures and are encased in flammable plastic, are similarly filled with flame retardants. Dust both comes from and accumulates on TVs and computers, where it can easily come off on your hands. Shared rooms are also high traffic spaces, and the floors can be quite dirty, especially if your house doesn't have a no-shoes-inside policy (see page 119). For all of these reasons and more, the dust cocktail in the family room can be quite toxic. Most of the chemicals found in any living room are the exact ones found in bodies via biomonitoring blood tests.

While it is impossible to avoid dust altogether (PBDE dust from an old couch, for example, will remain in your living space for a long time after the couch is removed), there are ways to minimize your exposure to it—ventilating, vacuuming, and wet-dusting. Do this carefully and frequently, since your family rooms are where you and your children may spend a lot of time.

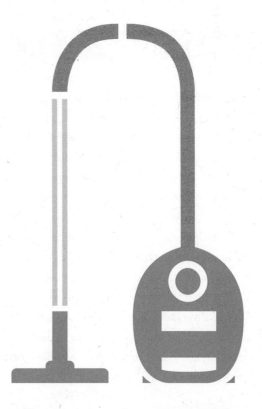

FIREPLACES

Wood is a renewable resource, but not all of it is created equal: some is sustainably grown and harvested, some isn't. And burning any wood adds carbon monoxide and particulates to the air and generally pollutes. The components in wood smoke are similar to cigarette smoke—it contains known and suspected carcinogens like formaldehyde, carbon monoxide, sulfur dioxide, polycyclic aromatic hydrocarbons, and may even contain dioxins. It can increase the risk of lung infections and harm developing children. Fireplaces can also be a significant cause of outdoor air pollution; burning wood releases all the pollutants described above into our neighborhoods and beyond.

At this point in time, most of us use traditional wood fireplaces because they're pretty, dramatic, and relaxing, but as a method for actually warming a home, they're extremely inefficient. That said, there are some advanced combustion fireplace and EPA-approved woodstoves on the market that reduce smoke and pollutants, and you can also retrofit your traditional fireplace to make it safer and more efficient. If you have a fireplace, either don't use it, use it only on special occasions, or upgrade it. Make sure to clean out the ashes and have the chimney checked regularly for buildup that could lead to a chimney fire.

Fireplace Safety

* Crack open a window whenever you're having a fire to help ventilate the room.

* Install a carbon monoxide detector close to the fireplace.

* If you prefer artificial fire logs to wood, use an environmentally friendly version. The conventional products burn especially dirty and may contain petroleum-derived wax, among other things you don't want to be breathing.

* If you burn candles instead of wood in your fireplace, keep in mind these also add to air pollution. Always choose synthetic- and fragrance-free natural versions with metal-free wicks.

* For more information, check out epa.gov/burnwise.

Renovations

High-traffic rooms get a lot of wear and tear. Maybe someone zoomed into the baseboard on a scooter a few too many times on a rainy day, chipping paint and possibly even putting a hole in the wall. Perhaps other small people—or four-legged friends—tore, stained, or otherwise ruined a couch. Or after years of guests and use, the wood floor is scuffed and dulled to a point you deem unacceptable. Whatever needs redoing, it's far better to fix than to demolish, remove, and start over from scratch. For touch-ups, or if you do pull the room apart, be sure to source the greenest materials you can find— ones that won't off-gas hazardous chemicals into the environment and that are safe for you and your family. And don't forget to reuse any of the old gutted materials if possible.

PAINT, LEAD, AND PRECAUTIONS

The paint on your walls presents a myriad of potential health and environmental hazards. If your home was built before the mid-1970s, it is likely to have paint containing durable, moisture-resistant lead pigment—usually under layers of newer coats of paint. Lead may be naturally occurring and versatile for a whole host of uses, but environmental health experts say no amount of it—no matter how small—is safe. It wreaks havoc on the youngest among us, but isn't great for adult bodies, either. Lead sticks around in our systems for years after we're first exposed to it. It's now banned from new house paint but can still be found in the dust created during the demolition and renovations of older houses. Paint chipped through wear and tear or just age also gets into dust and can remain in homes for years. Children crawl through it, then put their hands in their mouths, and pets doze on and otherwise roll around in it.

If you live in an older home with chipping paint or windows and doorjambs that look worn, use a home test to check for the presence of lead. These aren't 100 percent accurate, so if you're renovating rather than just painting,

you may want to call in a professional to do an assessment. If the swab is positive, take steps to repair or remove the paint. Usually all you need to do is paint over it with an unleaded product, although this isn't a long-term solution. A professional inspector can help with that decision, too. For more information, head over to EPA.gov/lead.

New paint may be lead-free, but unfortunately it might contain formaldehyde, benzene, ammonia, toluene, and xylene. Some of these VOCs are worse than others, but across the board these are neurotoxins and have been linked to cancers. They serve different purposes in

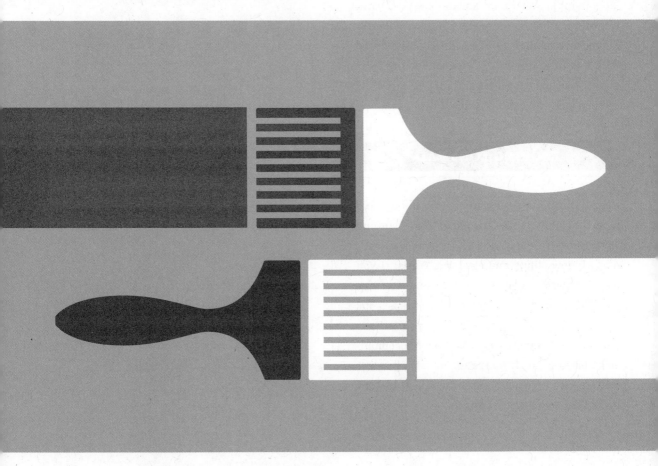

paint, but generally speaking VOCs are useful because they evaporate to aid drying. It's an absolute must to use no-VOC paint. These are now widely available (caveat: they will take longer to dry). Always read the fine print on what "no" actually means in any particular paint you're considering buying; oddly, some no-VOC products do contain VOCs. The best are petrochemical-, preservative-, and biocide-free. In homes where moisture and mildew are problems, homeowners may want a paint that can help minimize them. Be especially careful when shopping for these; the oil-based ones tend to be very high in VOCs. A low-VOC water-based latex paint is preferable. No- and low-VOC paint is not only better for your family, it's better for the environment. But even if you've painted with a natural product, it's a good idea to clear out of your home for a few days if you can while the product dries and any smell dissipates.

LOOKING FOR LEAD

Lead can also be found in common household items including toys, the pipes our drinking water flows through, and items made of PVC, like window blinds and electrical cords. If you have a choice, choose lead-free versions of any household products. And always wash your hands before eating, especially if you've been plugging and unplugging cords or on a computer before a meal. If you're unsure if a product contains lead, you can purchase a lead test kit to test for lead on any surface.

REDUCE VOCs

Paints, stains, and other coatings, plus cleaning and personal care products, collectively are widely considered to be the second-largest source of VOC emissions, after automobiles. Do your part to reduce this number by only using no-VOC products.

A bare wood floor with an unbacked washable cotton rug is as good as it gets in any room in the home. But what if you want to resurface that floor? Stains can be as bad as conventional paints when it comes to high VOC levels. Just think of how powerful a newly refinished wood floor smells. There are better, greener products on the market that are safer for the family and the Earth. Choose these.

If you need to put in an entirely new floor, there are many eco-options, including bamboo, cork, sustainably grown or certified hardwood, natural linoleum, tile, and even "green" wall-to-wall carpets. All glues, underlayment, and related installation materials should be as eco-friendly as the new floors themselves. For ideas, check out greendepot.com or ecohaus.com. Take the time to make sure whatever you're introducing into your home is the safest version available. You'll be living with your decision for a long time to come. The fumes and emissions from stains, glues, and new materials can fill the entire house and stick around for years.

Furniture and Fabrics

REPAIRING AND REPLACING FURNITURE

Upholstered furniture, which is usually foam-filled, contains flame retardants just like conventional mattresses, unless there is some declaration to the contrary. A new sofa might have that sort of labeling, but there's no telling which kind of flame retardants an antique or a hand-me-down contains. If there is any exposed foam on your couch, it needs to be recovered. If said foam is crumbling, it should be replaced with a new, greener foam or an otherwise cushy material, then slipcovered or reupholstered as soon as possible. The flame-retardant-filled dust from the crumbling foam

is quite toxic and not something you want to be exposing the family to.

If you're not interested in repairing, slipcovering, or reupholstering what you already own and are going to buy a new couch, love seat, or upholstered chair, seek out items being sold as eco-friendly. Not all of these will be as green as they claim to be, but they're preferable to their conventional counterparts. Some companies are crafting pieces out of FSC-certified solid wood. Look for these. If you see something labeled Sustainable Forestry Initiative (SFI) certified, buyer beware; their standards aren't as credible. Other natural furniture materials that promote good air quality include cotton batting, wool fill, water-based glues, foams containing soy, natural latex, natural twine and webbing, recycled-content metal springs, plus free-range down and feathers. As with anything, how these are grown, extracted, processed, and manufactured can make them more or less pure.

New furniture containing these materials isn't only made by tiny collectives; some of the larger, well-known stores are now offering one or two eco-friendlier options. It's preferable to buy from the completely green companies if you have access to them. A so-called green couch can be pricey, but remember that an upholstered piece can last for decades. Choose the purest, most durable version you can afford. If you're short on cash but really want a pure and comfortable place to sit, a sustainable hardwood frame with a natural (foam-free) futon mattress is a wallet-friendly option.

FABRICS 101

What covers your sofa and chairs is as important as what lies beneath. Natural, biodegradable materials (like wool and organic cotton) colored with nontoxic heavy metal–free dyes are preferable to synthetic fabrics or heavily sprayed cotton. There are fabric-certification standards like Oeko-Tex 100 (www.oeko-tex .com) that shoppers can rely on to make the most conscious choices. Whatever fabric you choose, make sure it will hide stains and dirt well, and that it can be cleaned easily. Avoid materials that have been chemically stain-proofed, and just say no when a couch salesperson offers to throw in stain guarding as part of your deal. Some of these products contain the same perfluorinated chemicals used in nonstick pans (see page 39). As these are being phased out, new ones are now being made with silicones, among other things. These are better. But it's even better to not stain guard at all.

As for reupholstering, re-covering antique ottomans with eco-friendly fabric is the sort of DIY project anyone with a staple gun and a steady hand can attempt. To redo something more elaborate, look for an eco-reupholsterer, a small but growing breed. Or ask a conventional reupholsterer to use green materials for your project.

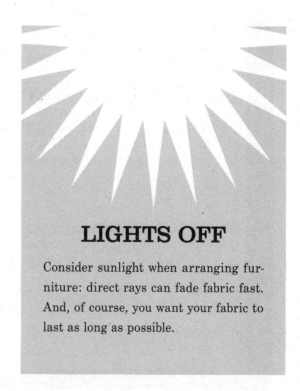

LIGHTS OFF

Consider sunlight when arranging furniture: direct rays can fade fabric fast. And, of course, you want your fabric to last as long as possible.

OUT WITH THE OLD

When upgrading a piece of furniture, make sure to give your old one a new life:

* Put it in another room of the house where it might still be useful, like a guest room.

* Donate it to the Salvation Army, Goodwill, or a similar organization.

* If you live in a busy city, put it out on the sidewalk where someone else might consider it a find. There are whole apartments that have been decorated with street finds. What you don't want is for it to wind up in a landfill or incinerated— think of the flame retardants that will be released into the air.

Media

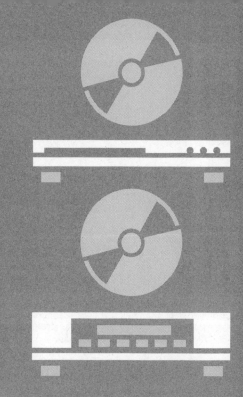

Some families choose not to watch any media at all, or at least ban it from the shared living spaces. Others only watch movies or shows recorded on DVR rather than live television. Still others love to gather to watch TV together or play video games. Gently monitoring, directing, and limiting what your young children do and don't see on television isn't a bad idea; the data is available—and quite damning—on the harmful effects of excessive media exposure. But this only works until a certain age. Once a child has unrestricted access to a television or computer, all bets are pretty much off. Anything can be seen online or on late-night TV.

If you'd prefer your children watch only a small amount of television, lay the foundation when they're young by stimulating interest and passion in other things: reading, hiking, playing instruments. If your kids are showing a keen interest in video games, try (re)introducing real games—chess, checkers, cards, and board games, as well as activities like ping-pong. And if you're looking for something to do together, why not turn on the radio or play a CD? Listening to music is a great activity to share.

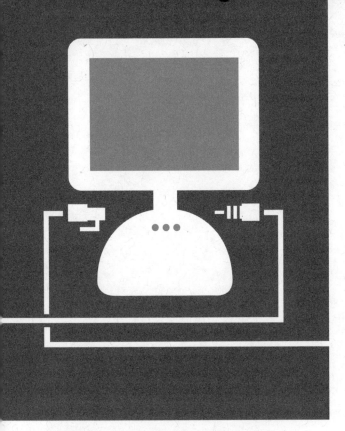

ELECTRONICS

Wherever your family falls along this to-TV-or-not-to-TV spectrum, your home will likely contain a television, plus a VCR or a DVD player, even if they're rarely used. And you probably have some sort of music system—a CD player, turntable, an MP3 player docking station, or all three—and speakers. Depending on what you have, these may be energy efficient or energy hogs. Electricity costs money, and people tend to only focus on their monthly bill. But remember also that coal needs to be burned to create most of that energy. Consuming less electricity directly affects air quality. So try these energy-saving techniques:

* With any TV, new or old, adjust the brightness to cut power use.

* Plug your CD player, TV, and all of its related gadgets (cable box, DVR, DVD) into a power strip. Switch this off whenever they're not in use. All plugged-in electronics draw a phantom load even when turned off, and remote-control-operated devices like TVs, VCRs, and DVDs draw more than most. This can be a considerable amount of wasted energy depending on your makes and models.

* If you're shopping for a new TV, projection screen, or any sort of media room electronic device, check out the equipment of interest on EnergyStar.gov; these products use about 30 percent less energy than standard units.

* Use common sense as you shop. Smaller LCD TVs consume the least amount of electricity, and giant plasma monsters, even if Energy Star rated, are the biggest energy consumers. The Energy Star site states that there are about 275 million TVs currently in use in the United States, consuming more than 50 billion kilowatt-hours of energy each year—or 4 percent of all households' electricity use. Buying a more-efficient model can help reduce that figure.

* Also check out cnet.com, consumerreports.org, and nrdc.org for "greener" and more energy-efficient TVs.

TUCK THE TV AWAY

Try placing the TV in an out-of-the-way spot, or at least house it in an armoire so it's not the focal point of the family room. This will also keep it out of direct sunlight, which can shorten its life span. If you have the space, put it in a separate media room.

GET OUTSIDE!

There's no need to spend all family time inside. Get outdoors together. The same sense of community you create at the dining room table or sitting around the living room can happen planting bulbs, raking leaves, or just wandering in the woods or urban parks. Establishing a relationship with the natural world early on will instill in kids a sense of empathy toward nature, which will make them want to protect the Earth later on in life.

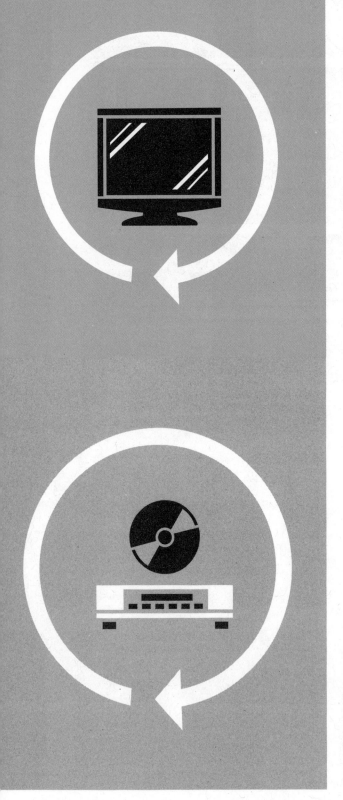

Many resources go into creating electronics. Keeping old versions for as long as you're willing to use them reduces both the consumption of these resources and e-waste. When you're truly through with an item, try to reuse before recycling. Move an unwanted VCR and your old VHS tape collection into a guest bedroom, where it might delight a visitor. Give your out-of-favor TV to a relative or friend who could use it, or donate it to an organization. If all else fails, take it to an electronics recycling event.

Whatever you do, make sure it doesn't wind up in a trash heap. Older CRT TVs contain lead and other toxic chemicals—not something we need more of in our landfills. The Electronics TakeBack Coalition (ElectronicsTakeBack.com) is a good resource for locating responsible recyclers in each state. Unfortunately, not all recyclers are trustworthy, and some don't handle your electronics as they claim they're going to. TakeBack maintains a list of TV companies with take-back programs. Earth911.com also helps connect conscious consumers to electronics recyclers.

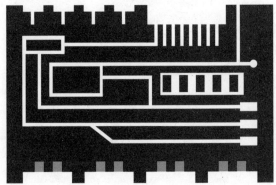

Working Out in Front of the TV:
Do You Know What's in Your Equipment?

Generally speaking, getting exercise outside is the best. But if the choice is between turning on a yoga DVD or a 30-minute "burn" tape while the kids do their homework nearby and not working out at all, there's clearly nothing wrong with stretching, kicking, or lifting weights in the living room. If your windows are open and allow for a nice air-exchanging breeze, and the couch nearby contains neither brominated flame retardants nor is treated with a toxic stain guard, then spreading a PVC yoga mat on your bare wood floors or lifting PVC-covered weights doesn't make much sense. Always consider what sports equipment is made of before bringing it into your home. Yoga mats can be found in natural rubber versions, and there are plenty of hand weights available that aren't encased in colorful, flexible plastic. Choose these, then resume your sit-ups.

Beyond the Basics: Pets

Greening your pet is a great idea for him or her, for the planet, and for all family members. Pet food made from conventional animals raises all the same red flags as human food. And dousing an animal in a conventional toxic flea bath or very fragrant shampoos isn't safe for the pet or the people it crawls into bed with. Give your pet the same natural care you give yourself.

PEST PROOFING

Dips, powders, sprays, and shampoos all contain pesticides to prevent or rid pets of fleas and ticks. But these nervous-system-disrupting poisons can harm animals and humans, too. For a more natural way of keeping your pet flea-free, add small amounts of brewer's yeast and garlic to its food. Some people repel fleas by rubbing fur with essential oils (like clove, citrus, or eucalyptus). Try applying one drop of lemon oil and one drop of rosemary oil on your pet's collar to repel fleas and ticks. Or put a few drops of one or more of these oils into the palms of your hands, rub hands together, and run fingers through your pet's fur around the neck and legs. You can also put 10 to 20 drops of essential oils in a dark-glass spray bottle with 2 cups of water and use it to mist your pet's fur, bed, and crate. Repeat weekly. Keep in mind that just because something is natural doesn't mean it's always safe. If you're considering using essential oils on your pet, check with your veterinarian first.

SLEEPING

If your dog or cat has been walking on city streets or across a neighbor's heavily sprayed lawn, you might want to wipe its paws before it curls up with your toddler. If your pet is dozing mainly on a pet bed or your couch, offer a foam-free spot—studies have shown that cats have high levels of PBDEs in their systems because they sit on couches filled with them all day long, then lick themselves clean. If the cat adores a specific upholstered chair, try placing a wool blanket over it as a barrier of sorts. Wall-to-wall carpeting, especially new, can be similarly dangerous. These surfaces are more harmful to pets than humans since they're spending so much time lying around on them.

Unwelcome Guests

If, come spring, your living room has more bugs than you'd like to see, convince them to leave in a nontoxic fashion. Pesticides have no place in the home. For a natural ant killer, mix 1 part Borax and 3 parts sugar (granulated or powdered) with enough water to give the mixture a soupy consistency. Pour the mixture into one or more containers with lids. Punch eight to ten holes in the lid(s) big enough for ants to access and place containers in infested areas. Caution: Keep out of reach of children and pets. Borax is harmful when ingested.

FOOD

Most pet food is made from the remnants of conventionally raised animals that weren't deemed fit for human consumption. It's the grimmest of the grim, full of questionable additives and chemicals. And the cans the wet food comes in are likely lined with the hormone-disrupting chemical BPA. We all know good food can help foster health. This pertains to pets, too. There are families who feed their cats and dogs raw organic or pastured meat, as well as other concoctions they cook at home.

If you're willing to do this, great; if not, an entire industry has sprung up offering ready-made organic or at least minimally processed pet food devoid of hormones, antibiotics, and anything genetically modified or overly artificial. Serve the food in stainless steel or glass, change the bowls often, and offer your pets the same filtered water the rest of the family drinks. If you've recently mopped the kitchen floor with a toxic cleaner or had a pesticide application, do not place your pet's water or food dish there. If you have a cat that goes outdoors and you have a garden, why not plant a (organic) catnip patch in a sunny spot? It will be like kitty heaven.

WASTE

Animals create waste. And their plastic-bagged waste clogs landfills, or, unbagged, can become runoff. There are some eco-friendlier ways of handling this conundrum. If you live in an urban environment that requires you to scoop your dog's poop, use newspaper or bags with recycled plastic content for the task, or ones that break down if you compost the waste. Don't compost pet waste anywhere near a vegetable garden, as it isn't safe to eat.

Cat owners should use unscented litters made from wheatgrass, pine, or recycled paper, some of which are even safe to flush, instead of highly fragranced clay varieties. Clay dust isn't great for feline or human lungs, and fragrances can linger on cats' fur, which is harmful for them and the people they cuddle with. Clumping litters should be avoided; they may cause digestive problems if swallowed. Ingestion happens frequently, as cats lick the litter off their paws when cleaning themselves.

TOYS AND GEAR

Just as it's dangerous for a baby to teethe on PVC, it's dangerous for a puppy, too. Offer your pets toys made from safe, sustainable materials. Look for recycled fiber leashes and collars. When animals get dirty, wash them with safe shampoos and soap.

Cleaning Your Family Room

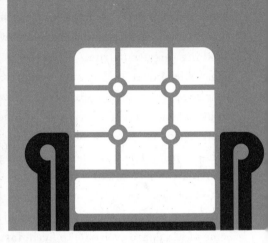

Vacuum with a machine containing a HEPA filter every few days or at least once a week in order to reduce dust and keep your living spaces clean and pest-free. Even if you did it yesterday, your bare feet will inevitably discover and pick up crumbs near the coffee table today. Vacuum all upholstered items with an attachment, as dust is constantly migrating from them. Flip and rotate cushions when you vacuum to evenly distribute wear and tear. Rugs should also be vacuumed weekly and washed when they need it. If you have carpet, there are likely years of accumulated dirt in it. You won't get rid of this by vacuuming, but you will minimize the new dust that has been generated since you last vacuumed.

WIPE-DOWNS

Wipe-downs are essential in the living room. A coffee table might require a daily wipe, especially if there is a spill or popcorn residue from movie night. Once a week, wet-dust all surfaces, especially those near open windows or where sticky hands might have lingered. For glass tables, spray natural glass cleaner or vinegar on newspaper and wipe. Use a damp cloth sprayed with natural furniture polish for wood items. Warm soapy water does wonders for just about everything else. Book spines and art frames can be wet-dusted weekly, too.

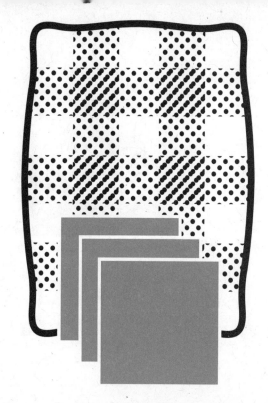

DUSTING ELECTRONICS

Dust particles cling to television screens; they generate static, which attracts it. Once a week, wet-dust screens and consoles with a soft cloth sprayed with a little all-purpose cleaner or warm soapy water. And don't allow small children to touch TV screens.

DEEP CLEANING

Every once in a while your couch or rug will need more than vacuuming and spot cleaning. Slipcovers and rugs can be sent out to a cleaner specializing in alternatives to dry cleaning (wet or CO_2 methods—see page 117). But chairs, sofas, and carpets should be steam cleaned. It is increasingly difficult to find someone who steam cleans without solvents and heavily fragranced detergents. Call around. If you cannot find a company that uses real steam rather than a mist of chemical water, try to locate one that uses, or is certified to use, low- or zero-VOC fragrance-free cleaners—or rent your own machine. Keep in mind that the dust you're vacuuming weekly is more hazardous to you and your family than the soils you're hoping to remove by steam cleaning.

COPING WITH PETS

Pets are hairy, their dander can trigger allergies, and they tend to be pretty dirty. Vacuum often to reduce the hair and dander that accumulates in your living spaces. Clean up muddy paw prints, hair balls, and other messes with natural cleaners. Warm soapy water will suffice. If your cat wanders onto the dining room table after a litter box visit, something stronger might be in order. Try an all-purpose cleaner containing hydrogen peroxide or a thyme-based disinfectant.

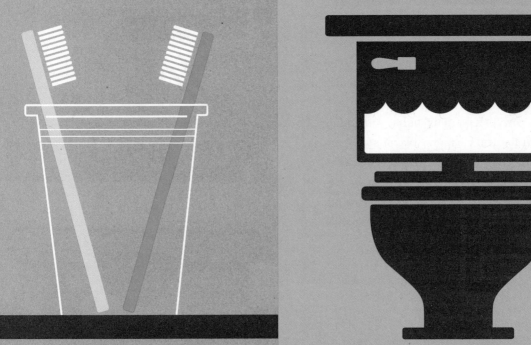

the
BATHROOM

The Conscious Ritual

The bathroom is tailor-made for conscious rituals, as it is already a place of daily rituals: it's where we brush our teeth and hair, wash and care for our bodies, and more. And there's much to appreciate here, especially the fresh, clean water filling your sink and tub. Water, which makes up more than 60 percent of our bodies, is as indispensable to life as the air we breathe, yet it's in limited supply.

Water is an essential communal resource that needs to be treated respectfully. What enters the drain isn't just going "down" or "away." It all winds up somewhere and, depending on what you're adding to the mix, has the potential to do harm. Certainly something to be mindful of as you rinse your face to greet the day.

The Conscious Components

It's probably a bit of a leap to think of your actions as part of a global ecosystem when you're in the most private place of the home: the bathroom. But even on the toilet, you're not alone, and everything you do matters. It may feel like this concept is being pushed a bit too far here, but hang on—take a quick peek around your bathroom and you'll see that this is undeniably true, from the residues that pour down our drains into our shared waterways, to the impact of our water use and the way our toilet paper is made. Keep the following components in mind for a healthier bathroom—and a healthier ecosystem.

Here's a handy checklist to help you remember the pieces that make up a conscious bathroom ➡

☐ Open windows for ventilation

☐ Retrofitted toilet that uses less water when flushed

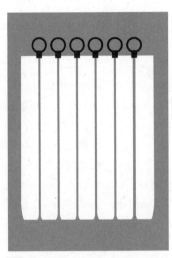
☐ A glass shower door, or a PVC-free shower curtain

☐ Carbon showerhead filter

☐ Small fan for windowless bathrooms to reduce moisture

☐ Green cleaning products, including hydrogen peroxide for minimizing mold

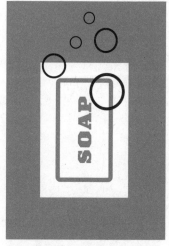

☐ Hand soap that doesn't contain antibacterial chemicals

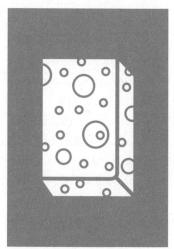

☐ Sponges and rags for cleaning instead of paper towels

☐ Postconsumer recycled toilet paper whitened without chlorine

☐ Dry and neatly stashed PVC-free bath toys

THE ISSUES

Most people think of germs—dirty toilets, filthy faucets—when they think of a bathroom. It's a room that instigates an unfettered desire to disinfect. But the most problematic issues in any bathroom are actually humidity and moisture, which can breed air-polluting mold, especially in an inadequately ventilated space. Air is necessary to dry up moisture, and most conventional cleaning products are supposed to be used in spaces with ample ventilation. Most bathrooms, however, are not sufficiently ventilated, so using eco-friendly products is especially important in reducing the potential harm of keeping your bathroom clean. Equally suspect are the conventional products we all use to clean our own bodies, and to hydrate them and style our hair post-bath.

Ventilation and Cleaners

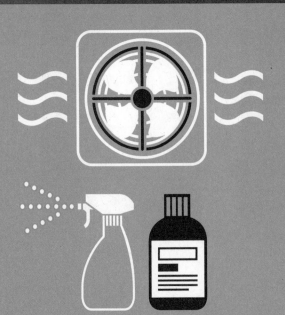

CLEANING SAFETY

Natural formulas are the only safe and conscious choice to clean any room, but this is especially true for the bathroom. That desire to disinfect what is perceived as icky and dirty means we tend to pile on the toxic products, using a wide array of conventional cleaners with chemicals that emit high levels of volatile organic compounds (VOCs) in an attempt to render tubs, toilets, and sinks sterile. Spraying cleaners with VOCs creates airborne particles and vapors that hang around in typically enclosed spaces where they cannot diffuse easily or become diluted. Breathing this heady cocktail of their relatively high concentrations can potentially damage your lungs, skin, and eyes whenever you're in the bathroom. Post-scrubbing residues also linger in or around the space well after the products have been used.

USING TRADITIONAL DISINFECTANTS IN SMALL SPACES

All traditional bathroom "disinfectants" are actually pesticides regulated by the Environmental Protection Agency. These are poisons and/or strong acids and solvents. Though most of their labels read "Use in well-ventilated areas," it's the rare consumer who reads these directions, and most warnings don't take into account that they're being squirted and spritzed in a five-by-seven-foot bathroom, and possibly one with no exterior ventilation. Even if an interior bathroom has a ventilation grate, it may just lead to a central duct with no actual ventilation. It therefore comes as no surprise that studies show hotel service workers who clean many bathrooms a day are exposed to chemicals in excess of the levels acceptable by the U.S. Department of Labor Occupational Safety & Health Administration (OSHA).

CONVENTIONAL DISINFECTANTS CAN HARM YOUR HEALTH

One in three cleaning products contains ingredients undisputedly known to cause harm to human health as well as contaminants that are known to negatively impact air and water quality. Data collected by Washington State demonstrates that 6 percent of janitors report a job-related injury from chemical exposure to cleaning products yearly.

Conventional cleaners also have the potential to damage and break down many of the surfaces in your bathroom, even extremely durable materials like porcelain and certain metals.

SAFE ALTERNATIVES

Just say no by avoiding the products altogether. Alternative cleaners derived from vegetable and other nontoxic sources are just as efficient as conventional cleaners. Hydrogen peroxide is known to either kill or disable just about anything you would need or want to in a bathroom. For a stronger natural cleaner that has been tested and proven to kill 99.99 percent of all types of germs, try a spray or wipe containing thymol, an EPA-registered botanical disinfectant. It's made from thyme.

OTHER INDOOR AIR POLLUTANTS

Besides cleaning products and mold spores, there are other materials and products in a bathroom that emit chemicals and contribute to indoor air pollution. This sounds like a setup for some bathroom humor, but unfortunately this is no joke—some are lung irritants, others are hormone disrupters. Be wary of vinyl shower curtains (see page 203), certain construction materials, synthetic perfumes in cosmetics and cleaners, and even your kitty litter. For felines, choose a natural, scent-free, preferably biodegradable non-clumping version—your nose, the cat, and the earth will thank you. (See page 178 for more pet care information.)

What Does That Warning Label Mean?

Traditional cleaners don't usually have ingredient lists on their bottles. If you truly cannot locate environmentally friendly cleaners or find yourself in need of something last minute in a store that doesn't stock them, use common sense. Always avoid products that have warning labels with skulls and crossbones on them or signal words such as "Danger," "Poison," and "Warning," which are used on product labels to describe the level of hazard of that product.

Cleaners that are labeled "Danger" or "Poison" are the highest in hazard and should be avoided. These warnings mean that the cleaner is highly toxic to humans, animals, and the environment, and may cause death or irreversible damage to eyes and skin.

Cleaners with the "Warning" label are lower in hazard, indicating they are slightly to moderately toxic if eaten, inhaled, or absorbed through the skin, and may cause minor skin and eye irritation. "Caution" represents the lowest level of concern.

Labels may include other safety warnings, such as "do not inhale"; "do not mix"; "avoid contact with skin, eyes, and clothing"; "use with gloves"; "wear safety glasses"; "use in areas with adequate ventilation"; and first aid responses should the product be swallowed, inhaled, or make contact with your skin or eyes.

Chemicals That Shouldn't Mix, Ever

Never mix ammonia with bleach. Because both chemicals are found in bathroom cleaners, they can cross paths, like when someone puts bleach in a toilet that is concurrently being scoured with a cleaner containing ammonia. When they do mix, the combination releases chloramine gas, a highly toxic and noxious material. There are several deaths a year as a result of this mistake. Also, never mix strong acids with bleach. Many toilet bowl cleaners contain strong acids. When they are mixed with chlorine bleach, they release chlorine gas. This also results in injuries and occasional deaths each year. One surefire way to avoid this: use products free of strong acids, ammonia, or bleach. And don't mix any conventional products ever; you never can tell what is in them or what the reactions might be.

Top 4

TOXIC CHEMICALS FOUND IN CONVENTIONAL BATHROOM CLEANERS

Traditional bathroom cleaners contain the most toxic chemical formulas of all household cleaners. Avoid—at all costs—products that contain (or are likely to contain) the following chemicals. You can read more about each of these chemicals in the Ingredients Guide on page 334.

1. Chlorine Bleach (found in household bleach and in products labeled "with bleach"): Household bleach is the most common cleaner accidentally swallowed by children. If it's mixed with ammonia- or acid-based cleaners (including vinegar), the combination releases highly toxic chloramine gas.

2. Glycol Ethers, like Butoxyethanol (found in all-purpose cleaners, glass cleaners, spray cleaners, and scouring powders): Some glycol ethers are reproductive- and neuro-toxins. They produce harmful VOCs, some of which are listed as Hazardous Air Pollutants by the EPA.

3. Triclosan (found in disinfectants, antibacterial hand soaps, and detergents): Triclosan is a synthetic antibacterial agent. It is non-biodegradable, irritating to the eyes and skin, highly toxic to aquatic life, known to accumulate in the breast milk of women and in the tissues of animals, and alters hormone regulation in animals.

4. Synthetic Fragrances (found in deodorizers, air fresheners, and other synthetically scented products): These chemicals release odorous VOCs into the air, many of which are secondary air pollutants like benzenes, aldehydes, and phthalates. Most are hormone disruptors. They are irritating to the skin, eyes, and lungs and may cause headaches, nausea, or asthmalike symptoms. They are also non-biodegradable and toxic to fish and animals.

Ventilation and Mold

AIRFLOW AND MOLD

Airflow impacts the presence of moisture in any given room. Bathrooms are hotbeds of moisture: they're small, filled with water and mist, and often poorly ventilated. Without adequate ventilation, moisture sticks around. This is a direct invitation for mold to grow. Mildew tends to be used generically to describe the musty odor that comes from mold growing in an overly moist room or area ("It smells mildew-y"). Technically, mildew refers to certain specific strains of mold, including some found in bathrooms lacking proper ventilation.

HOW DOES MOLD GROW?

Mold grows by the generation of spores, which are submicron particles carrying the genetic information needed for more mold to grow. It propagates like bunnies. Beyond being unsightly—darkened tub grout isn't pretty—some mold spores (but not all) can cause or trigger respiratory illness and even skin infections.

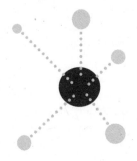

WHICH MOLD IS BAD FOR YOU?

The problem is that it's very hard to know which mold is bad for you and which is unsightly but safe. Unfortunately, the layperson can't easily make this distinction. That said, it isn't necessary to call in an expert the minute you see a bit of mold forming on the shower walls. The truly toxic versions are rare. Just reduce potential harm by taking simple steps to keep your bathroom drier (see pages 198–199). This will prevent the bad stuff from growing. Spores—safe or unsafe—will not progress to become mold on dry surfaces. It's a convenient cycle: if you don't have problems with mold, you'll never have the urge to reach for a harsh chemical to combat it in the first place.

Coming to Terms with Germs

Even with all of this talk about germs, don't immediately reach for a harsh chemical disinfectant. Remember that most of what surrounds us—including germs, bacteria, moisture, and mold—is perfectly safe. Our bodies have been exposed to these natural entities—some worse than others—for eons, and we have evolved and adapted to them. In some instances we have developed appropriate antibodies to protect ourselves against them; in other cases we live in symbiosis—our bodies host them, and in return they provide us with a variety of services necessary for our survival. Humans—like bathrooms—are not organisms in isolation. We are composed of 100 trillion cells, 90 percent of which are microorganisms living on and in us in harmony. These germs are far from bad—without them we could not live. We need them to help us to digest our food, generate nutrients, and fight off disease. Their balance is crucial to our health. This is why if we must take antibiotics, doctors might also prescribe probiotics, to maintain the equilibrium. Complete "sanitization" isn't possible or desirable.

Black Mold: What You Need to Know

There are many, many kinds of mold. As you eye your less-than-white grout suspiciously, it might be reassuring to know that there's a difference between the black or gray mold found in most showers and the far more uncommon toxic molds known to produce dangerous mycotoxins. These rare toxic-mold infestations tend to occur primarily on consistently moist material that contains cellulose (paper, wood, ceiling tile, etc.). The materials in showers and bathtubs typically do not contain cellulose, and therefore the dark-colored stuff growing on them isn't likely to be toxic. If you have black-colored mold growing on a material containing cellulose in your bathroom, especially if you've had a leak or water damage, it's prudent to test it. The EPA says mold sampling and analysis should be done by professionals. That said, there is a home test kit on the market approved by a leading respiratory hospital. Black mold can provoke severe reactions in people with allergies and isn't wise to have around people with other respiratory problems or growing lungs (i.e., kids).

LETTING THE AIR IN

While moisture reduction is simple, it's easier suggested than done in some bathrooms. Building codes only require interior bathrooms with no windows to have a small ventilation fan. And not all bathrooms are up to code—some have no ventilation at all. If you have sufficient ventilation, the surfaces in your bathroom will dry off relatively quickly post-shower. They should not stay wet day to day. If your surfaces remain moist or if you have leaks and visible pooling, it's time to take added steps to increase your ventilation and reduce moisture.

Even bathrooms with windows (aka exterior bathrooms) can have moisture issues. In winter, condensation can be found on windows. This rarely leads to mold but can cause cracking and peeling paint on the trim. This can be a serious problem if you have old paint containing lead. If your bathroom doesn't have a good moisture barrier, condensation can also form inside the wall.

YOUR BATHROOM WALLS

Paint and wallpaper do not protect against mold, and mold can certainly grow on wallpaper. If you're in the market for new paint or are considering putting up wallpaper, make sure either is specifically meant for use in high-moisture areas. (See page 345 of the Resources for suggestions.) And don't forget to double-check the materials they're made of—paint should have no (or low) VOCs. Avoid vinyl wallpapers; they contain phthalates and off-gas hormone-disrupting fumes.

THE GUNK THAT WON'T DISAPPEAR

Moisture problems are complex and usually take some engineering to resolve. If condensation isn't reduced through good ventilation—even by adding fans and wiping down walls and surfaces with a dry cloth post-shower—and you have very stubborn black gunk in your shower that seems to be coming from inside the walls, plus a strong musty, mildewy odor that concerns you, call in an expert set of eyes.

MILDEWCIDES

Yes, there are mildewcides available that promise to kill mold. But they typically contain a number of undesirable ingredients, including heavy metals—formerly mercury and now things like copper—that should be avoided. Look up the specific ingredients and the Material Safety Data Sheet (MSDS) of the product online before purchasing. A better option is to try using diluted natural essential oils, like tea tree or thyme. Hydrogen peroxide and thyme-based cleaners can also help eliminate mold.

10
WAYS TO REDUCE BATHROOM MOISTURE

Share this list with friends, family, neighbors, and colleagues who might not be aware of the potential hazards of a damp bathroom.

1. Shower with a window or door open and the exhaust fan on.

2. Take colder showers so the moisture doesn't condense as much on the walls. An added bonus: you'll save energy.

3. To prevent or reduce mold and/or mildew, wipe down the tub and walls with a dry cloth or a squeegee post-shower or -bath. Then hang the cloth to dry. Pay attention to horizontal surfaces and cracks—especially the spots where the bathtub and wall intersect—where moisture collects. Dry those areas a little more vigorously. An added bonus: wiping the tub will also remove hair, reducing the risk of clogs. It will also save you cleaning time later on.

4. Leave the shower door open post-use. If you have a shower curtain, make sure water doesn't remain in its folds. If you have a window in your shower, open it and leave the curtain closed. If you don't have a window, dry between the shower curtain folds, leave the curtain open long enough for the shower stall and tub to dry, then close it. It's easier to wash and remove mold from a curtain than it is from grout.

5. Check for leaks and fix them immediately (leaks can also waste thousands of gallons of water).

6. Clean up puddles and spills when they happen. Sitting water is a mold invitation.

7. If you have a toilet with a cold tank, check to make sure there is no moisture condensed on the tank, and if there is, make sure it isn't also dripping or pooling on the floor. This tends to happen in warmer, humid months. To combat this, try installing a toilet tank cover.

8. Wrap pipes with eco-friendly insulation if you see water condensing on or dripping off them.

9. Close the toilet lid before flushing to keep moisture droplets from spraying all over the bathroom (this also prevents the spread of bacteria those droplets might contain).

10. If you feel you don't have adequate ventilation, use a small fan to circulate the air and move it out of the bathroom.

Water

WATER FOR DRINKING

Before delving into how—and with what—to clean your bathroom, the issue of water must be tackled. It's pretty clear that water is a communal resource—not an individual one—but there are many personal health repercussions from water that has, say, high radon or lead levels. This is of particular concern in a kitchen, where cooking and most drinking water comes from. H_2O is addressed at greater length in Chapter 11. But it should be considered in a bathroom, too. And if you've ever lowered a baby into a tub of water you didn't feel entirely comfortable with, you already know why.

When it comes to the water in your bathroom, keep in mind that your exposure is pretty low. You don't actually swallow that much per day brushing your teeth or even taking vitamins and medicine. That said, unless you know your municipal or well water is safe, or you have a whole house filter, it's preferable to get your drinking water from a sink that has a filter (see page 316) or to install one in your bathroom.

WATER FOR BATHING

When bathing in unfiltered water, people infrequently develop skin rashes and even some respiratory irritation if their municipality chloraminates instead of chlorinates water to disinfect it. This means chlorine is used, followed by ammonia, which can produce small amounts of toxic chloramines. You can call your local government office to find out what your water is treated with.

WATER FILTERS

Charcoal filters placed on showerheads can help reduce your risk of inhaling vaporized disinfecting agents and whatever else might be in your water. The chlorine added to water becomes volatile when heated up and sprayed into the air during a shower. While the level of exposure here isn't huge, a showerhead filter does reduce levels of these volatile chemicals in a poorly ventilated bathroom, and it's simple to install one. Also, they're inexpensive and removable, which makes them an option for renters and owners alike. Absorption through the skin is less of an issue than exposure via drinking or inhaling vapors, so tub water is

typically unfiltered unless you have a whole house filter, which is a more complicated and expensive endeavor. If you have serious water concerns or aging pipes and you're bathing young children who, pound for pound, are more vulnerable to these chemicals than adults are, you may want to look into one.

WATER FOR CLEANING

Another concern when it comes to bathroom water is how it affects cleaning. Hard water is mineral heavy and tends to build up mineral deposits on tiles and porcelain surfaces, leading people to purchase more strident cleaning products they hope will wrest the deposits from their sight. Hard water also causes friction as you run your hand over your skin after washing. On the flip side, if water is very soft, it leaves skin feeling slippery. Soft water contains virtually no minerals at all.

CLEANING HARD WATER DEPOSITS

To combat hard-water deposits, some people with deep wells install water-softening systems to replace the calcium, iron, and magnesium with sodium. To remove deposits you may already have, try a natural tub and tile cleaner containing lactic or citric acid designed for that purpose, or vinegar (plus a considerable amount of elbow grease).

Materials and Maintenance

Construction materials can contain a whole host of chemicals you do not want off-gassing into your bathroom air, let alone the atmosphere. Glues, putties, grout, and more must be waterproof for use in a bathroom, but they can also be made with no or low VOCs. Check to see if they contain mildewcides or antibacterial agents, and avoid these if you have the choice. For the best possible versions, shop for these materials in stores that specialize in sourcing eco-friendly building materials (see page 36). If you do not have one near you, purchase online. Wherever you're buying, ask questions and read labels. You want products from manufacturers that willingly disclose "all" ingredients or that make their Material Safety Data Sheets easy to access on their websites.

TOWELS

The eco-friendliest towels are the ones you already own. But if you're in the market for something new, dye-free or eco-dyed organic cotton is a better option than bamboo. Bamboo, the green movement's fast-growing wonder plant, is actually very energy intensive to turn into fabric, which is too bad, because it's naturally antibacterial—a plus in a damp bathroom.

MATS

Bath mats with plastic backing may keep you from slipping but are often made of the worst possible plastics, which may even be infused with antimicrobial chemicals. Opt for mats without backing or search for ones that specifically say they're antibacterial- and PVC-free.

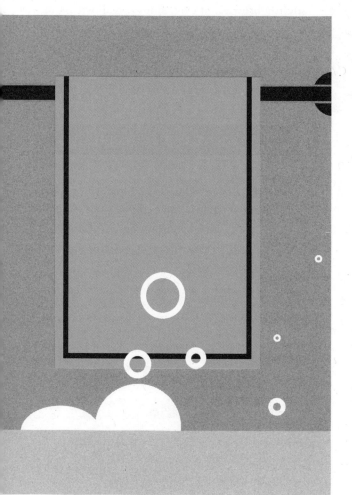

SHOWER CURTAINS

Speaking of worst possible plastics, that very familiar new-shower-curtain smell is actually PVC off-gassing toxic compounds like VOCs and phthalates into your bathroom. Vinyl shower curtains may also contain lead. While this is certainly of concern in a small, unventilated space, keep in mind that it's the communities with factories that manufacture PVC that report the highest health—not to mention environmental—toll. Thankfully there are alternatives. The safest would be to avoid curtains altogether and install a glass shower door. If this isn't possible, opt for a natural fiber like hemp. These do best in very well-ventilated bathrooms. If yours is not, or you live in a humid climate, choose a polyester curtain liner (preferably made from recycled plastic). Poly liners sometimes contain a small percentage of an antimicrobial chemical woven into their fabric. See if you can find one without. If not, this is still preferable to the plasticizers in vinyl. If you see mold starting to bloom on a fabric shower curtain, spray it with a peroxide cleaner or put it in the washing machine, adding $1/2$ cup of hydrogen peroxide along with your detergent. As for drying, if you can hang it outside, that's your best bet. Otherwise, line-dry in a well-ventilated room or tumble-dry in the dryer.

Bathroom Accessories

out of a plastic bottle. Just don't allow kids to chew on their bath toys, and avoid toys with drain holes—moisture always gets trapped inside them, making inviting little caves for mold to grow in. No matter what material your tub toys are, they should be towel-dried post-bath or lined up on the side of the tub until they're good and dry, then stored in a well-ventilated area so mold won't grow. Clean toys with soap and water and/or soak them in vinegar and water. If you already have a toy that seems a little grimy, or a wooden item that has turned slightly brown and even slimy, scrub with a little peroxide, then rinse. It will kill bacteria and mold but not the spores. Remember, though, that spores won't multiply on dry surfaces, so make sure the toys are thoroughly dried.

GROWN-UP BATH ACCESSORIES

Don't neglect grown-up bath accessories either. Exfoliating scrubbies, bath pillows, hairbrushes, and other items shouldn't be left damp and festering in the shower stall. The fewer accessories you use, the better—exfoliating, for example, can be done with a washcloth you can then dry.

GOT KIDS?

If you have children, grandchildren, or other kids in your life, take a moment to look at your tub toys. Are they moldy? What are they made of? Rubber duckies and the like should be safe and nontoxic, i.e., not PVC. In the market for new ones and not sure what's safe? Look up toys on healthystuff.org and goodguide.com. Unpainted hardwood boats float just as well as plastic and tend to be much safer. Parents looking to avoid questionable materials may worry about putting anything plastic in warm water, as high temperatures can cause plastics to leach their chemicals into surrounding water. Floating plastic toys in a lukewarm bath is actually less of a health concern than drinking

Bath Systems

Organic Baby Products and Chemical Disinfectants Don't Mix

Mothers and fathers tend to want the very best for their kids. Who can blame them? And in today's world, this means becoming self-educated citizen scientists on the lookout for BPA in baby bottles and can linings, and lead in birthday toys. The gateway to eco-parenting is typically organic food, and especially organic milk. From there, friends and articles usually tip parents off to hormone-disrupting chemicals lurking in sippy cups, food storage containers, and waterproof crib mattress barriers. Parents may even go so far as avoiding potentially harmful ingredients in creams and ointments slathered on babies by purchasing organic personal care products like those listed on page 345. But if you lower a child into a bathtub containing third-party-certified natural bubble bath with a high percentage of certified organic ingredients that was cleaned earlier that day with a conventional tub and tile disinfectant, all of that hard work and careful parenting is for naught. The chemical residue that is likely to end up on your child's skin will more than undo the benefits of using organic personal care products. Bathing is a system like everything else we do in our homes. Consider the whole of what you're doing, and don't let the system break down in the middle.

Pipes, Drains, and Toilets

If your sink or tub is clogged, do not resort to conventional chemical de-cloggers containing lye, which is toxic to you, plumbers, and waterways, and can even hurt your pipes. First, try to see if you can manually remove what's causing the backup with your hands. Or snake a wire clothes hanger down the drain to pull up the gooey mess that is the probable culprit. What you drag out will likely be black and gunky—a combination of mold, bacteria, and decomposing hair. Wash your hands after you're finished. Plungers can help if there is standing water. If you have a truly stubborn clog, try a product with natural enzymes and little else—read the ingredient list. These work slowly so are best used at night. Let them sit and finish the job in the morning.

ADOPT A CLOG-PREVENTION REGIMEN

Remember that prevention is always simpler than removing clogs, and keeping a drain clog-free means never having to resort to using a questionable chemical. Set up a regimen now to stop clogs before they happen. Place strainers in the drains. When wiping your tub daily to reduce the moisture, remember to remove hair and cosmetic residue before they have a chance to gum up the works. For added drain maintenance—once a month or so—try putting $1/2$ cup baking soda followed by $1/2$ cup vinegar down the drain. Allow this to foam up as it eats away at whatever might be in the drain, and then pour a few cups of boiling water to wash down the crud.

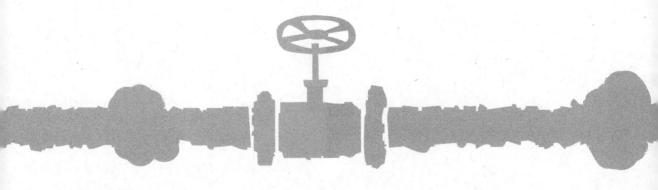

TOILET SPECIFICS

The toilet is one of the largest consumers of water in your house and presents a unique opportunity to conserve water. Older toilets may have 3.5-gallon or even 5-gallon tanks, whereas toilets made in the United States for home use after 1994 are required to consume 1.6 gallons or less per flush. Environmentalists flush them as little as possible, but even extremists should try to flush at least once daily (especially if said toilet has multiple users). One can go longer without causing any harm, of course, but the odor isn't great, and concentrated urine can stain. People who let yellow mellow may also find themselves battling clogs from time to time if too much of their 100 percent recycled, non-chlorine bleached toilet paper has accumulated. Keep an eye on the levels and flush before you reach a problematic clump. If you've got a clog, plunge it. Then clean your plunger by rotating it vigorously in a recently cleaned and flushed toilet. Store it where it can dry so it won't grow mold.

Odor Management

Don't use air fresheners or light any old candles to mask bathroom odors; there's no telling what they're made of, and more often than not they reek of phthalate-containing synthetic fragrance. Most candles are made of petroleum-derived wax and can even contain lead wicks—not the sort of smoke you want wafting into your breathing space. Beeswax and soy candles scented with organic or natural essential oils are preferable, especially if the soy isn't genetically modified, but the burning will still pollute the air. If you're going to light candles, do so infrequently, and make sure they have 100 percent cotton wicks.

You can concoct your own deodorizing spray by adding a few drops of your favorite essential oil to a few cups of water. Another way to disperse scent in a bathroom is to dab a few drops of organic essential oil on a light bulb. When you switch it on and the bulb heats up, it will diffuse into the bathroom. If what you're trying to mask is a musty or mildewy scent, pay attention to where it is coming from and work on ventilating and dehumidifying, not perfuming.

RETROFITTING YOUR TOILET

Another way to conserve water is to retrofit your toilet so it uses less water per flush. There are several ways of doing this, from the very DIY (put a brick or a water-filled half gallon plastic jug of water with its cap closed in the tank to physically reduce the amount of water being used) to more high-tech solutions (there are dual-flush toilet retrofitters you can purchase for less than $100—this gives you the option of a small flush for liquid waste or a full flush for solid). If you buy a dual-flush kit,

follow the manufacturer's installation instructions. If you're going the DIY route, be careful not to reduce the water level too much or the toilet won't work well and you might wind up flushing several times in a row to get the job done, defeating the purpose. If this happens to you, it's simple to fix: just use a smaller jug—like a one-liter soda bottle—or a brick. A little trial and error will get you what you need; this isn't an exact science, and much depends on the size of your tank.

SHOPPING FOR TOILETS

If you're in the market for a new toilet, choose a dual low-flush model—the liquid flush option usually uses 0.8 gallons of water. If you live in an area with chronic water shortages, you might consider replacing your current toilet with a low-flush model. This could be considered wasteful, but toilets are generally used for a long time, and they're not very hazardous in a landfill (though there might be some lead in that white finish).

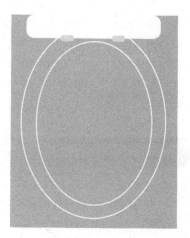

Toilet Paper

Toilet paper can be made from either virgin trees and then chlorine bleached—both environmentally destructive—or from dye- and fragrance-free post-consumer recycled paper whitened without chemicals containing chlorine. Chlorine is a highly toxic chemical and a widely used whitening agent that can irritate your lungs and eyes. In waterways, chlorine reacts with organic matter to produce a carcinogenic by-product. Amazing how something so seemingly innocuous—buying toilet paper—is actually a choice that affects the ecosystem of a house as well as the entire municipal system and beyond: dioxin from pulp mills using chlorine bleach circles the planet and has been found in the fatty tissue of polar bears. A good reminder that nothing exists in isolation.

Feminine Care

CHOOSING CONSCIOUSLY

Despite the fact that half the population menstruates monthly, not many women think about how feminine care products impact the environment and their own bodies. It's good common sense to choose tampons and pads made of certified organic cotton grown without pesticides and that has not been bleached with chlorine, dyed, or perfumed with fragrance.

CONVENTIONAL TAMPONS

According to the National Research Center for Women and Families, approximately 43 million women in the United States use tampons. And no one knows the cumulative health effect of using conventional feminine care products. While the boxes on most drugstore shelves aren't required to list ingredients, most tampons are cotton or a cotton-rayon blend with scent. Fragrance can contain hormone-disrupting chemicals and can also be irritating to skin, especially in such a delicate area.

Conventional cotton often comes from genetically modified seeds and has been sprayed with pesticides, which is bad for farmers and the environment. According to the Sustainable Cotton Project, cotton farming uses about 25 percent of the world's insecticides and more than 10 percent of the pesticides. These pesticides used on cotton happen to be among the world's worst: Five of the nine most commonly used have been identified as possible human carcinogens. Others are known to damage the nervous system and are suspected of disrupting the body's hormonal system.

Highly absorbent rayon is manufactured from wood pulp, a process that involves bleaching with chlorine-containing substances. The eventual product may contain chlorinated hydrocarbons as well as dioxin residues. Highly absorbent synthetic fibers can be a breeding ground for the bacteria that cause toxic shock syndrome. Although some synthetics have been banned, the FDA still allows the use of viscose rayon in certain amounts in tampons. Dr. Philip Tierno, author of *The Secret Life of Germs,* director of clinical microbiology and diagnostic immunology at the New York University Medical Center, and a leading expert on the health risks of tampons, says that rayon can still create a breeding ground for toxins. All-cotton tampons present the lowest risk.

BLEACHING

Chlorine is currently the predominant bleaching agent used in the manufacture of feminine care products. The bleaching process creates highly toxic dioxins, which are both released into the environment as a by-product and left in the product as a contaminant. In 1994, the Environmental Protection Agency declared that dioxins are known to cause cancer in animals and likely trigger the disease in humans. The EPA has also determined that people exposed to high levels of dioxins may be at risk for immune system damage, increased risk of pelvic inflammatory disease, and reduced fertility. Recent research has also linked dioxin exposure with an increased endometriosis risk. Given this, the EPA has declared that there is no acceptable level of exposure to dioxins and says the real dangers of dioxin exposure lie in repeated contact. Using approximately five tampons a day for about a week every month for some 40 years certainly constitutes repeated contact. Oddly, the FDA directly contradicts the EPA, saying that the low levels of dioxins found in conventional tampons pose no risk. Peter de-Fur, research associate professor with the Center for Environmental Studies at Virginia Commonwealth University, doesn't accept the FDA's position. He says that if "a sensitive area such as the endometrium is exposed to dioxin, there would be a near 100 percent absorption of the chemical. It is taken up, transported, and stored."

ORGANIC COTTON TAMPONS

The best tampon options are those made of dye- and fragrance-free organic cotton bleached with hydrogen peroxide, which is far safer than chlorine. Buying these over your

lifetime can make a difference to your health and the health of the planet. To locate a supplier near you, go to letstalkperiod.com. Most tampons and pads are individually wrapped to make them easier to carry around in a purse. If you're interested in reducing waste, choose applicator-free tampons.

REUSABLE OPTIONS

If you'd like to avoid anything disposable, you can buy a reusable menstrual cup, which is usually made of silicone or natural rubber, or washable pads.

SMALL CHANGE, BIG IMPACT

If every woman of menstruating age replaced one 16-count package of regular absorbency conventional cotton tampons with organic cotton ones, we could prevent 17,000 pounds of pesticides from polluting our rivers, lakes, and streams. For super absorbency, that number is 21,000 pounds of pesticides, and for super-plus, it goes up to 24,000 pounds.

Fixtures 101

MATERIALS

You may not have any control over the fixtures in your bathroom, but you should know what they're made of so you can care for them properly, and make them last. And if you're gearing up to renovate, choose only the greenest, safest, most durable materials. Most toilets are made from a mix of clays called vitreous china, and toilet seats are either plastic or a blend of wood and plastic. Sinks tend to be ceramic, vitreous china, glass, or a blend of acrylic polymers (though some old sinks are enameled steel or even stainless steel). Tubs can be cast iron or steel covered in porcelain, acrylic, or fiberglass. Shower stalls are usually fiberglass or acrylic, with tempered glass doors. Acrylic and fiberglass are the least desirable of these materials and should be avoided if you have a choice. Eco-friendly cleaning products can be used on any of these materials, and they won't cause acrylic or fiberglass to break down or off-gas their chemical components into your bathroom and beyond. Nor are they likely to damage the softer surfaces of acrylics or fiberglass. Interestingly, the best-known home-keeping experts agree with the eco-interested in not recommending the harshest chemical cleaners (or any abrasive sponges or tools) for bathrooms. These are extremely tough on the materials you want to keep looking their best.

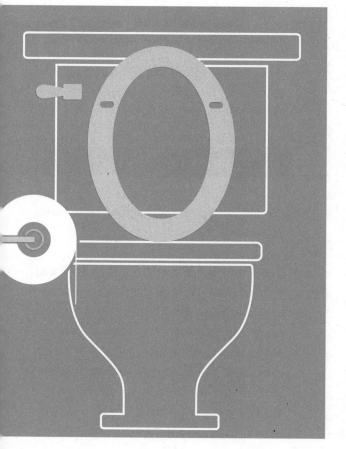

When things aren't looking their best, repair rather than replace whenever you can. Unfortunately this sometimes involves hazardous materials. Reglazing an old tub, for example, means spraying it with synthetic porcelain, a toxic, extremely stinky, and headache-producing experience for all involved—the repair person, the atmosphere, and you and yours. Green construction and building materials are constantly being developed. Don't automatically go for the most common conventional repairs—always do the research and ask around to find the newest, greenest repairing methods. One exception to the rule of repairing versus replacing is if you have carpeting in your bathroom. Carpet harbors moisture, which, as you know, is a breeding ground for mold. It's also not easy to clean. Look into removing it and replacing it with an easy-to-wash, eco-friendly surface like ceramic tile. Make sure to seal it with a low- or no-VOC product.

Cleaning a Bathroom

A bathroom should be cleaned with products containing eco-friendly substances that do the job without the added environmental harm or health concerns associated with conventional disinfectants. Eschew everything else—unless you want to make your own cleaning solutions. Here are some good ones for the bathroom:

* **Diluted vinegar:** Use to remove mineral buildup from toilets, dissolve soap scum, and clean glass.

* **Hydrogen peroxide and tea tree oil:** Use as sanitizers.

* **Baking soda:** Use alone to scrub a toilet or combine with liquid soap to make an excellent scouring paste.

THE MUST-HAVES

Here's the nitty-gritty on getting your bathroom perfectly clean:

* Glass cleaner can be used on windows and mirrors (and on sinks, tubs, showers, and counters if you don't have or don't want to use a separate product). Paper towels aren't required: use a clean rag (an old T-shirt works well) or newspaper for streak-free mirrors and windows. A sponge is fine for all other surfaces. To clean sponges used with natural cleaners, you can do several things,

including boiling them in hot water, placing them in the microwave for a minute, and spraying their surface with hydrogen peroxide.

* Use a tub and tile cleaner that contains natural lactic acid to break down soap scum in your bath or shower stall.

* If you see any mold forming, particularly at the bottom of your shower curtain or on that hard-to-keep-dry crack between the tub and the wall, use a cleaner containing hydrogen peroxide or plain old 3 percent hydrogen peroxide. Keep in mind that peroxide is good at killing active mold, not mold spores. The gray color won't go away immediately or sometimes ever (this usually comes from mildew that has gone deep into porous grout). It can't hurt to spray this area daily if you have a perpetual mold issue.

* For inside the toilet, use a green toilet cleaner and a brush. The surfaces—including the seat—can be wiped with glass cleaner or an all-purpose cleaner and a sponge. For deeper cleaning, use a peroxide or a thymol cleaner.

* For removing rust stains, try oxalic acid, a poison found in milkweed and rhubarb. Look for a natural version (oxalic acid can be made synthetically), and use with caution. Conventional rust removing products contain hydrochloric acid or phosphoric acid and should be avoided. If the stain is on porcelain, try a homier remedy: pumice stones. These volcanic rocks won't hurt the surface and will scrub the rust right off.

Our Drains

Conventional cleaning product and cosmetic residues go down the drain and into our shared waterways, wreaking havoc on the ecosystem. Male fish can turn into female fish because some of the hormone-disrupting chemicals we pour down the drain—including alkylphenol ethoxylates (APEs), a common surfactant ingredient—mimic estrogen. Those residues feminize male fish, making them produce eggs.

Basic Cleaning Timeline

If you're not sure what to clean and when, here are some thoughts.

Daily

After bathing, wipe down surfaces with a dry cloth to reduce moisture. Spray your faucets with a product containing hydrogen peroxide or thymol, or something you've made with vinegar or tea tree oil; these handles are touched before hands are washed, so they harbor more bacteria than their surroundings. Wash your hands often. If you are going to bathe—or bathe a kid—in the tub, rinse or lightly clean it with the mild soap you use on your baby or a DIY scrubbing paste of ecological dish soap and baking soda before filling.

Weekly

Your sink and mirror could stand to be cleaned once or twice a week, or when you see spots from tooth brushing on the mirror. If you're scrubbing your bath daily, a deeper cleaning once a week is more than sufficient. If you're not, weekly is a good idea. Swish your brush around the toilet with some cleaner once a week, especially if you only have one toilet and several people in your household. Low-traffic toilets can go longer.

Monthly

Good news: diligently wiping up water after a kid splashes around in the bath can count as mopping. But once a month or so—whenever you're mopping your kitchen floor—drag the same bucket of diluted multipurpose cleaner into your bathroom and give the floor a real rinse with some elbow grease. Do this with whatever tool you prefer—mop or rag—as long as it is reusable, not disposable. A cotton mop head is less likely to contain the hidden antimicrobial agents many squeeze mops harbor. Scrubbing with a rag avoids that concern altogether. Whatever you use, pass a dry cloth over the floor once it's clean to remove any lingering moisture.

Infrequently

When you think of it, or when your paint job looks dulled by sprayed water and steam, wipe down your walls and even your ceiling with a rag and whatever cleaner is handy.

Cosmetics

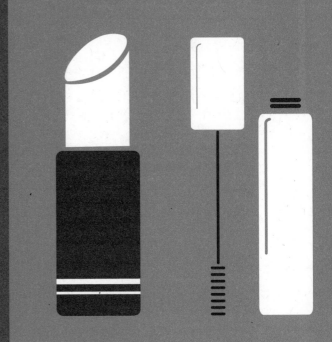

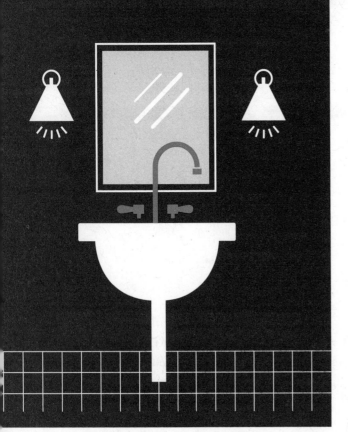

The beauty and personal hygiene products we use on a daily basis are filled with a host of questionable chemicals: hormone disrupters; skin, eye, and lung irritants; reproductive toxicants; and carcinogens (actual, probable, and possible). These chemicals are sometimes derived from petroleum, and many have been (cruelly) tested on animals. Some have been found in various concentrations in the blood or the breast tissue of humans and have even been linked to birth defects. Though the skin is not as direct a route of exposure as eating or inhaling, there is no disputing that what goes on it gets into our bodies—think about the nicotine patch. This is all the more troubling when you consider the fact that no one knows what the cumulative effects of these ingredients are.

Exposure to this unknown cocktail of potentially harmful ingredients is especially unwise during periods of growth, which makes using conventional cosmetics particularly controversial for women in their reproductive years, pregnant women, babies, young children, and teenagers. Teenage girls tend to use more cosmetics than most. The Environmental Working Group (EWG) did a study showing that they use an average of nearly 17 personal care products each day, while adult women use 12. Common chemicals in these products include phthalates, triclosan, parabens, and musks, and the EWG found them all in the blood and urine of adolescent girls across America. The EWG report states: "Emerging research suggests that teens may be particularly sensitive to exposures to trace levels of hormone-disrupting chemicals like the ones targeted in this study, given the cascade of closely interrelated hormonal signals orchestrating the transformation from childhood to adulthood."

It's hard to understand how cosmetics filled with largely unrestricted and untested chemicals are allowed to line store shelves. Personal care companies are subject to very broad regulations set forth by the federal government, though these are not well enforced, and the cosmetics industry is largely left to self-police. But that doesn't mean consumers need to be the guinea pigs. There are safe—or at least safer—versions of just about every lotion, elixir, and treatment on the market (see page 345 of the Resources). One caveat: those of us who rely on chemicals to regrow thinning hair, whiten teeth, or polish nails may be out of luck. Some things are too toxic to replace naturally. (See the Cosmetics Chart on page 340 for what to avoid.)

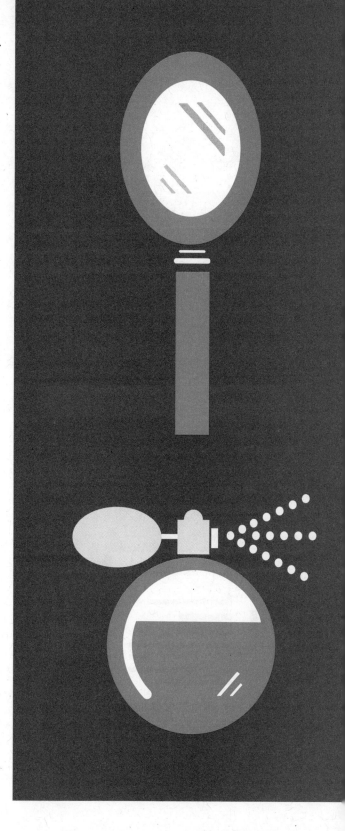

How to Choose Safe(r) Cosmetics

When it comes to choosing cosmetics, it's buyer beware. Read labels. Rely on watchdog groups. And remember that less is more. That conventional mascara may not be worth its weight in heavy metals and irritants. Seek out a more natural version, or dare to go bare. If you're wearing a product on your lips, keep in mind that you are actually ingesting it. Lipstick doesn't evaporate—it gets swallowed. The things we put on our skin daily can really make an impact on our health—and the planet's—over time.

Cosmetics Consumer Guide

1. **Shop for cosmetics at the same places you shop for conscious food.** Health food stores, farmers' markets, online specialty retailers, and even some mass market and grocery stores have special sections for "natural" products. But you should still read labels to be sure the ingredients are as safe as possible.

2. **Rely on certifications.** There is an incredible amount of greenwashing in the natural product arena. Companies stick one organic ingredient in an otherwise toxic face cream and then market themselves as "organic." Look for the following third-party certifications, which are widely found organic and natural labels on cosmetics: USDA Organic (ams.usda.gov/nop), NSF (nsf.org), Soil Association (www.soilassociation .org), BDIH (kontrollierte-naturkosmetik.de), Eco-Cert (www.ecocert.com), and National Products Association (npainfo.org). Some are stricter than others. Go to the websites to learn each organization's criteria.

3. **Rely on watchdog organizations and businesses that help consumers make better choices.** Bookmark these sites and check products and ingredients on them before or while you shop: the Environmental Working Group's Skin Deep Cosmetic Safety Database (cosmeticsdatabase.com) and the Campaign for Safe Cosmetics (safecosmetics. org). The Good Guide (goodguide.com) is also helpful.

4. **Be a smart consumer.** Make sure you know who owns the company that makes the shampoo you like and decide if you'd like to support it. Get to know the ins and outs of the certifications and watchdog groups. Many truly natural products get worse ratings than they should on CosmeticsDatabase.com, for instance, because they list their essential oils as "fragrance" or "parfum." EWG always takes that to mean hormone-disrupting synthetic fragrance and therefore gives it high hazard scores.

5. **Be wary of fragrances.** Cosmetics are required by law to list their ingredients. But there's a giant loophole in the federal law: companies are not required to disclose their secret fragrance mixtures on their labels. Synthetic fragrances should be avoided, as they can contain hormone disruptors and neurotoxins and may trigger allergies. Look for products with natural essential oils—preferably those that are USDA-certified organic or Demeter-certified biodynamic.

6. **Think before you polish.** There are many nail polishes now on the market claiming to be free of the three worst substances found in those little glass bottles: formaldehyde, dibutyl phthalate, and toluene. But nail polish still contains chemicals that make it harden; it still has color (some synthetic, some mineral derived); and people—including nail salon workers—are still inhaling VOCs when it's being applied and removed. In this world, we all choose our poisons, so ultimately it's up to you if red toenails are worth the risk. Proceed with particular caution if you are pregnant or trying to get pregnant. And think twice before painting kids' nails. Nail polish isn't a child-friendly product—far from it.

7. **Just because it's "prescription" doesn't mean it's safe.** If you have a skin condition like acne or eczema, you might turn to a professional for help. Try to find a dermatologist interested in CAM (complementary and alternative medicine) to work with you on determining the underlying cause of the symptoms. Some people find success in treating eczema, for example, by changing their diets. If you feel that you truly need what the doctor prescribes, just be sure to read labels. Some steroid creams come only in a base of petrolatum and nothing more, while others contain preservatives and even fragrance. Always get the version with the fewest additives. Also consult Medline Plus (nlm.nih.gov/medlineplus), a service of the National Institutes of Health that provides helpful details on the side effects of prescription medications.

8. **Carefully screen your sunscreens.** The best bet is to choose a mineral cream with an SPF above 15 and below 30 that does not contain nanoparticles. Hats, shade, UVA-blocking sunglasses, protective clothing, and just plain staying out of the sun when it is strongest (10 a.m. to 4 p.m.) are also excellent—and safe—precautionary steps. Avoid chemical sunscreens, which may disrupt the body's hormone systems, among other things. Oxybenzone is the main chemical used in these. To learn more, check out the Environmental Working Group's Sunscreen Guide at ewg.org.

Hair and Skin Treatments
You Can Make at Home

If all of this label reading and seeking out third-party certification is too much work or too confusing, you can always make your own products. That way, you'll always know exactly what they contain. They can be highly effective and inexpensive, too. Just follow these recipes:

* **Conditioner:** After shampooing, rinse hair with a mixture of 1 tablespoon apple cider vinegar and 1 cup warm water.

* **Deep-conditioning hair treatment:** In a bowl, mash 1 peeled and pitted avocado and 2 tablespoons organic honey. Massage into hair and leave for 20 to 30 minutes. Wash hair as usual.

* **Deodorant (powder):** Combine 1 part baking soda and 6 parts cornstarch in a resealable container and shake until powders are thoroughly mixed. Using a cloth, cotton ball, or cosmetics pad, dab a small amount of the powder onto clean armpits.

* **Dry-skin face mask:** Mix ½ cup cooked plain oatmeal with 2 teaspoons honey. Apply to face, let sit for ten minutes, and rub off. This mask is both moisturizing and cleansing.

* **Exfoliating face scrub 1:** Combine 4 teaspoons powdered brewer's yeast, 2 teaspoons plain yogurt, 2 teaspoons almond meal, and 1 teaspoon organic honey and mix well. Rub gently over face, then rinse with warm water. Use immediately; do not store in the refrigerator.

* **Exfoliating face scrub 2:** Mix 1 teaspoon baking soda, a dab of mild, plant-based liquid soap, and a few drops of water. Rub evenly over face and rinse with warm water.

* **Shampoo:** Combine ½ cup baking soda with 3 cups warm water in a bottle. Rub a small amount of the mixture into hair and rinse. Or, for one-time use, rub ⅛ cup baking soda into hair and rinse.

* **Toothpaste:** Combine 2 parts baking soda and 1 part fine table salt. Put powder on damp toothbrush, brush, and rinse with water.

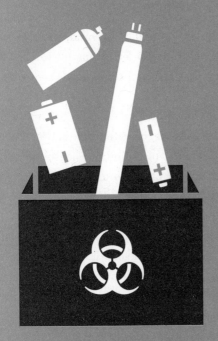

the UTILITY ROOMS
Attic, Garage, Mudroom, and Basement

The Conscious Ritual

Utility rooms are the unsung heroes of the home: the places where you store your most treasured keepsakes, your daily clutter, and the emotionally important junk you can't bear to part with but never actually use or look at, plus all of the equipment needed to run a household and maintain the grounds. So be grateful for all the things your attic, garage, mudroom, and basement hold, as well as the tasks you're able to accomplish because you have the room to store items like tools, sports equipment, and mementos. Even if you live in a small apartment, you can still marvel at what a well-organized utility closet can contain and be thankful for not being able to hoard unneeded stuff.

The Conscious Components

We all have stuff to store. Some of it is seasonal: sweaters and blankets get squirreled away to make room for bathing suits and sandals. Some of it is for special occasions: tablecloths, silverware, and holiday decorations. Then there's the gear and equipment: weed trimmers, drills, skis, snow boots, hockey sticks, high chairs, cribs, car seats. But the mtajority of what fills the garage, attic, or basement is unneeded junk and materials deemed too unsafe to leave elsewhere. A conscious utility room is well ventilated and safely insulated. It contains only the least hazardous chemicals available, which are well marked and placed out of the reach of kids and pets. It's a well-organized space that's prepared for leaks or floods.

> Here's a handy checklist to help you remember the pieces that make up a conscious utility room ➡

☐ Attic clutter kept to a minimum and stored in sealed containers to protect against dust and leaks

☐ Items stored in the basement kept off the floor and in waterproof containers to prevent water damage

☐ Open windows or fans for ventilation

☐ Rooms cleaned with natural products

☐ Low- or no-VOC paints in their original containers

☐ Any hazardous materials kept to a minimum, clearly labeled, stored in a detached garage or disposed of properly

☐ Dehumidifier to prevent basement moisture

☐ Eco-friendly insulation such as cellulose, fiberglass, or cotton fiber

☐ Basement root cellar to store fruits and vegetables year-round

☐ Holes closed up to prevent pests

THE ISSUES

Despite our best intentions, the extremities of the house are where the worst of the worst is dumped and lumped, usually without much thought. But these rooms deserve thought. Garages—attached or not—are where the most dangerous chemicals in any household tend to be kept. In homes without garages, these items are often relegated to the basement, or in a small apartment, to a closet or a cabinet—spaces that tend to be poorly ventilated. This mix of clutter and household hazards is unique to utility rooms, and the two don't commingle harmoniously. What's stored is often ruined by leaks and humidity and can be tainted by those chemicals. Clutter is very hard for people to part with. Making sure the spaces where we store our stuff are safe—even the mudrooms where we kick off our shoes—is important.

The Attic

FIRE SAFETY

Attics can be hot and dry, and many have exposed incandescent bulbs. These can get excessively warm and, if the attic is filled with clutter around the bulb, catch fire. Improperly installed recessed ceiling fixtures in the rooms below the attic can also cause attic clutter or insulation to ignite.

INSULATION

Attic insulation can be asbestos-containing vermiculite (dangerous) or cellulose (mainly innocuous), among other materials.

* Vermiculite is a mineral used in many consumer products, including potting mixes, sound insulation, and fireproofing. It was sold as insulation from 1919 until 1990. Most of this came from a mine in Libby, Montana, where a deposit of asbestos

contaminated the vermiculite. If you suspect your attic contains asbestos, seek out images online so you know what to look for—it resembles brownish chips and gives off dust. Thankfully, we don't spend much time in our attics, so if you have it, your exposure is low. But check epa.gov for advice on dealing with it, or speak with an asbestos expert to find out if it should be removed or encapsulated. In the interim, wear a dust mask when up in the attic.

* Cellulose (this looks like gray, ground-up newspaper) is usually quite safe. Sometimes it contains boric acid—which is generally nontoxic but can be a male reproductive toxicant—to control pests and mold.

* Fiberglass insulation contains a formaldehyde resin, which is far more stable and therefore safer than the version of formaldehyde found in composite woods.

* Cotton fiber insulation—sometimes made of recycled blue jeans—can be a great option, but only if your roof doesn't leak. Once wet, it has no insulation value and can grow mold.

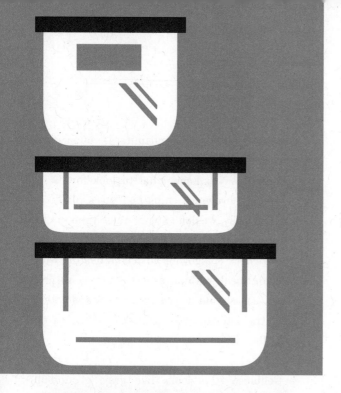

Leaky roofs should be fixed immediately. But there are other ways for humidity and moisture to enter an attic. Sometimes bathrooms are vented into them, pouring humidity into the space. These vents should be redirected outside of the home. Ventilation can help with humidity, and also with dust and heat. The sun beating down on a roof can make an attic and the floor below it hot. An exhaust fan in the attic will cool the whole house, especially if you have grilles mounted in closets and staircases. These permit the fan to draw air from below, all the way through the attic, and send it outside.

STORAGE

Anything stored in an attic needs to be placed there carefully and deliberately and not just tossed out of sight.

* Items should be sealed in storage boxes to protect against chemical dust and roof leaks.

* Attics are good places to store items that shouldn't get damp, like books and clothing.

* Beds and furniture need to be stored in protective coverings in case of unexpected leaks.

* Consider installing a cedar closet for wool storage. Do not fill it with mothballs, which are far too toxic for any household, especially in poorly ventilated spaces.

PESTS

Squirrels and other animals can enter through holes in your attic, make their homes, and even chew wires. Regularly check for and seal any openings.

WHAT LIES ABOVE?

You may not know the exact makeup of your roof, but most are asphalt shingles with a chemical on them to add durability. The shingles may or may not have a PVC membrane, a layer of sheathing that provides additional insulation and protection. Metal roofs are becoming increasingly popular and can be considered a greener option. They're durable and cost-efficient but energy intensive to make and transport and can be very loud when it rains. If you're installing a new roof, cedar shingles are considered environmentally friendly but can be cost-prohibitive—sometimes two to four times more expensive than asphalt. Pay attention to the coating on any roofing material, because it is usually high in volatile organic compounds (VOCs). Although roofs are obviously well ventilated, VOCs aren't good for the environment. Seek out the greenest version you can find via the eco-building supply resources on page 345. If you have solar panels, be mindful that the bolts used to puncture the roof and secure them are installed carefully and don't cause leaks. Leaks can also be an issue with green—aka living—roofs covered with vegetation. These are great for absorbing runoff and keeping homes cool but can cause trouble if a drainage system backs up.

The Garage

There is no shortage of VOC-filled substances stored in a garage: paints and paint removers, stains and stain removers, pesticides, and gasoline. This is usually where you find the largest accumulation of toxic and VOC-emitting chemicals in any house. And if you have an attached garage, these fumes, plus car exhaust, have a direct route into the home. Therefore, it is crucial to exercise caution in the garage. The best way to minimize exposure to these hazards is to not use them in the first place. There are ample ways to enjoy your lawn and garden without pesticides. Avoid solvents and oil-based paints and favor no- or low-VOC paints. If you do use a product with a high VOC content, buy the smallest amount to cover the job. As soon as you finish the project, dispose of such containers, especially any corroding ones, at a hazardous-waste collection site. Also, if you have a lot of electrical equipment and tools in your garage, make sure you have three-prong grounded outlets for them to minimize the risk of shock.

* Only store hazardous chemicals if you know you're going to be using them shortly or if they're required for the upkeep of crucial equipment like cars and generators. Make sure all bottles and cans are labeled well and placed out of reach of children and pets.

* Keep clutter to a minimum.

* Make ample room for recycling bins, and recycle all that you can in your municipality. This doesn't only mean plastic bottles; screws, nails, and old keys are generally fair game. Call your town's recycling center to find out what is recyclable where you live.

* Keep tools well organized and accessible.

VENTILATION

Maintain an air exchange in the garage by leaving windows open, even in the winter. If you're doing woodworking or automotive work, open the door, too. Even better: take the project outside. And wash your hands well after working in the garage. A mat (preferably one without PVC backing) between an attached garage and the house is a perfect place to take off your shoes before entering the home without dragging the outdoors in with you. Never run your car with the garage door closed, and after you start it, pull out immediately. Carbon monoxide exhaust can kill.

FLUIDS AND BATTERIES

Automotive fluids tend to be toxic, but, unlike cleaning products, there are rarely green versions. Vinegar and water may be adequate to clean your mirror, but they can freeze and therefore won't work for your windshield. An exception: standard antifreeze (ethylene glycol) can and should be swapped for a propylene glycol version. The latter is biodegradable and safer for aquatic life.

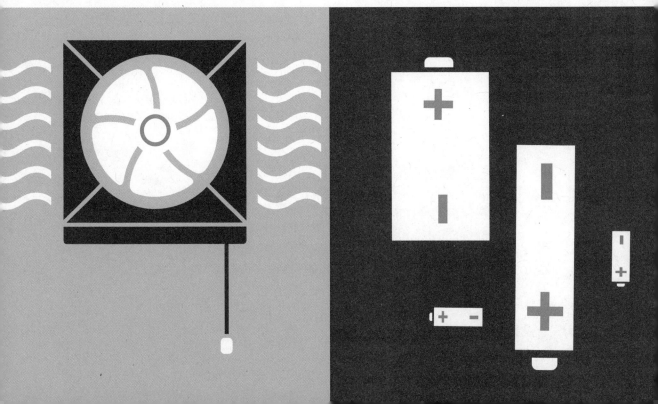

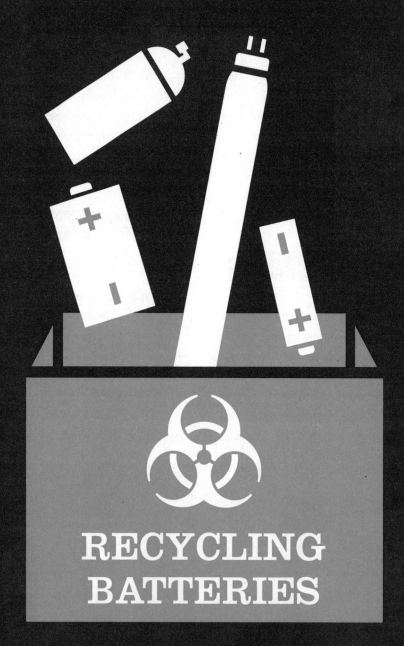

RECYCLING BATTERIES

Hazardous fluids aren't the only materials that must be carefully recycled. Batteries—little and big, conventional and rechargeable—are also highly toxic and require special care. You can often return batteries to the stores where you purchased them, or look on Earth911.com for recycling centers that take them near you.

The Mudroom

Mudrooms, usually located in hallways or alcoves near back entrances to homes, are great places to leave daily clutter, like coats, book bags, umbrellas, hats, gloves, mail, reusable shopping bags, and even gear like skates and scooters. But don't let this area become a pigpen. Line the walls with coat hooks and the floors with bench-topped cubbyholes. Leave a few towels here for wet dogs and children, and even a metal or plastic tray for really wet footwear to contain the moisture.

Taking off your shoes before entering a house is the public-health equivalent of washing your hands. A large majority of the dirt in any home arrives on the soles of our shoes, and removing them will help keep your house cleaner. Mud, water, snow, and animal feces are not pleasant, but the real issues here are the invisible ones: pesticide residues if you live in an agricultural area or if your neighbors spray their lawns, automotive exhaust, and chemical contaminants from your workplace. You do not want these substances in your home.

If you don't like walking around barefoot, invest in a funky sock collection or comfortable slippers. And ask guests and visitors to remove their shoes before entering your home. The more people encounter and learn about shoe-free homes, the more likely they are to institute similar policies in their own. Some families choose to provide slippers to guests. If you have maintenance workers who decline to take off their boots, keep some protective booties on hand for them to wear into the house. Don't feel strange about asking them to do this; their shoes might have just come from an asbestos-dust-filled basement.

The Basement

A basement brings up many of the same concerns as any storage room: hazardous materials, including conventional cleaning products and pesticides, dust, and poor ventilation. Even though this is an area of the home where you might have some extra, underutilized space, it's not a good idea to set up an office or workspace here; there's just too much down here you don't want to be breathing on a regular basis. Basements also present unique concerns: moisture, radon, and asbestos.

Because basements have a tendency to flood and harbor mold, anything stored in a basement should be kept at least several inches off the ground. This can easily and inexpensively be accomplished with some repurposed two-by-four pieces of wood. If you know your basement floods, or you're moving into a new place and there are telltale signs of moisture—a sump pump or water stains three to four inches above the floor—store your valuables elsewhere. Papers, books, and old photographs deteriorate over time in a moist environment. If you have nowhere else to store items, opt for waterproof containers over cardboard boxes. And don't store your wine next to the furnace: damp works; heat doesn't.

MOISTURE

Along with rain, clogged roof gutters and watering shrubs too close to a home can lead to basement flooding. Moisture can also enter a basement via drips and leaks from pipes and boilers, so check them from time to time to make sure all is in working order. Keep the whole house system running smoothly and you'll be less likely to have a wet basement. For general dampness, a dehumidifier can help. Be sure to dispose of the water it collects and to wipe off the coils from time to time.

Your Own Root Cellar

If you're trying to eat locally and seasonally, a cool basement is the ideal place to set up a root cellar, an underground spot that keeps foods like apples, potatoes, carrots, winter squash, and more cool and crisp throughout the winter. However, most modern basements have furnaces or heaters, so you may need to section off a corner of your basement to keep it as cold and humid as possible. You can increase humidity by covering the floor with mulch or wood chips.

Root cellars need to be well ventilated. Do what you can to increase air flow to the space. Keep in mind that the air lowest to the floor will be coolest and dampest, while the air near the ceiling will be warmer and drier. Vegetables keep best in high humidity, and fruits last longer in lower humidity. So store potatoes, onions, and other root crops in perforated containers, such as mesh bags or punctured cans, near the ground, and place fruits and veggies on shelves.

What's the Temperature?

Your root cellar must be able to maintain a temperature of 32 to 40 degrees at 85 to 95 percent relative humidity to be effective, so it's important to buy and install a thermometer. The cold temperature slows the release of ethylene gas, stopping the growth of microorganisms that cause crops to decompose. The high humidity level is important to prevent the loss of moisture, which causes crops to wither.

Don't forget to place a screen and bars over basement windows to block unwanted guests. Closing up all holes in the basement will also go a long way toward keeping out small animals and bugs.

Radon is a naturally occurring radioactive material that causes lung cancer. If you live in a part of the country that is known to have radon, it can enter your house via the basement and diffuse upward into the atmosphere. So do a home test, available at most hardware stores. To eliminate radon, ventilate. Opening a small window tends to be enough, but in bad cases you may need a fan to force ventilation.

Garage Systems

After having converted your garage to an eco-safe environment by carefully disposing of unused paint and gasoline cans, getting the dust off the floor, and making sure all the power tools are unplugged so that they don't phantom electricity, you head out for a family picnic. With everyone loaded in the car, you open the garage door and start the car, then notice that the rear door is ajar. You jump out to open and re-close it while the car is left running. As you open the door, a breeze blows the toxic fumes from the car's exhaust into the vehicle. Then you shut the car door, locking those fumes inside for your family to breathe. Remember, the garage isn't suddenly a sanctuary because you've consciously greened and cleaned it. You still need to use common sense and caution to minimize your exposure to air pollution and more.

Additional air pollution can come from the furnace. There can be carbon monoxide (CO) from improper combustion, so make sure your house is equipped with a CO detector. The basement is also where whole-house air systems tend to live. If you're concerned about dust, pollen, or mold spores, putting an electrostatic filter on the air conditioning/heating unit is a good way to minimize these throughout the house. Just be sure to change the filter often. If you're very sensitive to dust, wear a mask when doing this task.

ASBESTOS

Check to see what is insulating the pipes that line your basement. It might be asbestos, which is pervasive because it's inexpensive and non-flammable. This naturally occurring material—most of it mined in Libby, Montana—wasn't recognized as carcinogenic until World War II workers who had sprayed it on walls of ships started to develop various lung diseases 20 years later. You'll know it when you see it: asbestos is a dust-covered white material wrapped around pipes, often with two metal bands holding it in place. On a furnace it looks like hard plaster. It can usually be safely encapsulated in a plastic nonpermeable membrane and left in place. Or you can have it removed by a certified contractor. If you have it, and especially if you're renting your home and don't have much say in how it is being maintained, the basement isn't a great place for children to play.

FINISHED BASEMENTS

All that said, if you're reading this in your comfortable family room in a finished basement, don't run frightened up the stairs. These can be perfectly safe, especially if they're well ventilated and not prone to flooding. If you're finishing a basement space, avoid wall-to-wall carpeting, which will trap moisture and dust, and is likely to grow mold in a high-humidity area. If you do laundry in your basement, turn to Chapter 9 for tips on maintaining a conscious laundry room.

Cleaning Your Utility Rooms

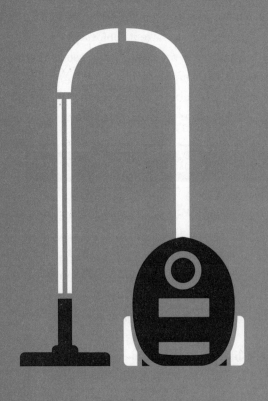

Lazy housekeepers rejoice: utility rooms rarely need scrubbing. In fact, most of us treat them more like outdoor spaces than indoor. A finished basement will obviously need to be cleaned more frequently and treated like a living room. But an attic where you go three times a year doesn't need to be cleaned more than once a year, and sometimes less frequently than that. Basically, you only need to get the dust out and wipe down the spots you touch most often: doorknobs, countertops, and appliances.

THE ATTIC

It's the rare and fastidious person who cleans an attic more than once a year or at all. This should mainly involve wet-dusting any buildup on storage containers and sweeping the floor. If you can get your HEPA-filter-containing vacuum into the attic, use it.

THE GARAGE

Throw open the windows and give the garage a ritual cleaning every spring. During the winter, garage floors—typically concrete—fill up with dust, dirt, mud, and (if you live in a cold climate) ice melt residue. Put on a dust mask if you're sweeping, as that dust can be a heady mix. A sprinkle of water will help

windows, put on a mask, dampen the floors to suppress the dust, then sweep or vacuum and mop. Go around with an all-purpose cleaner and wipe shelves and storage bins. A finished basement should be cleaned like a living room.

A mudroom should be cleaned weekly. Ideally you have machine-washable rag rugs laid out where you're taking off and stashing your shoes. Wash these when you do the laundry, and mop as they're drying. Remove shoes from cubbies and wet-wipe these down from time to time, too. Shoe dust harbors a whole host of unsafe chemicals, which is why you're taking off your shoes in the first place. You don't want it to accumulate in your mudroom, either.

suppress it. Or vacuum and mop with a soap and water mixture. For greasy car drippings, sprinkle powdered natural laundry detergent on the spot, leave it for a few days, and then sweep it up. The oil will transfer to the powder. Then scrub the spot with a wet brush to remove any remaining residue. If you're wiping off shelves, be careful of what is stored there. Moving around corroding paint cans can result in some unanticipated and hard-to-clean messes. Far better to take them to a hazardous waste center.

THE BASEMENT

An unfinished basement with concrete floors can be cleaned much like a garage: open

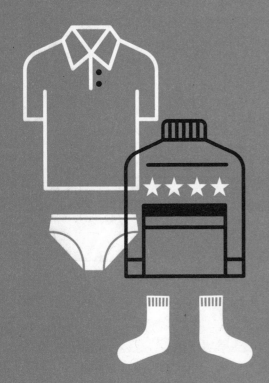

9

the LAUNDRY ROOM

The Conscious Ritual

If you're the type who refers to laundry as an art, you're probably already pausing to appreciate what you enjoy most about the process: knowing just the trick to remove any stain, pinning wet sheets outdoors to dry in the sun, or folding towels just so. Or if washing your clothes is such a chore that you've excused yourself from it entirely by relying on another family member or a professional cleaner, you are surely thankful for their work. Either way, the next time you pull on your freshly laundered favorite jeans or giddily notice that the stain from last week's greasy dinner came out of a new shirt, take a moment to acknowledge the tremendous resources involved in cleaning each and every load of clothes— water and energy—and the potential health and environmental effects of any synthetic detergent or whitening agent used.

The Conscious Components

It's a conundrum: laundry must be done, and yet it's so resource-intensive. The energy required to heat water is one of any home's largest contributions to global warming. To make your laundry room a more conscious one, you need to take steps to mitigate washing and drying's environmental footprint. Wash loads in cold water, use the dryer as little as possible, and rely on natural, unfragranced detergents, whiteners, and spot cleaners.

Here's a handy checklist to help you remember the pieces that make up a conscious laundry room →

☐ Open windows for ventilation

☐ Full loads conserve water and reduce energy use

☐ Hand-washing instead of dry-cleaning, or eco-friendly wet- or CO_2-cleaning when necessary

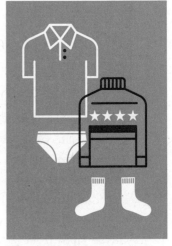

☐ Clothing and other items washed only when necessary and treated gently so they last

☐ Energy-efficient washers and dryers

☐ Natural laundry detergents, either fragrance-free or scented with essential oils

☐ Chlorine-free bleach

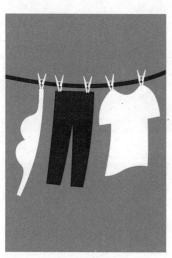

☐ Line-dried clothing, outdoors or in

☐ Clothing washed in cold water

☐ Dryer sheets without synthetic fragrance

THE ISSUES

The main concerns in any laundry room are energy use, water use, and chemicals, which impact environmental and human health. And what is better for the environment is better for fabric, too. Washing in cold water with a gentle yet cleansing natural detergent and without chlorine bleach, then drying outside or only minimally in a machine, will make your clothing last longer.

Water and Washing Machines

HOT VS. COLD

Believe it or not, about 90 percent of the energy used in doing laundry—including the costs associated with making detergents and the energy used by the machines—is making water hot. It's hard to conjure up the image of a coal-fired power plant and the pollution it creates—the greenhouse gases and the mercury residue in our waterways and seafood—when you reach your finger toward the hot water button on your washer. But try to. We may be home alone washing doormats, jeans, and rags, but our actions always affect the world beyond our walls. Washing in cold will reduce that impact and minimize your dirty laundry's footprint.

By using cold water, you will also reduce your indoor air pollution: heating water blasts volatile chemicals, including chlorine in municipal water, into your breathing space. If you're using heavily fragranced conventional synthetic detergents, all of those vapors are also released when heated. Cold water is truly all you need to

clean, and some natural detergents are specially formulated to remove soils and stains in it. Cold also prevents stains from setting, colors from bleeding and fading, and wools and silks from shrinking.

SET YOUR FURNACE FOR SUCCESS

No one needs scalding water; you just wind up cooling it with cold—a big waste of energy. Set your furnace lower—125°F will suffice—and you'll use less hot water when you choose warm on your washer. If you have a choice, an on-demand or tankless water heater is best, followed by a high-efficiency gas version. With electric, the heater itself is efficient, but the production and transmission of energy is not.

When You Want to Be in Hot Water

It's hard to understand why we still overwhelmingly choose hot water for our laundry when we know the environmental repercussions and are well aware that cold really cleans. That said, there are a few instances that call for warm or maybe even hot water. If you or your children are allergic to dust mites, washing bedding in hot or warm will kill them. If your whites are turning gray, an occasional warm-water wash with non-chlorine bleach can help brighten them; the heat cleans dirt efficiently and helps make peroxide more effective. A truly filthy load will benefit from heat as well. And if someone in your household is sick, heat helps kill germs. If your machine offers the option, rinse a hot load in cold water to cut some of the energy use.

WATER CONSERVATION

Front-loading or HE (high-efficiency) washers use less water and electricity than their top-loading counterparts. They also don't require as much detergent and are easier on clothes because they tumble rather than agitate loads. If you have a choice between the two machines—at a laundromat or when buying one for your home—always choose the front loaders. The only downside to a front loader is that they tend to be less versatile—you can't only soak a load or stop it midcycle.

With or without a front loader, there are several ways to save water:

* Reduce the amount of laundry you do weekly. Things like jeans can be worn a few times or longer before washing.

* Only do completely full loads.

* Washing machines leak waste water while also filling the laundry room with unwanted moisture that can lead to mold growth. Check the pipes often and be vigilant about fixing them.

WASHING MACHINES

Most people do laundry at home in machines that have been around for a while; when treated well, they're quite durable. So even if you're interested in saving water with a front-loading washing machine, don't run out and replace your current machine. Any new appliance has the energy and resources it took to manufacture it embedded in the manufacturing cost. When you swap out a perfectly good machine with a new one, you may be saving electricity immediately, but it takes many years to break even on the environmental cost. If a new-ish machine is broken, attempt to repair

it before replacing it. Consumer Reports' greenerchoices.org says to skip any repair that costs more than half the price of a new product. The data show that it may not pay to fix a top-loading washer that's more than four years old, or a front-loader more than seven years old. Ask the store where you're buying a new machine if they recycle old ones, or call the manufacturer directly and ask them for recycling advice.

Detergents, Fragrances, and Whitening Agents

Good news! Laundry (and dish) detergents tend to be less toxic than other conventional household cleaners. But that doesn't mean the chemicals used in most laundry rooms are safe for humans or the environment; in fact, they pose both immediate and chronic hazards. You can easily and significantly reduce the potential danger in your laundry room by choosing to clean and whiten with natural products and better chemicals. Use common sense and avoid any bottle labeled "danger," "corrosive," or "skin irritant." Store any laundry cleaners out of reach of children and pets. And whatever you use, don't use too much of it. It's a waste of detergent and money, and extra residue will actually attract dirt to your clothing.

The point of a detergent is basically to transfer dirt and stains from clothing into the water. This cannot be done in water alone. Water and oil don't mix. So something—the surfactant in the detergent—needs to help the two mix so the greasy stains can disperse into the water and come out when rinsed. Historically this was done with soaps derived from animal fat, then vegetable oils, but there was a shortage of both during World Wars I and II. Synthetic surfactants were created to fill in, and they stuck around. Nowadays conventional detergents contain petroleum-derived surfactants, while natural products contain vegetable-derived ones. Animal-based soaps are still on the market, but these create soap scum and dull-looking laundry when washed in hard water.

The petrochemicals in conventional detergents are among the many ingredients that are bad for both the environment and for people. Though it's the rare conventional detergent that lists its ingredients, they likely contain several irritants that can result in rashes. Among them are hormone-disrupting synthetic perfumes and optical brighteners, which put a residue on clothing that reflects light and tricks the eye, making it appear brighter—but essentially you're dyeing your clothing. If you have optical brightener residue on your skin and go out in the sun, it can cause reactions. Furthermore, optical brighteners don't biodegrade, so they slip through wastewater treatment facilities, wreak havoc on aquatic life, and wind up in sludge that is then used to augment fertilization at farms. Conventional detergents may also contain alkyl phenoxy ethanols—surfactants that act as hormone disrupters.

A natural product, on the other hand, tends to contain readily biodegradable surfactants, natural fragrance made from essential oils, and no dyes. But don't just take the bottle label's word for it. Read ingredient lists and only buy a product that readily discloses all the ingredients it contains.

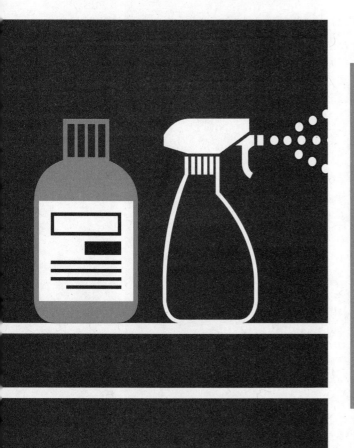

SHOPPING FOR A NEW WASHER OR DRYER?

Consult these organizations to find the most efficient replacement:

Consumer Reports: *consumerreports.org*

Consumer Reports Eco-Labels: *greenerchoices.org*

Energy Star: *energystar.gov*

Fragrance: The Essential Truth

Scent-induced skin rashes can be uncomfortable, but the real reason to avoid synthetic fragrances is because they contain hormone-disrupting phthalates. We breathe them in the laundry aisle at the supermarket, when we open the cap, when clothes come out of the dryer, and for months beyond that. Lungs are a fast route for chemicals to enter the body. If you've ever stashed away a freshly washed item in a drawer in the fall and noticed it smells just as strongly in the spring, you can be certain this is a synthetic fragrance. Keep in mind that even something labeled "free and clear" might contain an odor-masking agent to cover up the scent of the ingredients. If you want to avoid synthetic fragrances, use a product that specifically says it only uses natural plant-derived essential oils. Look for a label that says it is free of masking agents as well as fragrance.

FRAGRANCE

It can be frustrating to wash laundry in communal machines where people wash their clothes in highly fragrant detergent. Not only does the laundry room smell—some people report headaches from the fragrance, plus chlorine bleach fumes—but some of the residue will make it into your clothing. While this is unavoidable, take solace in knowing that your exposure is far less than it would be if you were using a similar detergent yourself.

BABY DETERGENT 101

Consumers see baby-specific detergents and immediately assume they are made specifically for gentle infant skin. They're not. These detergents are formulated to be more effective at removing kid-related stains and aren't any healthier than their adult counterparts; though they may be fragrance free, young skin is typically sensitive to perfume and prone to contact dermatitis. In the natural-product arena, a baby detergent might contain more stain-fighting enzymes than the regular version.

WHITENING AGENTS

There have been entire books written on the hazards of bleach (check out *Pandora's Poison: Chlorine, Health, and a New Environmental Strategy*, by Joe Thornton). Here's why you should avoid it:

* Bleach is a severe irritant and a carcinogen precursor.

* It can damage fabric.

* Bleach isn't safe to have around children.

* Chlorine bleach can form carcinogenic dioxins, furans, trihalomethanes, and other toxins when it's released via wastewater and comes into contact with natural materials in soil and water. It can also do this in our machines, when combining with organic matter like the dirt in our clothes. When you open the machine post-wash, you can inhale these toxins.

Natural whiteners are safer and gentler on the environment and on fabric. Many products marketed as "natural" bleach or "color safe" are just hydrogen peroxide (also called oxygen bleach). This sanitizes and whitens without producing chlorinated by-products. Read the label to make sure it has no additives or surfactants.

It may be cheaper to just buy 3 percent hydrogen peroxide at the drugstore and use that when laundering. Add $1/2$ to 1 cup (depending on load size) of 3 percent hydrogen peroxide to the bleach section of your washing machine. If your washing machine does not have this section, let the washer fill to the load level and pour the hydrogen peroxide directly into the water. Allow the washer to agitate a few minutes to evenly distribute the peroxide before adding clothes.

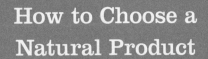

How to Choose a
Natural Product

Because there is no standard definition of "natural" or "nontoxic," it can be hard to know what to look for. Following these rules of thumb should eliminate most of the unnatural detergents in any given store:

* Seek out products that aren't covered in danger warnings.

* Look for bottles that list all their ingredients, and read the ingredients. These should be complete lists.

* You should see a disclosure about the use of vegetable-based surfactants.

* Always check to see what kind of fragrance is in a natural product. It should be 100 percent essential oil.

* For help, check out GoodGuide.com or Seventh Generation's Label Reading Guide, which you can download to a computer or a cell phone for free: seventhgeneration.com.

Do-It-Yourself Laundry Solutions

Borax

You can find Borax (sodium borate, a naturally occurring mineral composed of sodium, boron, oxygen, and water) in the detergent aisle of most grocery stores. Add $^1/_2$ cup of Borax to your regular detergent (liquid or powder) to give it an extra boost. Borax will help to improve the cleaning power, whiten, and remove stains and odors. You can also soak clothes in water with Borax (1 tablespoon per gallon of water) before washing. When using on delicates, add $^1/_4$ cup to your regular detergent instead. Exposure to Borax can be harmful in high amounts, so avoid inhalation and ingestion.

Baking Soda

Adding $^1/_2$ cup of baking soda to the usual amount of liquid detergent at the beginning of the wash cycle will improve the cleaning power of your detergent. To help eliminate odors, add $^1/_2$ cup of baking soda during the rinse cycle.

White Vinegar

Add $^1/_4$ cup of white vinegar during the last rinse cycle; it removes yellowing, acts as a fabric softener, and inhibits mold and mildew.

Cornstarch

Make your own starch spray by mixing 2 tablespoons non-GMO cornstarch with 2 pints cold water in a spray bottle. Shake well before each use. For laundry starch, stir $1/2$ cup cornstarch into 1 cup cold water. Add boiling water (2 quarts for heavy stiffness, 4 quarts for medium stiffness, and 6 quarts for light stiffness). Dip newly washed clothes into starch mix and dry. Sprinkle lightly with warm water and iron as usual.

Lemon Juice

Boost whitening power naturally by adding $1/2$ cup of lemon juice to the rinse cycle. Do not use lemon juice with hydrogen peroxide or chlorine bleach. If lemon isn't enough, add 1 cup of club soda to your wash as well. For a pleasant scent, add a teaspoon of lemon juice to the wash cycle of any load.

Washing Soda

Use washing soda (sodium carbonate, a highly alkaline chemical compound) to help make the switch from conventional detergents to natural soap laundry cleaners. First-time loads should be washed once with $1/3$ cup of washing soda only. This will eliminate residues left by other detergents, which may react with soap, causing fabrics to yellow. For all subsequent washes, add $1/3$ cup of washing soda to water while the machine is filling. Add clothes and 1 to $1^{1}/_{2}$ cups of natural laundry soap. You can also add $1/4$ cup of white vinegar during the rinse cycle to improve cleaning if your water is hard.

Laundry Systems

Going Halfway

It doesn't make sense to spend good money on organic cotton sheets and then send them out to be laundered in hot water, conventional detergent, and chlorine bleach. Similarly, it doesn't make sense to wash your own clothing with a natural detergent if you're also dumping chlorine bleach into the mix. Minimizing exposure to synthetic fragrance, optical brighteners, and petrochemical surfactants is a good idea, yes, but you'll be drastically weakening your efforts if you're using household bleach to disinfect and whiten at the same time.

Swap out that chlorine bleach for something better at home, and if you're outsourcing your washing and folding, choose a laundromat that uses natural detergent. If you're using starch when you iron, keep in mind that the bottle may contain an environmentally destructive propellant, plus additives. It's a much better idea to do without, or to add real starch to the rinse cycle.

Packaging

Thanks to California and Oregon state laws, detergents now come in bottles made of a minimum of 25 percent recycled plastic. But not all companies disclose this information on their packaging, unfortunately, because they can't or won't guarantee the percentage of recycled content. Sometimes you can tell by looking at the bottle—it may contain specks and be a slightly off-white color. Some bottles now contain a mix of recycled plastic and bio-derived plastic. This sounds good, but many municipalities don't recycle them yet, and some bio-plastics are made with genetically modified corn and copious amounts of pesticides and petroleum-based fertilizers. Not very green.

Seventh Generation's 150-ounce laundry detergent containers are made of 80 percent recycled content, and their 25-ounce dish liquid is packaged in 96 percent recycled content HDPE bottles. Choose detergents sold in bottles that have as much recycled content as possible and that you can recycle in your town. Powdered detergent is a good option, because you are avoiding the high-energy costs of transporting liquid, which is heavier, and the packaging will be cardboard rather than plastic.

Washing and Caring for Clothing

How you shop for clothes is an important part of a conscious laundry room. Don't buy anything that can't be washed or that requires special laundering or must be dry-cleaned. Certainly you never want to buy anything for a kid that cannot be tossed in the washing machine. Paying attention to fabrics and treating them well—along with using cold water and safe, natural detergents—will make your washables last as long as possible.

The first step to caring for your washables is not overlaundering, which reduces the life of clothing, sheets, towels, and anything else you wash on a regular basis. Ideally we should be doing laundry as infrequently as possible while still maintaining an acceptable level of cleanliness.

Some guidelines:

* **Underwear, undershirts, and socks:** Wash after one use.

* **Shirts:** Wash after two or three uses unless you spilled on them or were very sweaty.

* **Pants:** Wash only when dirty. Some makers of pricey denim claim you almost never need to wash jeans.

* **Wool sweaters:** Wash only when necessary, and never machine-dry.

* **Bedding:** Wash weekly especially if you're concerned about dust mites and allergies.

* **Soiled and stained clothing:** Wash immediately, especially animal and kid messes and anything illness-related.

WORK CLOTHES IN THE HOME MACHINE

If you or a family member work with hazardous materials that contaminate your clothing—pesticides, solvents, automotive fluids—you need to be mindful of your dirty clothes when you come home. If you can, wash these items outside the home. If not, remove them at work, seal them in a bag, and change into clean clothes to wear home. When you reach the washing machine, do a small load of work clothes that doesn't contain any other household items (kids' clothes, towels, etc.). There have been studies of men working in asbestos mines who brought the toxic substance into their homes via their clothing, sickening other family members. If you take your work clothes to a commercial laundry, warn them as well.

If you tend to toss your gardening clothes into the washer and wait until the machine fills up to turn it on, make sure to warn other members of the household that your clothing might have poison ivy oil on it.

WASHING TIPS

If you have a grandmother who wants to share her tricks of the trade, listen to her. Laundry is something of a lost art. There are housekeeping guides that will inform you to turn jeans inside out before washing to keep them from fading, to sort clothes by dirt content as well as color (gardening gloves and sheets don't mix),

and to hand-wash things like silk and wool so as not to overagitate the fabric. There are stain-removing formulas, most of them largely natural, that require only cornstarch, vinegar, lemon juice, cool water (warm water sets stains), elbow grease, and hydrogen peroxide. But knowing what to use when (i.e., sprinkling an oil stain with cornstarch) can be impossible if you don't speak the language.

Thankfully, there are many solid guides online, and *Better Basics for the Home,* by Annie Berthold-Bond, is full of good information.

Use laundry as a teaching tool, sharing both the knowledge and the task with your children. Helping with sorting, loading, hanging, and folding is an excellent and engaging ritual (okay, chore) for kids of any age.

Drying

AIR-DRYING

Using the elements—air, sun, and wind—to dry your laundry makes sense for a host of reasons:

* It's gentler on clothes, provided you don't leave them in direct sunlight for hours a day (the sun can fade colors).

* It's extremely environmentally friendly—dryers use 10 to 15 percent of domestic energy in the United States.

* Sunshine is great at killing bacteria, fungus, and mold.

* Indoor racks can help humidify dry indoor spaces.

There are some obstacles to air-drying outdoors. Oddly, some towns have bans on laundry lines as they're considered unattractive. But many people flaunt municipal rules and hang lines regardless. A Vermont-based nonprofit, Project Laundry List, is working to change the rules and to encourage people to air-dry (laundrylist.org). If you'd like to sign a petition allowing line-drying where you live, go to right2dry.org.

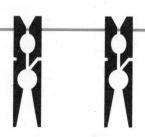

When line-drying your laundry, keep in mind:

* A line needs to be strong—nylon or fiber—and installed correctly so hems don't touch the ground.

* Try to hang laundry shortly after it is washed; if you let it sit in a wet lump, mold can form, and clothes start to smell.

* If you don't feel comfortable putting your underwear on public view, or you have no outdoor space, there's no reason you can't dry inside, preferably in a well-ventilated space.

* There's an art to air-drying, and it takes a little while to master. Be patient. Invest in the right racks and lines for your space, and ask friends who are already doing it for their tips.

* Check the weather before you wash, and try to do laundry on sunny, lightly breezy days.

* In case of rain, have a backup indoor plan, or keep your laundry in a sheltered outdoor spot.

for a vent tube to leak, the hose can disconnect behind the dryer. Usually you can feel the humidity in the air and see condensation on the walls when this happens. Take immediate steps to fix this if it does.

All of this means any room with a dryer should be well ventilated. If you have windows, open them. If you don't, fans and dehumidifiers may be in order. Cleaning dryer screens of lint after each use and checking dryer hoses for clogs is crucial for boosting the efficiency of your dryer, and also for preventing fires.

CONVENTIONAL DRYING

A conventional dryer uses energy to remove moisture from wet fabric. This moisture has to go somewhere. Typically it is vented outside of a home through ducts, though there are also ventless dryers on the market. These types of dryers can take longer to do their job, requiring more electricity than those with vents, and the collected moisture must be completely and frequently disposed of to avoid creating a breeding ground for mold. Any dryer hose can get clogged with lint or dryer sheets. It can also contain high levels of heated-up VOCs from the municipal water, the synthetic fragrance residue from conventional detergents in the clothing, and those dryer sheets. While it is rare

WHAT NOT TO DRY

Don't put anything flammable in your dryer. The heat can make it ignite. Items with plastic or rubber backing and rags soaked with solvents must always be air-dried.

DRYER SHEETS

Dryer sheets, designed to soften clothes and reduce static, tend to be made of unrecyclable petroleum-derived synthetic material and are saturated with hormone-disrupting synthetic fragrances that transfer onto your clothing. Like fragrance in detergent, these can cause contact dermatitis (rashes) and off-gas into the air for a considerable amount of time post-dryer tumble. There are free and clear dryer sheets on the market, as well as natural versions scented with 100 percent essential oils, though people used to conventional dryer sheets will notice that the natural fragrance dissipates very quickly. Sheets made out of unbleached wood fiber can be composted but also tend to wind up in the trash. And keep in mind that softening fabric can decrease the absorbency of things like cloth diapers and towels.

A better way to reduce static is to not overdry clothing. Or, to soften clothes without using dryer sheets, add some baking soda to the wash cycle—¼ cup per load should suffice.

There's nothing eco-friendly about a machine made of metal, rubber belts, and plastic parts that uses energy to heat and evaporate water. But if you are in the market for one, keep the following in mind:

* Gas dryers are more efficient than electric.

* Dryers need regular maintenance (remove the lint from the filter after every load and clean the exhaust pipe from time to time) and should be repaired when necessary.

* Energystar.gov and consumerreports.org can help you make the right choice for your home.

REDUCING ENERGY WHEN MACHINE DRYING

To use a dryer correctly, clothing should be removed when it still has a bit of moisture in it and feels supple. This will help it last longer and reduce wrinkles. The best way to do this is to use the automated moisture sensor if your machine has one. If not, dry clothing in two short stages: test it when the first timer goes off, and then continue drying for just a bit longer if needed. This also reduces the amount of ironing you'll need to do. Remove items you normally iron when they're still damp and hang them on hangers. Use your hands to smooth the fabric and reshape pieces, then allow them to dry.

COOL DRYING

Another way to dry less is to set your dryer for a heat-free cooldown period. The residual warmth in the clothing will help dry the remaining damp spots as it tumbles.

CLEANING THE LAUNDRY ROOM

The room you do your laundry in warrants cleaning from time to time as well. You can do this when you're doing the wash.

1. Wet-dust lint from the top of the dryer and washing machine.

2. Wipe up any laundry detergent spills as they happen.

3. Leave washing machine doors open after use to allow the water to evaporate so mold doesn't grow. (If you accidentally leave wet clothes in the washing machine overnight and they smell, rewash.)

4. Wipe the interiors of your washer and dryer from time to time, and especially after a very dirty load, with a damp cloth.

5. If the machine smells like mildew, run it empty on the hot cycle with one cup of white vinegar or hydrogen peroxide.

6. If you see anything else that needs wiping or cleaning, warm soapy water will suffice. You don't want to spray cleaning products into the interiors of a washer or a dryer.

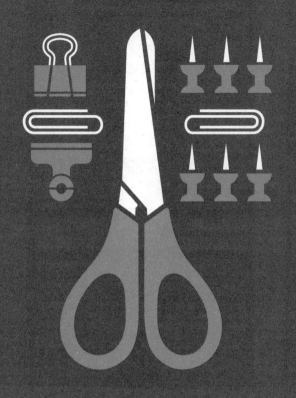

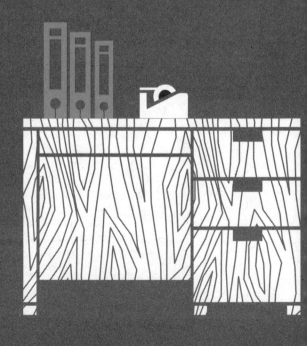

the HOME OFFICE

The Conscious Ritual

One of the most challenging rituals in any home is maintaining a sustainable work-life balance, especially if you have an office at home. Try whenever possible to set attainable boundaries. Commit to shutting off the computer nightly by 8:30 p.m. or all day Saturday, so your whole life won't be entirely about looking at a screen. If you can't help but check your gadgets every time they ring or buzz, turn them off, too. If you're going to work on weekends, consider working in the kitchen or the living room so you're at least visually present to other family members, not locked away behind a door. Behind that door, personalize your home office so it will be a place for reflection. Maybe this means lining the shelves with a shell collection from your favorite beaches, family photos, or books collected over the years. If you have a window, situate your desk so you can draw creativity and inspiration from your surroundings.

The Conscious Components

Beyond being a space set off from the rest of the home for contemplation and work, ideally a conscious home office is low-impact, with minimal electronics, paper, and distracting clutter. It's smoke-free, well ventilated, and free of any hazardous chemicals.

Here's a handy checklist to help you remember the pieces that make up a conscious home office →

☐ Open windows for ventilation

☐ Plants for air filtration

☐ Electronics plugged into a power strip that can be turned off when they are not in use

☐ Independent or progressive telephone, Internet, and electricity providers

☐ Hardwood antique or used furniture

☐ New furniture made of sustainable hardwood or eco-friendly materials

☐ Computers, printers, and scanners chosen for their durability, recyclability, and efficiency

☐ Reusable food and beverage containers for lunches, snacks, and coffee

☐ Eco-friendly office supplies

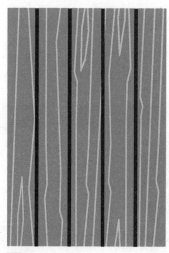

☐ Bare floors

THE ISSUES

We're generally aware of the conventional hazards in a traditional home office. Most of us know to use grounded outlets and to avoid overloading any given outlet with tons of equipment, especially in older houses, to avoid shock hazards or circuit fires. And we tend to be mindful of the physical issues an office presents: repetitive stress injuries from using a keyboard, as well as back and posture issues from bad seating. We know we need to stretch or move around from time to time. It's the environmental and personal health issues that tend to go overlooked.

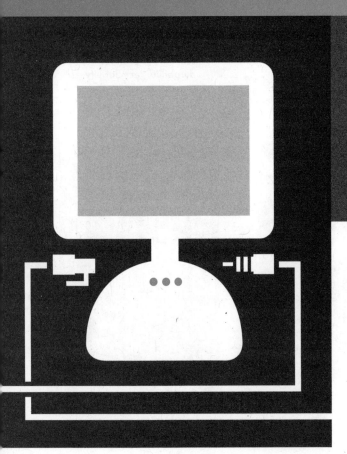

Working from Home

SAFETY

Safety issues arise from many of the same hazards found in the rest of the home—lack of ventilation, conventional cleaning product fumes and residues, construction materials, off-gassing carpets some of which are amplified in this arena. Offices tend to be crammed with flame-retardant-filled electrical equipment, which gives off unique particulates that lurk in spots like hard-to-remove keyboard dust, mazes of electrical wires, and thick carpeting. Copy machines and certain printers can generate air-polluting ozone. Office furniture is often made of composite wood containing formaldehyde glue and chairs with stain-guard-treated foam cushions, which may also contain flame retardants. Not everything in an office overlaps with whole-house concerns, though. There are some unique-to-an-office issues to be aware of, including the safety of various office supplies, the disposal of electronics when you upgrade, and the importance of going as paper-free as possible.

THE GOOD NEWS

Before delving into what can go wrong in a home office, a few words on what's great about them.

* **The Commute:** If your daily commute involves padding from one part of the house to another, you save a lot of resources.

* **Coffee, Lunch, Snack:** Most office workers buy drinks and (not very conscious) food in nonreusable containers several times a day, five days a week, tossing out countless coffee cups, plastic utensils, and individual packages. The amount of waste this creates is staggering. Working at home means access to your own drinks and food, as well as reusable glasses, mugs, plates, and silverware.

Both the money saved and garbage reduced are considerable.

* **Clothing:** Working at home often means working in pajamas or casual clothes. This keeps a tremendous amount of perchloroethylene, the highly toxic chemical used in most dry cleaning, out of the environment. Even if you work for someone who insists on video conferencing, that only means getting dressed from the waist up.

* **Schedule:** Inevitably you will have to commute somewhere for a meeting. But if you work from home, you tend to have the option to travel during nonpeak, traffic-free hours.

Ventilation

Throw open the windows in any home office to improve the indoor air quality. Remember that the air outside is likely to be much cleaner than the air inside, even in a city. To purify air—and make the home office look nice—add plants, which are natural air purifiers that can absorb formaldehyde, benzene, and other chemicals that aren't great to breathe. Plants won't filter everything, but every little bit helps. To be most effective, use a lot (a NASA study recommends 15 to 18 good-sized houseplants in six- to eight-inch-diameter containers to improve air quality in an average 1,800-square-foot house), and don't forget to water them.

Your Houseplants Can Work for You

The plants that filter out the most unwanted chemicals are:

* Boston fern

* Areca palm

A few other great bets and the gases they absorb:

* Aloe vera (formaldehyde)

* Ficus (formaldehyde)

* Spider plant (carbon monoxide)

* English ivy (benzene, formaldehyde)

* Bamboo palm (formaldehyde, benzene, and trichloroethylene)

* Rubber plant (formaldehyde)

* Peace lily (alcohols, acetone, formaldehyde, benzene, trichloroethylene)

For more, check out *How to Grow Fresh Air: 50 Houseplants That Purify Your Home or Office*, by B. C. Wolverton.

Office Systems

When Your Home Office Is Nontraditional

The majority of home offices involve a conventional setup: desk, computer, phone, and maybe a printer. But not everyone works this way. Perhaps your home office is a darkroom or an art studio, or maybe you cut and dye hair and paint nails in part of your home. Most workplaces with more than 50 people are government-regulated by the Occupational Safety and Health Administration (OSHA). But if it is just you and a few clients, there are no mandatory protections in place for you or your workers. Epidemiologically, certain workers—including artists—have higher incidences of some diseases than other people in the population due to exposure to hazardous chemicals or materials. So take precautions:

* Educate yourself on the safety of the materials you're working with. Be mindful that you don't expose yourself to solvents. If you're unsure of what a material contains and it doesn't have ingredients listed on the bottle, look up its Material Safety Data Sheet (MSDS) online.

* If you're working with toxic materials, set up your home office in a space that doesn't share air with the rest of the home. An outbuilding is best.

* Ventilate well.

* If harmful substances get on or otherwise permeate your clothes, make sure to take them off—and leave any rags behind—before entering your home, especially if you have young children. All other precautions won't matter much if you're helping the kids with homework in the living room wearing turpentine-soaked clothing.

Electronics

There's a lot of electrical equipment in the home office: computer, printer, scanner, copy machine, phone, maybe a fax machine, possibly a shredder, perhaps a camera or two. And then there are all of the cords that go with these, plus cell-phone chargers, docking stations, and more. The first question for any conscious home office is: What do you actually need? How can you simplify this sea of energy-hogging plastic items that will be obsolete almost as soon as you get them home from the store? One example: most of us who live in urban areas don't need a printer at home and can easily go to a copy shop for the infrequent times printing and copying are necessary.

When in the market for a new electronic gadget, vote with your dollars and buy from a company that is actively working to address environmental concerns. Check out the best manufacturers at greenpeace.org/electronics. Consumers can and should participate in the organization's online petitions.

ELECTRONICS RECYCLING

Try to use what you own for as long as possible. Repair what you can. If something is truly past its useful life, part with it carefully. The constant desire for new electronics has caused an abundance of electronic waste, or e-waste, which is filled with hazardous substances that aren't easily recycled and shouldn't be thrown out. Electronics may contain lead, mercury, and flame retardants (which are added because they generate heat that can lead to fire when housed in flammable plastic), among other dangerous materials, and extra steps are necessary to ensure they'll be refurbished and reused or recycled. When tossed in a landfill, their toxic components leach into the groundwater; when incinerated, they pollute the air and can harm workers.

Many electronics also contain precious metals—everything from gold to tantalum to palladium—used for their good electrical properties. Cell phones might contain copper, iron, silver, zinc, and platinum. These require energy to manufacture, and stories of horrifying labor conditions abound. When you toss these, they're wasted, and then more precious metals must be mined and manufactured in highly destructive ways. These should be recouped and reused.

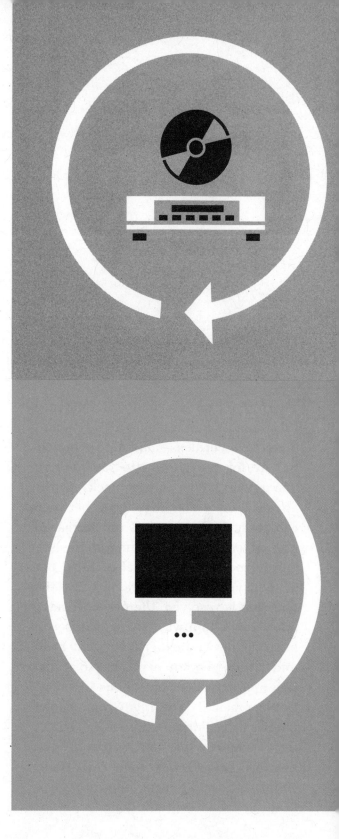

TO HEADSET OR NOT TO HEADSET?

There's a growing body of evidence that speaking on a phone all day long— a cell or a cordless—may not be entirely safe for your brain (to say nothing about what it does to your neck). In the absence of a definitive link between cell-phone radiation and an increased risk of certain brain tumors, the scientific community has yet to hand out a specific recommendation. Until the question is resolved, the precautionary approach is to always use a headset to keep the device farther from your head and minimize your exposure to radiation and/or to use your phone less. The Environmental Working Group ranks phones by radiation levels and has links for consumers to take action to tell the FCC and FDA to modernize their cell-phone radiation standards. Go to ewg.org/cellphone-radiation.

✳ Your laptop may not be useful to you any longer, but could someone else use it? Donate it to a family member, friend, school, charity, or any other organization that might be happy to have it.

✳ See if the manufacturer will take an item back and reuse parts and recycle others. Many companies do this now, and some even accept items they didn't make. (Take the proper steps needed to ensure that any personal information is removed from a computer or cell phone before recycling.)

✳ Check to see if your municipality recycles electronics.

✳ Search epa.gov or 1800recycling.com for organizations near you that might recycle electronics.

✳ Don't forget about batteries: these can and should be recycled, too.

Too Wired?

There has been much speculation about the safety of being in a room for hours a day with so many electronics, or sitting for long stretches with a laptop perched on your lap. The science is inconclusive, but if constant exposure to these fields concerns you, opt for cable over wireless for your Internet service and a dedicated line over cordless for your phone to minimize your risk. Bonus: cable can be faster than wireless.

Energy Hogs

Electronics use energy even when they're not turned out. To stop this phantom draw, unplug all electronics from the wall when you turn them off. Or you can plug them into a surge-protecting strip and throw that switch off when the electronics are not in use, and overnight.

Furniture and Floors

As in any room of the house, your best desk and bookshelf options are hardwood, not particleboard. Hand-me-downs and antiques work well for offices, but if they have chipping paint, test for lead with a home kit. Antique chairs aren't always the most ergonomic ones, and they might contain flame-retardant-filled (crumbling) foam. Filing cabinets tend to be metal and are often available secondhand—a good choice. If you're in the market for a new chair, a desk, or whatever else you might want in your office, make sure the material is safe and sustainable.

CARING FOR FLOORS

Floors should be left bare and vacuumed frequently. Vacuuming is especially crucial if your office has wall-to-wall carpeting in it. If you want a rug, use an unbacked cotton throw that can easily be laundered. Natural latex skid pads are far preferable to PVC.

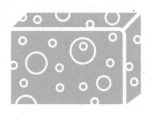

Beyond the Basics: Office Supplies

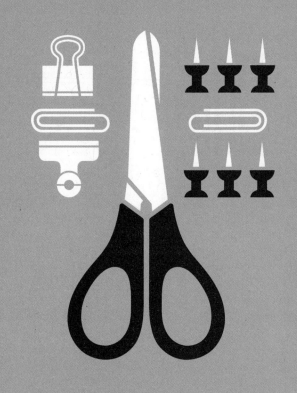

Office supplies—ink, corrector fluids, toner, and the like—can harbor various toxins and air pollutants. This is particularly of concern if you set up a home office in a corner of your bedroom rather than in a separate, well-ventilated room you don't sleep in. Here are some supplies to avoid or at least minimize exposure to. Thankfully there are plenty of places online to find greener versions, like TheGreenOffice.com. (Turn to page 346 for more suggestions.)

TONER AND INK CARTRIDGES

The dust from laser toners is quite toxic; when inhaled it can lead to respiratory issues. Most new printers and copiers use the comparatively safer ink jet technology. If you have an old printer, be careful when changing the toner or removing excess toner. You may want to wear a mask. Wipe up dust with a damp cloth, and wash your hands afterward. Always return your empties and buy refilled ink cartridges rather than new ones. Some companies now offer soy ink as an alternative to petroleum-based versions.

PERMANENT MARKERS, GLUE, CORRECTION FLUID, AND TAPE

Look for water-based permanent markers and correction fluid to avoid VOCs. There are also water-based, solvent-free tapes on the market. Traditional white glues and glue sticks tend to be safer than other versions. Use your nose to guide you.

PENS

The average pen doesn't contain highly volatile inks—you can tell this by smelling it. The scent is pretty faint. But since it's hard to find out if your pen contains a harmful dye or if it's water-based, don't let your kids write on their skin. (Don't do it yourself, either.) To reduce waste, look for pens with replaceable cartridges rather than disposable ones.

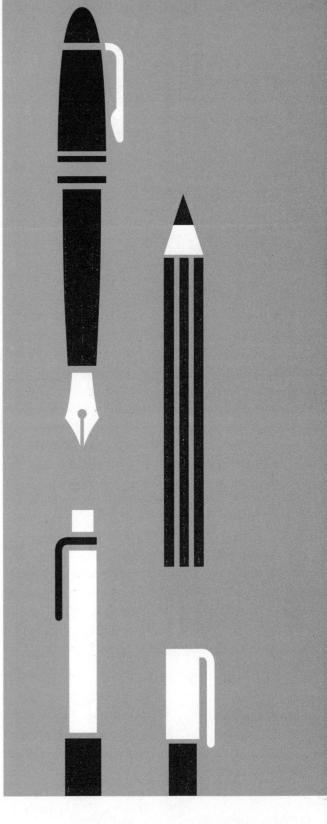

Reducing Paper

The most conscious home offices are paper-free. This isn't possible for everyone, but you can certainly reduce the amount of paper you use:

✳ Print only when absolutely necessary.

✳ Use high-recycled-content, non-chlorine-bleached paper, and print on both sides.

✳ Ask colleagues to send you e-mail documents rather than printed or faxed ones.

✳ Read maps on a GPS.

✳ Have your name taken off junk mail lists to reduce the amount of paper arriving at your office. There are a number of online databases you can register with. A good one is the Mail Preference Service of the Direct Marketing Association (dmachoice.org), or you can google "stop junk mail." You can also contact catalog companies directly to be removed from their mailing lists.

✳ Reuse any paper that does come into your office as scrap.

✳ Have eco-friendlier business cards made on recycled paper using safer inks.

A Note About Sticky Notes

Sticky notes are highly convenient and do come in recycled-paper versions, but the glue on some of them creates havoc in the recycling process. If you have ever looked at recycled-content paper towels or tissues and seen a hole in them, it's likely from sticky-note glue that made it through the process—it pulls the paper off an opposing sheet and forms a hole. If you're going to use sticky notes, rip the adhesive part off and throw it out prior to recycling.

PHONE, CABLE, AND INTERNET PROVIDERS

Have you ever truly considered your phone, cable, or Internet company? Did you know that in some parts of the country you can still find a local telephone provider, possibly even a small, family-owned business? If you're the sort of person who shops locally for produce, try doing the same for your phone company and Internet provider. We all need to value the ability of independent businesses to survive, especially in industries that have largely been taken over by big multinational companies. The best providers treat their employees well, invest their cash in a socially conscious manner, and protect your privacy. To find these, ask neighbors, search online, or look in the local telephone book. One of the largest phone companies offering an alternative to the multinational ones, Working Assets, has shifted its focus to cell-phone service and now operates under the name CREDO. It's well worth a look. You can also choose to buy heat and power from independent or cooperatively owned energy companies.

LIGHTING

Try keeping the light in your office off entirely if you don't really need it—often the glow of a laptop or natural light suffices. However, completely relying on natural light can create eyestrain, so make sure the lights in your office are outfitted with LEDs or CFLs for when you need them.

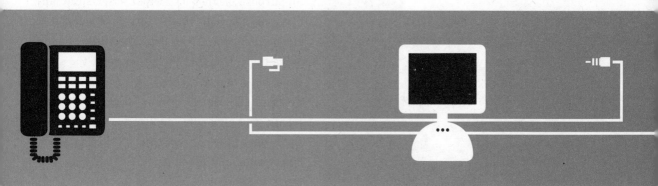

Cleaning Your Office

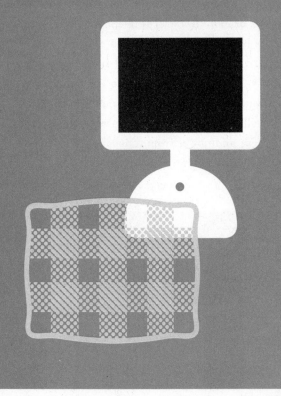

The best way to keep a home office clean is to avoid clutter. This means setting aside a daily, or at least weekly, moment to go through mail, papers, and notes. Keeping clutter from accumulating helps you stay on top of your work. There are no hard and fast rules on how best to clean a home office. All that's needed is a weekly wet-dust and vacuum (with a machine containing a HEPA filter), plus a surface wipe-down with a warm soap-and-water mix or a natural all-purpose cleaner. If you have a lot of books, give their spines and exposed surfaces a wet-dust or vacuum while you're at it. Once a year, pull them out entirely for wet-dusting and wipe out the shelves.

COMPUTERS

Always turn a computer off before you clean it. Products sold specifically for computer-screen cleaning tend to be far from natural. When a screen needs it, dampen a soft rag with a soap-and-water solution or a natural all-purpose cleaner and wipe. Never spray any cleaning solution directly onto the computer, as you don't want it to drip into the keyboard. Wipe the casing and the keyboard at the same time, but avoid using those spray cans of compressed air, which usually contain environmentally unfriendly additives. Try turning the keyboard over from time to time to shake out crumbs and other particles that may have fallen in there.

WASH YOUR HANDS

One of the most important things to clean in any office is your own two hands. Dust from your keyboard isn't the sort of thing you want to be swallowing with your afternoon snack. Of course, one of the bonuses of working at home is not having to eat at your computer.

PHONES

Most office electronics can be cleaned in a similar fashion to computers, but as your phone is in contact with your mouth and face all day long, you should disinfect it from time to time with a hydrogen peroxide or thymol-based cleaner, or vinegar, especially if you have a cold.

CORDS

Piles of cords make for dust. Slide a cloth dampened with a soap-and-water solution or a natural all-purpose cleaner around the length of a cord to clean it, especially if you see dust clinging to it. Do this while wearing gloves, or wash your hands afterward; cords typically are made of PVC and can contain lead, creating lead dust.

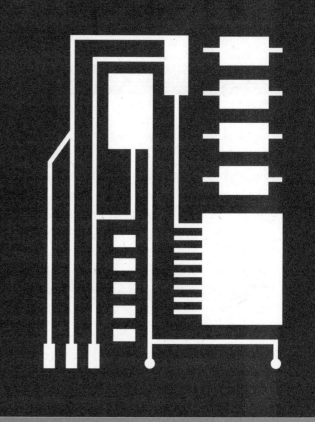

the
BIG PICTURE
Protecting Your Home and
Your Planet

Any conscious home is a small part of a much larger system; what you do at home can impact the world around you, and the world around you can impact what you do at home. Now that you've tackled the necessary nitty-gritty of creating and maintaining a conscious home, you're probably wondering what else you can do beyond your own walls to effect even broader change. It's great to switch your lightbulbs to CFLs—they use 75 percent less energy than incandescents—but to truly slow down global warming and minimize the harm we're collectively doing to our air, water, and earth, we must fully understand these bigger systems we're all a part of and advocate for necessary structural and political change. The combination of personal change plus political influence is how we as a community can protect and maintain our most vital resources for generations to come.

Understanding the Connections

A system is a very basic thing—but it's always more than the sum of its parts. Thinking about systems—focusing on the whole and trying to understand how all of the parts in any system influence one another—is difficult. When trying to visualize the whole, it helps to think metaphorically: drop a pebble in a pond, and it ripples outward in even larger circles. We as a society largely focus on the dropping of the pebble rather than the ripples that flow from its impact. We think about grocery shopping, diaper changing, and gardening without considering their connections to the systems they are a part of, or the unintended consequences of our actions and choices. Many of us simply don't know where our electricity comes from when we turn on a light, or how our wastewater treatment actually works when we drain the bathtub.

Everything we do ultimately touches everything and everyone else. Light a candle and it warms a room, creates smoke, and releases that smoke into our shared air. In isolation, something like ethanol sounds great—what could be better than a fuel made from vegetables? But when you look at it from a systems perspective, you quickly see that creating vegetable fuel involves massive amounts of genetically modified seed, petroleum, and pesticides. If corn is being used, its price can shoot up and, among other things, tortillas are suddenly unaffordable in Mexico. We're all members of an intricately and endlessly connected community.

challenge is to maintain these connections to all of the systems running your home and throughout your life, to literally picture the flow of energy as it moves into and out of your house.

TAKE ACTION

Once you're aware of these whole-house systems, you'll be better positioned to minimize their environmental impact. We can all cut consumption—of stuff, of water, of electricity—and repair, reuse, recycle, and compost. But to make the broadest gesture, we must also get political. Ultimately, legislative action carries more weight than individual action and is necessary to improve and more permanently change these often unsustainable systems. So it's crucial.

Most of us can't sign a bill into law, but we can vote, send e-mails, make phone calls, spread the word to family and friends, and join organizations lobbying to protect our water, create cleaner energy, and conserve our land. We must work together to influence people in charge—of government, of businesses—to bring about systemic change.

KNOW YOUR COMMUNITY'S SYSTEMS

The first step in making broader change is to get to know exactly how our homes and our actions are part of this much larger system, to see the sequences of interrelated events that are needed to make and maintain a household and its contents. Visualize these systems: Where does your garbage go? What's the impact of blasting your air conditioner in the summer? If you've ever experienced a power outage or an issue with your municipal water, or had an insurance claim denied or had problems with a home oil delivery, you know exactly how directly you are connected to those systems. The

Power: Electricity, Heating, and Cooling

On the most basic level, power rules our daily lives. Electricity gives us light. It entertains us, giving life to our phones, televisions, and gadgets. It helps us work, charging our computers, our printers, our cell phones. It feeds us by chilling and freezing our food. It keeps us and our clothes clean by heating up water. It cools us, too. Yet research shows that 90 percent of Americans don't know where the energy that runs our homes comes from. And certainly most of us aren't as aware as we should be that the resources we use to power our lives are finite, and that we will eventually run out of them. Many of us don't recognize that these resources are environmentally destructive to extract, transport, and burn. We're not alone in our homes generating light. Power plants affect the quality of all of our lives and our health.

Our homes hum with this electric power, and our neighborhoods are scattered with the poles and wires that deliver it to us. What's less visible is the air and water pollution this system produces. Generally speaking, the burning of nonrenewable resources creates greenhouse gases, including carbon dioxide, and emits mercury, nitrogen oxide, and sulfur dioxide that dissolve in rain particles and fall to earth (this is known as acid rain). The mercury contaminates fish in our waterways that we then catch and eat, poisoning ourselves. Even if you don't live near a coal power plant, the pollution travels. New England forests are being harmed by mercury smog from power plants in the Midwest, and there is evidence now that emissions from Chinese power plants are reaching the West Coast of America. That's quite a system.

Where Our Electricity Comes From

Most U.S. homes are on the electric grid. The power on the grid is produced in large stations, centralized by regions, and comes mainly from coal, but also from natural gas, nuclear energy, or other sources. These resources are burned to generate steam, which in turn generates electricity.

*Source: U.S. Energy Information Administration, Electric Power Annual (2010)

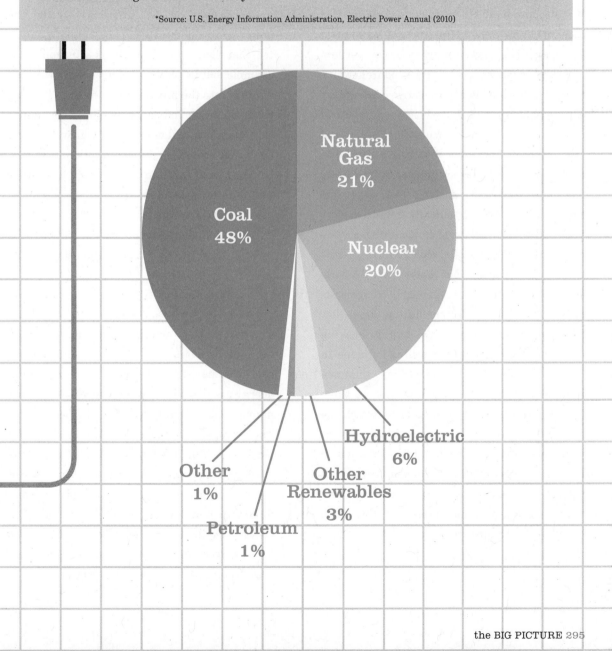

Natural Gas 21%

Coal 48%

Nuclear 20%

Hydroelectric 6%

Other 1%

Other Renewables 3%

Petroleum 1%

WHAT THE FRACK?

Depending on your home, your heating and cooling might or might not be coming from the same source as your electricity. When it comes to heating, natural gas burns cleaner than oil. We also produce it domestically. To use it, a home must have the infrastructure for natural gas, which is common in urban areas, but less common in rural areas. But all nonrenewable energy sources come with negative consequences to our health and the environment. Natural gas is usually extracted from deep wells, and fairly recently it was also discovered trapped in a layer of porous bedrock about 3,000 to 9,000 feet below the earth's surface. To release this, the shale must be hydraulically fractured. This process, called "fracking," is done with a toxic and proprietary mix of chemicals that sickens workers and pollutes our waterways. As a result of that potential danger—and tremendous pressure from environmental groups—New York and Pennsylvania have halted fracking for the time being. But it's still being done in 34 states, so it's a good idea to join the environmental groups working to stop it. To learn more about fracking and its effects, watch the documentary *Gasland*. And get in touch with your representatives to let them know you'd like natural gas to be extracted in a way that cannot contaminate our drinking water, and that gas companies must protect us from harm in the event of a mishap.

SO WHAT CAN BE DONE?

Choose Cleaner Energy

Depending on where you live, your electric company may offer the option of purchasing cleaner energy that they will distribute through the power grid. Choose this. They cannot guarantee that your actual energy is wind only, for example, but by purchasing greener power, you put that into the mix on the grid. And choosing cleaner energy indicates to power companies that there is a real demand for renewable energy. It may cost more than conventional options, but the higher cost can be mitigated by savings from taking measures to conserve energy in your home. Turning to renewable energy reduces pollution and helps protect the environment—and you can't put a price on that.

The Cost of Cleaner Energy

The cost of clean energy varies depending on the options available in your region. You can choose to purchase a percentage of your total energy use from a renewable source or buy a set number of kilowatt-hours (KWh) per month. The average home uses 920 KWh of electricity per month. Purchasing 100 KWh of renewable energy (offsetting more than 1,400 pounds of carbon dioxide per year) would add less than $2 to your monthly bill. Some Green-e Certified energy suppliers can even save you money—up to 30 percent in certain areas. Find clean energy options near you at green-e.org.

Alternative Energy Sources

Homeowners who have the space and where-withal can install solar panels. Or, if you live in the country, you might even be able to erect a wind turbine. People building new houses can also set up a geothermal system (it's rarely cost-effective to do this with existing struc-tures). Such a system pulls warmth from the soil and water in the earth to heat your home and takes the heat out of your home and depos-its it into the earth to cool it. Some states pay subsidies for these eco-upgrades. And if you make enough energy with your panels or wind turbine, you may be able to sell it back to power companies by putting it into the grid.

Individual actions can truly add up. They also create awareness. But even if we're opt-ing for "green" power, we're still depending on an energy system that involves coal. To make the necessary bigger impact, we must ask our politicians to change the systems that generate and regulate industry.

Act Up

✔ *Start Small*

No one can individually stop power plant pollution. But if we all conserve, we could actually eliminate the need for any new power plants to be created.

☐ Turn off lights during the day and when not needed.

☐ Buy energy-efficient appliances.

☐ Use compact fluorescents instead of incandescent light bulbs.

☐ Unplug items that constantly draw electricity, like cell-phone chargers, and equipment with standby circuitry, like televisions, when not in use.

☐ Get a home-energy audit (or perform your own following the steps listed on energystar.gov) to see what other changes you should make.

☐ Opt for renewable energy if your electric company offers it.

☐ Use less hot water when bathing, showering, and washing clothes.

☐ When it comes to using heat, turn down your home thermostat as low as you can tolerate. Most people prefer 65°F at night and 68°F to 72°F during the day. See how you do setting it at 56°F while you are away at work, 64°F when you come home, and 56°F again overnight. Adjust accordingly.

☐ Maintain your systems for optimum efficiency. Clean filters on hot-air systems and air conditioners frequently.

☐ Insulate your home. This includes windows. Make sure whatever plastic, double-sided tape, weather stripping, or caulk you're using is as low-VOC and nontoxic as you can find.

☐ Resist the urge to turn on an air conditioner; use fans and open windows instead. If you must turn on your air conditioner, set it at 75°F or higher, and make sure the filter is clean. When it has reached the end of its useful life, dispose of it properly; the Freon needs to be recovered.

☐ Take advantage of the natural heating and cooling of the earth: draw shades and close windows during the day and open them at night.

✔ Get Involved Where You Live

☐ Let your energy provider and local representatives know you want more alternative and renewable energy initiatives.

☐ Work with neighbors to reduce communal energy use, especially if you live in a large, multiple-dwelling building, like a co-operative or a condo.

☐ Educate and create awareness about energy via community groups, organizations, and schools.

✔ Get Involved Beyond Your Community

☐ Let your state and national representatives know you want more alternative and renewable energy initiatives.

☐ Sign up for action alerts from organizations working on alternative energy sources. When they e-mail you, take action by filling out forms, signing petitions, enlisting friends, writing letters to and calling your representatives, and donating to support their work. You can begin with the websites listed below.

Greenpeace: *greenpeace.org*
Natural Resources Defense Council: *nrdc.org*
Public Interest Research Group: *pirg.org*
Rocky Mountain Institute: *rmi.org*

Waste: Garbage, Recycling, and Composting

With population increase and rising living standards, our waste problem only continues to grow. There are more than 3,000 active and more than 10,000 inactive landfills in the United States. According to the EPA, landfills are the second-largest human-related source of methane emissions in the country. Food and yard waste and materials like paper biodegrade only when they have access to a combination of air, water, light, microbes, and enzymes. But these communal garbage pails are so overstuffed that biodegradable material doesn't have access to these, cannot biodegrade, and thus emits methane. The EPA now requires landfills over a certain size to recapture this potent greenhouse gas and use it as energy.

But it's not just what is getting thrown away; it's where those materials came from. Everything thrown away was first mined or grown from the earth, was processed by people and machines, and required energy and water to make. We have invested so much in it. Is it okay to just throw that investment away?

Every item we think of as waste affects all the other systems on earth. To reduce this impact, we have to reduce the amount of resources we consume, and reuse, recycle, and compost as much as possible. We also have to get political.

Reduce Garbage

The first step in reducing garbage is awareness. Start thinking about shrinking your trash way before it's headed for the pail; do it when shopping. Ask yourself if a product you're considering purchasing is made of recycled material. Look at how much packaging was used, and see if there is a less packaged and more durable version to buy. Then, the next time you put something in the trash, remind yourself that nothing gets thrown "away." Waste can either be reused, recycled, or composted, but if it goes in a garbage pail instead, it's either landfill fodder or it gets shipped off to other countries like China to be incinerated. This sounds absurd, but it's true: we export our garbage. Depending on what is being burned (certain plastics, like PVC, are much worse than others) and how carefully (in a closed system or just out in the open), this is a catastrophe for the atmosphere and for the health of the workers charged with the unenviable task. And for us, too, as those pollutants slowly spread across the earth. Essentially we are spoiling the home we live in. If we remember this fact each time we toss something, it will motivate us to buy less and to reduce what we send to the landfill. Part of the problem is that we live in a country so vast that we're able to locate our landfills in places we can't see. And you know the drill: out of sight, out of mind.

Set the bar high: give yourself a goal of zero garbage. It's impossible in this modern world to send nothing to a landfill, but taking steps toward that lofty goal is very doable.

Reuse

Repair and reuse items as long as you can before recycling them and take steps like using plastic you already have as garbage bags. Buying new plastic bags for trash doesn't make sense. (Neither do new bags treated with fragrance and antimicrobial chemicals. Garbage is inherently smelly and germy; it doesn't stay long in your home, so it doesn't need to wear perfume or be kept free of germs.) If you do buy garbage bags, look for ones made of recycled plastic.

Recycle

Recycling mitigates global climate change because making a new product from recycled material, rather than virgin material, always uses less energy. Recycling also reduces what winds up in our landfills, what gets incinerated (in the United States), and what gets shipped off to foreign countries to be put in landfills or incinerated.

Despite the fact that not every municipality collects all plastics, wax-covered paper, or wire hangers, everything can actually be recycled. During the Depression, and as part of the war effort in the First and Second World Wars,

everything was recycled: glass, aluminum, cotton, rags, even foil from gum wrappers. Resources were that scarce. But as technology progressed, it became cheaper to extract new materials from the earth, and recycling sadly became less advantageous due to its expense and inconvenience. It cost less to buy new and throw out the old than to reuse and recycle what you already had. Recycling is one of those foundational pillars of the environmental movement. Environmentalists began to trumpet recycling in the 1960s and '70s, but the municipal efforts most of us now know as reality didn't get under way until the 1980s, and even then they were fairly ineffective. To this day, there are places that don't recycle and states that don't pay for the bottle deposits widely proven to incentivize Americans to recycle.

Get to know your local program. Then, when shopping, pay attention to packaging and choose the materials—preferably recycled or containing some recycled content—that your hometown accepts for recycling.

Recycled materials need to be considered more valuable, and the infrastructure to collect them must expand. We can all let manufacturers know we want recycled materials by seeking them out, and we can vote with our dollars by purchasing them. It's hard for us at the grocery store to make the connection between the plastic we're buying and global climate change, but it's a reality.

Plastic

Plastic is everywhere: wrappers, beverage containers, shampoo bottles, TVs, toys, phones, and much more. And despite the fact that it comes from petroleum—an unsustainable, nonrenewable resource—virgin plastic is often cheaper than recycled plastic. Most municipal facilities only recycle a couple of kinds of plastic, and there are a lot more than that in the product and waste stream. Those great garbage patches floating around in the Atlantic and Pacific oceans are terrifying reminders of what happens when people throw plastic "away."

Using recycled materials means eliminating most of the steps along the processing chain. To make a plastic bottle, you have to have an oil well in the ground or the ocean, build a platform to extract it, transport the extracted oil, and refine the oil to turn it into plastic. If we recycle all of our plastic and use it to make new plastic, we don't need this oil and all of its trappings, risk, and emissions. Latest estimates indicate we're using 331 million barrels of petroleum and natural gas per year in the creation of virgin plastic. That's nearly double the amount we use to make gasoline.

Paper

Virgin paper is also often cheaper than recycled, because our government spends a billion dollars a year subsidizing road construction resulting in a surplus of cut-down trees. Paper can and should be recycled. It makes no sense to bury it in a landfill when tremendous resources were required to convert trees into paper in the first place.

Metal

The same goes for metals; it takes a monumental amount of energy and pollution to mine raw material from the earth and refine it into metals. Recycling it is much less intensive. Melting and re-forming aluminum, for example, takes a mere fraction of the energy necessary to mine then convert bauxite into virgin aluminum.

Recycling can be pretty confusing. Some towns take hangers and milk cartons; others don't. Some take plastic #1 and #2 but not #3 through #7. Familiarize yourself with what your town takes and sort carefully. Many of us throw things in the recycling bin without knowing if they are recyclable in our municipalities or not. This drives up the cost of recycling because someone has to manually re-sort everything, and it can contaminate the stream of material. Donate unrecyclable plastic items like furniture or kids' toys to Goodwill, or organize a swap with friends and members of your community.

Hazardous Materials

Despite the fact that most of us toss batteries, electronics, and more without even thinking about it, it is usually illegal to do so. If it isn't, it should be; these products contain harmful substances that leach into our groundwater. Set these items—plus things like paint and other construction material remnants—aside in your home. Every once in a while, make a trip to your town's hazardous waste collection center. Some states now have producer responsibility laws: it's up to manufacturers to dispose of hazardous items. Over time we will continue to see the burden of disposal shift from consumers to manufacturers. This will inevitably motivate companies to design more recyclable and fewer disposable products.

COMPOSTING

Composting food scraps and yard waste is good common sense. It's easy if you live in a rural area, but it can and should be done in cities, too. You don't even need a yard or a balcony to compost; it can be done indoors in worm bins or electric composters, which use minimal wattage to break down food scraps quickly. Many community gardens have their own compost bins and will accept scraps from garden members or neighbors. For urbanites with no access to plants or outdoor space, compost can be given to friends and family with access or (furtively) placed around city tree trunks or plants in parks. Composting is always preferable to using a garbage disposal, as putting too much food down a disposal can add a burden to municipal waste treatment plants. Once you start composting and see how emaciated your garbage is, you won't believe you didn't start earlier. Bonus: your garbage will hardly smell.

Act Up

✔ *Start Small*

☐ When shopping, seek out items and packaging made from recycled materials.

☐ Buy items that can be recycled in your municipality. So-called biodegradable plastic sounds good, but if it ends up in a landfill, it can't biodegrade.

☐ Repair and reuse before recycling.

☐ If your town doesn't recycle a certain type of plastic, a local store might. Look for ones that take back plastic #4 shopping bags or #5 containers.

☐ Reuse plastic shopping bags as garbage bags.

☐ Donate items you're no longer using to organizations like the Salvation Army or Goodwill that can use or resell them. Or post them on websites like craigslist.org or freecycle.org.

☐ Take batteries, CFLs, electronics, and old paint to hazardous waste collection sites. Look them up on earth911.com and 1800recycling.com.

☐ Start a compost bin. There are many websites devoted to composting, and the EPA maintains a page devoted to it at epa.gov/compost.

✔ *Get Involved Where You Live*

☐ On a municipal level, support structural changes that make recycling mandatory and put bottle bills into effect, if they aren't already law in your community.

☐ Petition your municipality to put in a facility that can handle more than a few kinds of plastic.

☐ Ask your municipality to charge for garbage by weight and to collect compost. San Francisco, Seattle, Toronto, and others are already successfully gathering food scraps.

☐ Organize a communitywide e-waste drive or hazardous waste drive.

☐ Organize a neighborhood yard sale or a community toy or clothing swap.

☐ Get active with local composting groups to help educate others.

✔ *Get Involved Beyond Your Community*

☐ Put pressure on officials to enact broader, tougher recycling laws, fees for garbage disposal, and better regulation of what's leaching into the ground from landfills.

☐ Ask the companies you purchase from to use recycled materials.

☐ Get involved with organizations working to ameliorate the waste situation:

The Ecology Center: *ecologycenter.org*
GreenBlue Institute: *greenblue.org*
Greenpeace: *greenpeace.org*
Zero Waste America: *zerowasteamerica.org*

Water

We are water. Literally. It makes up more than 60 percent of our body weight. We cannot live without it. Perhaps more than any other natural resource, it connects us to our environment, and our misuse of it is both monumental and easy to see. Water comes into our homes from lakes, rivers, and underground aquifers. We send it back to those same sources burdened by a multitude of contaminants. On the most basic level, every day we actively pollute the very water we drink: we flush our waste into our tap water. We also pollute our drinking water with agricultural runoff, pesticides, factory waste, and wastewater treatment plant sludge. It's not just big companies polluting what we sip; individuals play a huge role in this system. Everything we pour in our drains, flush down our toilets, or spray on our lawns comes back to us via our faucets.

TAP WATER

Some potable water, like the H_2O that flows out of the taps in New York City or Boston, comes from protected water sources—runoff from mountains, dammed up—because city planners more than 150 years ago recognized the need for independent water supplies. But towns and cities along the Mississippi, including St. Louis, use the mighty river as both sewer and water fountain. Water from unprotected sources is either taken from the points in the waterways where currents keep it cleanest, or from somewhere less pristine. And before people can drink this mix from any source, or bathe in it, it must be treated.

Water treatment involves filtering out organic matter—animal droppings, leaves, and the like—then disinfecting with chlorine, or chlorine plus ammonia. The latter, chloramination, is an increasingly popular method said to lower toxic disinfecting by-products, which are regulated by the EPA. There are alternatives to both that are safer, but only a handful of water-treatment plants use them. Disinfection is necessary, so these chemicals—which have problematic ramifications—are present in our drinking water at low levels that are considered safe by the government. But drinking them day in and day out may have health effects down the line. Studies suggest the possibility of elevated miscarriage rates for heavy drinkers of chlorinated water in the first trimester of pregnancy.

Most of us don't know how our municipalities filter our water. It's worth asking. We can't change how they're doing it, but having that knowledge means we can choose our own filters to remove or at least decrease those substances. Home filters can also remove or decrease lead and other substances the water encounters as it journeys through pipes from the treatment plant to our faucets. But they can't totally eliminate our exposure to harmful substances in water. The lettuce we eat is still irrigated with it, and the fish we dine on are still swimming in it. It's a systemic disconnect that we don't see all of the food we eat as part of this water system. What do you think our cows are drinking?

Filters are helpful, but really we need to stop putting bad substances in our water in the first place. The Environmental Working Group (EWG) claims that water utilities spend 19 times more on water-treatment chemicals every year than the federal government invests in protecting lakes and rivers from pollution. There has been recent focus in the media, for instance, about the pesticide atrazine, which is banned in the E.U. but allowed in the United States, in our drinking water. Atrazine has been linked to cancer and associated with birth defects. There is widespread concern about this one pesticide in the water, but not about the corn it's usually sprayed on, through which it not only gets into the groundwater and waterways but enters our food supply via myriad avenues (corn and its derivatives are ubiquitous).

EWG, the nonprofit consumer watchdog, has done a drinking-water-quality analysis of about 20 million records obtained from state water officials. From its research, it found that more than half of the chemicals detected in our tap water aren't subject to health or safety regulations and can legally be present in any amount. The EWG also reports that our government has not set a single new drinking water standard since 2001 and is calling for a national assessment of drinking water quality, along with new safety standards, pollution-prevention policy, and consumer education and outreach.

BOTTLED WATER

Given all this, it's no wonder the bottled-water industry has thrived. Fear of tap water sends us to the store. But studies have shown that bottled water is no safer than municipal tap water, and sometimes it is more contaminated. The EPA standards are stronger and more regulated for tap than the FDA's are for bottled (strangely, they're not overseen by the same agency). And here's the rub: most bottled water, as it turns out, is actually municipal water. We buy it to avoid tap, but it *is* tap. Several documentaries have been filmed on the topic (like *Flow* and *Tapped*). The bottled-water industry is finally registering its first decreases in sales as a direct result of the organizations working to spread the truth about bottled water.

PET Plastic

Most plastic water bottles are made of PET #1 plastic, which has long been considered safe. But some are starting to question that belief. Reports are surfacing that it leaches hormone-disrupting phthalates into its contents under certain circumstances, including high temperatures and prolonged storage, though it is more likely to leach into liquids like vinegar and soda than water. When the bottles end up in the ocean, PET breaks down into small plastic pellets. Fish ingest these, then we ingest the seafood.

Other reasons to avoid bottled water:

* You're paying up to 2,000 times as much, depending on the brand of water, for what's essentially free in your own home.

* Most bottled water is chlorinated, a fact that is not required to be mentioned on the label.

* Bottled-water manufacturers are not required to disclose the results of their contaminant testing to their customers.

* Bottled water comes in a petrochemical-derived plastic bottle that you use for a very brief period of time. Sure, you can recycle that bottle, but the Government Accountability Office says that 75 percent of water bottles are actually just thrown in the garbage, not the recycling bin. They're overwhelming landfills: it takes 1,000 years for a plastic water bottle to biodegrade. These bottles are also swirling about garbage patches in our oceans.

* That bottle of water was also likely transported either across the country or across the world to reach you, wasting precious fossil fuels on its journey.

THE BOTTLED WATER LIFE CYCLE

75% of bottles end up in landfills

Water is transported from a remote source

You buy it, drink it, then toss it

Water is processed and packaged in bottles made from unhealthy and unrenewable petrochemicals

Bottles are warehoused and then delivered

Bottles are packaged and shipped around the globe

SO WHAT CAN BE DONE?

You can find out about your own water, test it inexpensively for contaminates, filter it accordingly, and drink it in reusable glasses at home and reusable (preferably stainless steel) bottles when on the go. And you can also advocate for cleaner water for all. There are safeguards at the municipal level that are invisible to us until they stop working—like when a water main breaks. But they don't have to be so invisible.

Every municipal system providing water to more than 50 people is required by the EPA to issue an annual report on the quality of the water. This report, sometimes called an annual Consumer Confidence Report, or CCR, will include the compliance and/or failure of your water to adhere to government-set standards. The CCR lists the level of contaminants that have been detected over a certain period of time and shows how these levels compare with the EPA's drinking water regulations. If you're not a toxicologist or a chemist, these reports might be difficult to read. Keep in mind that the contaminants mentioned in the reports are, generally speaking, in the water at very low levels. There may be no immediate threat, but there is concern about what might transpire over a lifetime of exposure. These water reports are good references to have and consult when choosing a home water filtration system and when advocating for safe water.

If your water is highly contaminated, your municipality legally has to provide you with an alternative. You can also have your water tested to reveal what contaminants might be introduced when it leaves the treatment plant and comes out of your tap. Some municipalities offer this service for free. For more information, go to epa.gov/drink.

LOOK IT UP

The Environmental Working Group maintains a database on drinking water quality: ewg.org/tap-water. Type in your zip code to see how your municipal water fares. This is also a helpful tool if you're traveling and curious about the tap water where you're headed. In addition, some water suppliers post their annual CCR reports on the EPA's website: epa.gov. If you cannot find yours in either place, you can request it by calling your water utility. Alert your neighbors and community members if you find out something they should know.

Wells

If you have well water instead of municipal water, testing it is a must. Do you live near any large industrial farms? Do you live in a part of the country where radon is a concern? Deep wells do tend to be sheltered from contamination by a layer of bedrock that isolates the drinking water. Soil also acts as a filter. Fracking, a method of natural gas removal involving highly toxic chemicals (see page 296), can disrupt that layer and inject hazardous waste into well water. Fracking (or hydraulic fracturing) is an operation of the natural gas industry that is regulated by the State. Find out if fracking is being done near where you live—complaints have come from people living as far away as 60 miles from a drilling site. Thankfully, completely contaminated well water is rare, but if you do have it, you will, for once, need to rely on bottled water until you can identify the source of contamination and have it removed. This isn't an easy task. If your groundwater has been contaminated with a pesticide, the manufacturer may legally be required to install a water filter in your home.

Filters

Installing a home filter is a prudent precaution; even if your water gets a stellar report, things can enter it on its way from the plant or the well to your faucet. Old pipes, leading to or inside your building, may contain lead. On any given day, there could be extra contamination at the source, a spike in the amount of chlorine used, newly corroded pipes, or any number of contaminants that aren't removed at treatment plants. These can be reduced if you use an activated carbon filter, which is what most common pitcher filters contain. Activated carbon is an inexpensive option and works well for most issues. But there are other, more expensive filtering options for your sink or your whole house that will remove more contaminants from your water than carbon does. Be sure to maintain or change all filters diligently. Filters have a capacity, and as you approach it, they may reintroduce pollutants to your water.

The following description of the types of filters on the market comes from the NRDC's Consumer Guide to Water Filters (nrdc.org/water/drinkingfilters.asp). All filters should adhere to the joint National Sanitation Foundation (nsf.org) and American National Standards Institute (ansi.org) Standard 53, which covers drinking water treatment filters. They do independent testing to ensure that the pollutants a filter claims to minimize are actually being reduced under specific conditions. Take a moment to learn about the company that manufactures your filter, and make sure you want to support it.

Activated Carbon Filter

How it works: Positively charged and highly absorbent carbon in the filter attracts and traps many impurities.

Used in: Countertop, faucet filters, and under-the-sink units.

Gets rid of: Bad tastes and odors, including chlorine. Standard 53–certified filters also can substantially reduce many hazardous contaminants, including heavy metals such as copper, lead, and mercury; disinfection by-products; parasites such as giardia and cryptosporidium; pesticides; radon; and volatile organic chemicals such as methyl tert-butyl ether (MTBE), dichlorobenzene, and trichloroethylene (TCE).

Cation Exchange Softener

How it works: "Softens" hard water by trading minerals with a strong positive charge for ones with less of a charge.

Used in: Whole-house, point-of-entry units.

Gets rid of: Calcium and magnesium, which form mineral deposits in plumbing and fixtures, as well as barium and some other ions that can create health hazards.

Distiller

How it works: Boils water and recondenses the purified steam.

Used in: Countertop or whole-house units; can be combined with a carbon filter.

Gets rid of: Heavy metals such as cadmium, chromium, copper, lead, and mercury, as well as arsenic, barium, fluoride, selenium, and sodium.

Reverse Osmosis

How it works: A semipermeable membrane separates impurities from the water. (Note: this filtration technique wastes a substantial amount of water during the treatment process.)

Used in: Under-the-sink units, often in combination with a carbon filter or ultraviolet disinfection unit.

Gets rid of: Most contaminants, including certain parasites such as cryptosporidium and giardia; heavy metals such as cadmium, copper, lead, and mercury; and other pollutants, including arsenic, barium, nitrate/nitrite, perchlorate, and selenium.

Ultraviolet Disinfection

How it works: Ultraviolet light kills bacteria and other microorganisms.

Used in: Under-the-sink units, often in combination with a carbon filter and sediment screen.

Gets rid of: Bacteria and parasites; class-A systems protect against harmful bacteria and viruses, including cryptosporidium and giardia, while class-B systems are designed to make non-disease-causing bacteria inactive.

AVOIDING PLASTIC

Most pitcher filters are plastic. If you don't want to store your drinking water in plastic, install an under-the-counter or faucet filter. If you like your water cold, you can fill a glass pitcher with filtered water and place it in the fridge. If a plastic pitcher is your only option, look for one made of #2 or #5 plastic, and gently hand wash it when you're changing the filter.

Chances are if you live in a part of the country where there is a water shortage, you're already practicing conservation methods. But even if you currently aren't lacking for water, conservation is still wise. Here are some thoughts beyond taking short showers, running only full dishwashers and laundry machines, and never letting the tap run when washing hands or brushing teeth.

* Did you know that it takes 250 liters of water to make one liter of soda when you factor in the water needed to grow the components, like the sugar? Drink water instead.

* When planning your garden, take irrigation and watering into account. Don't choose plants that will need more water than Mother Nature can provide, and water early or late in the day to avoid the sun's evaporating effect.

* Buy rain barrels that collect rain from your gutters to be used for watering your garden.

* Check for leaks. An unusually high water bill can clue you in to one you might not see. Even a small leak in a hose or an outdoor faucet can waste hundreds or thousands of gallons of water over time.

Drain No!

There are some substances that should never go down your drain, like leftover hazardous liquids found in your garage, certain hormone-disrupting cosmetic residues, and even your leftover pharmaceuticals. These get into our waterways but are not specifically treated by municipal plants, though most of them can be reduced by an activated carbon filter. Be part of the solution, not the problem, by using only certified natural cosmetics and by disposing of your drugs properly in the first place. You can take them back to most pharmacies, or you can follow safe disposal instructions at whitehousedrugpolicy.gov. Share what you learn with friends and neighbors. If we're all educated about what not to put in water in the first place, we will reduce the cost of removing it down the line, and end up with better drinking water.

Act Up

✔ Start Small

☐ Test your tap water and filter accordingly.

☐ Ask your water utility for a copy of its yearly report; this will keep you informed, but it also lets the utility know citizens are paying attention.

☐ Ask your municipality how it disinfects your water.

☐ Avoid bottled water. Drink filtered tap water out of glasses at home and stainless steel reusable bottles on the go.

✔ Get Involved Where You Live

☐ Support organizations working to preserve your local waterways and bring attention to water contamination and conservation issues.

☐ Share what you know about your own water with neighbors, friends, and family.

✔ Get Involved Beyond Your Community

☐ Clean water for all is the ultimate goal. The following organizations are some of the many working to make that a possibility. Join them and support their cause.

Clean Water Action:
cleanwateraction.org
Corporate Accountability International:
stopcorporateabuse.org/water-campaign
Waterkeeper Alliance: *waterkeeper.org*

Indoor Air Quality

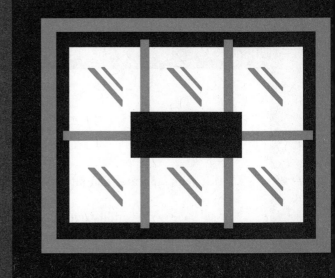

Historically we have worried about air pollution outside our homes. And with good reason: certain places are truly polluted. Stricter air-quality regulations have meant that cities like Los Angeles are now less polluted than they once were. It's time to start turning a similar focus on indoor air, which is getting worse even as progress is being made regulating outdoor air. In fact, the EPA lists indoor air pollution as one of its top five concerns and priorities.

The problems with outdoor air are also relevant indoors. There might not be a bus directly blowing exhaust into your bedroom window, but those same chemicals are bound up in the items we bring into our homes. We now know that, due to construction materials, furniture, cosmetics, cleaning products, and carpets, our indoor air, according to the EPA, is two to five times more polluted than outdoor air, even in cities. It has been calculated that in-

door air pollution results in $30 billion a year spent on treatment of health-related illnesses. Evidence abounds:

* As of 2009, the American Academy of Allergy Asthma & Immunology estimated that 40 to 50 million Americans have allergic diseases; more than half of all U.S. citizens test positive for one or more allergens; and more than 50 percent of our homes have at least six detectable allergens present.

* Allergies like asthma, chronic sinusitis, allergic dermatitis (eczema), and urticaria (hives) have become more prevalent.

* From 1982 to 1996, the prevalence of asthma in the United States increased by 49 percent, and 78.6 percent for children under 18.

* The number of people with asthma is expected to grow by more than 100 million by 2025.

* According to various surveys, 15 to 30 percent of Americans (37 to 75 million people) report that they are unusually sensitive or allergic to certain common chemicals such as detergents, perfumes, solvents, pesticides, pharmaceuticals, foods, or even the smell of dry-cleaned clothes. An estimated 5 percent of Americans have been diagnosed by a physician as being especially sensitive. Many of these people react so strongly that they can become disabled from very low exposures to common substances.

Still, people remain mostly focused on outdoor air. What we do inside affects outside air too. Tests show that in cities including Los Angeles, Denver, and Baltimore, household cleaning products, personal care products, paints, and stains are the largest sources of VOCs after cars. The California Air Resources Board estimates that cleaning products are the No. 2 source of VOCs in Los Angeles; in Baltimore they're No. 4; and in Denver, they're No. 5.

SO WHAT CAN BE DONE?

We take in ten times more air by weight when breathing than we do food when eating. If we're worrying about traces of pesticides in our food, we should also be worried about traces of contaminants in our air. One of the challenges to taking charge of our indoor air is that there is no systemic campaign on the issue of indoor air quality as a whole. Green builders and their organizations are focusing on construction and building materials. Parent groups focus on art materials and toys. Green cleaning product companies focus on cleaners. The EPA covers outdoor air. OSHA covers workplace air. This makes us the regulatory agency for our own homes.

As there is no true understanding of what happens when we're exposed, year in and year out, to accumulated pollutants from mattresses, cleaners, construction materials, and other sources, it's wise to take the individual precautions for each room described throughout the book. As we clean up the air in our own homes, we'll also reduce the amount of pollution we're responsible for adding to the outdoor air. Our indoor VOCs contribute to the smog and ozone affecting everyone around us.

We also need to get active and push for legislation that will reduce the amount of hazardous chemicals in general household products across the board. And we need to ask our elected officials for indoor air pollution regulations.

Act Up

✔ *Start Small*

☐ Reduce the amount of pollution you're adding to both indoor air and outdoor air by buying and bringing home only items that are the least likely to off-gas toxic fumes. Use green cleaners, natural cosmetics, no-VOC paint, and safe construction materials. Ventilate your home well.

☐ Use air filters or install a whole-house air filter.

☐ Reduce energy consumption. The energy we use to light and run our homes greatly contributes to air pollution, indoor and out.

✔ *Get Involved Where You Live*

☐ Spread the word to your community, especially schools, about indoor air pollution. Help committees like your Parent Teacher Association take steps to reduce indoor air pollution. Get local elected officials involved if needed.

☐ If you live in a co-op, condo, or rental apartment building, work with management to switch to green cleaners and make other choices to reduce indoor air pollution.

✔ *Get Involved Beyond Your Community*

☐ Sign up to get action alerts from the California Air Resources Board: arb.ca.gov.

☐ Let your elected officials know you want stronger reforms to block the toxic chemicals in everyday products that are polluting our air by signing up to get action alerts from the sites below:

The Environmental Working Group's
Kid-Safe Chemicals Act blog:
ewg.org/kid-safe-chemicals-act-blog
Safer Chemicals, Healthy Families:
saferchemicals.org

Outdoor Spaces

For those of us lucky enough to have outdoor space—a backyard or an apartment complex with a shared lawn—keeping it beautiful doesn't have to mean putting toxic chemicals on it. Not only are you poisoning the lawn for children, adults, and pets, but there is also runoff and volatilization of the fertilizers, herbicides, and pesticides that pollute the water and the air. Whatever you put on your lawn or grow in your garden is part of a much larger system. Pesticides sprayed on your neighbor's lawn don't just remain within his or her property lines; they permeate the whole neighborhood and beyond. Your dog can't read those pesticide warnings. He will run free and roll around in recently sprayed pesticides, then bound into your house, jump on your sofa, and cuddle with your children.

PARKS

Shared outdoor spaces are essential to healthy ecosystems, contributing to quality of life for all. Trees are cooling in urban spaces. Parks in the city are home to a whole world of bugs and birds not found elsewhere. We should all be supportive of our parks. Outside urban America, the preservation of large, open spaces is equally crucial. National parks deserve protection and shouldn't be opened up to mineral or oil exploration.

states away, a garden that requires heavy watering isn't doing anyone or anything much good.

* Perennials are preferable to annuals—it doesn't really make sense to buy something that only grows for one year and then must be replanted again the next.

* Always water early or late in the day, so the water will be absorbed rather than evaporated by the sun.

Lawns

* If you're willing, you can give up a lawn entirely, embrace gravel, and plant only things that don't need much water. Semi-wild outdoor spaces that don't require watering or cutting are becoming quite trendy.

* If you're not willing to give up your lawn, plant breeds of grass that need very little water and grow slowly so they don't need to be mowed often.

SO WHAT CAN BE DONE?

Gardens

To avoid polluting yourself, your neighbors, and the earth, care for your outdoor space naturally.

* Consult websites and lawn-care companies that are devoted to natural and organic gardening.

* When planning a garden, include only plants that are local or acclimated to your growing zone. Anything that needs a lot of water is a better choice for rainy New England than for parched Arizona. If you live in a part of the country where your water is sourced three

When it comes to mowing lawns or blowing leaves, use tools that pollute as little as possible. If you have a small space, a push mower might be an option. If you're using gas-powered equipment, crank it up as infrequently as possible. Those small two-stroke engines cause a disproportionate amount of pollution; they require that you add oil to the gasoline to run them. Using one for an hour is about the equivalent of driving a car 100 miles. Certain states are now passing laws requiring lawn-care equipment with four-stroke engines, which separate the oil from the fuel and burn more cleanly. When the time comes to replace a two-stroke engine mower, do so with a four-stroke version. Depending on what the old mower is made of, a scrap-metal place might be willing to take it, or you could try putting it on freecycle.org or looking up what to do with it on 1800recycling.com.

Consider battery- and electric-powered equipment, which pollutes less.

Parks

A park might not be your own yard, but you can still have influence over how it's tended, especially if it is a community garden. We can all advocate for the green spaces around our homes, buildings, schools, and playgrounds to be pesticide-free. Either join forces with the groups that physically plant and maintain local gardens or offer your time by making phone calls and sending e-mails and letters to support their protection and safe care.

Act Up

✔ *Start Small*

☐ Use natural lawn care. Look up alternative solutions at BeyondPesticides.org and Rodale.com.

☐ Plant perennials that do well in your climate.

☐ Rely on push mowers and hand tools, and minimize use of gasoline-powered machinery.

✔ *Get Involved Where You Live*

☐ Get involved with local government to ensure that good "Neighbor Notification" laws are in place. These require that ample notice is given to neighbors for certain commercial lawn applications.

☐ Work with local government to ban the use of specific lawn pesticides.

☐ Make sure you know when and if your town is spraying for seasonal pests like mosquitoes, and ask officials to use the least toxic chemical needed to get the job done.

✔ *Get Involved Beyond Your Community*

☐ Support and sign up for action alerts from organizations working to keep our parks, wilderness, and wildlife intact:

National Parks Conservation Association: *npca.org*
Pesticide Action Network of North America: *panna.org*
World Wildlife Fund: *worldwildlife.org*

Money

So you go out and get a great job working for, say, a nonprofit or a responsible business. You're working for a wonderful organization and doing good things. Life is swell. Your check for this excellent work automatically gets deposited in the bank. Then that well-earned money is used by the bank to finance a toxic chemical company, or invested in bad mortgages that end up throwing people out of their homes, or goes to support mountaintop removal mining. Your money, once in a checking or savings account, may be doing all kinds of things that might be contrary to your values, unless you put it in an institution that is aligned with your values. These institutions do exist. It could be a credit union or a bank that informs clients of the types of activities it loans to or invests in. But the majority of banks lack this transparency, as do most insurance companies.

Much has been said within the green community about "voting with your dollars." This usually only pertains to purchasing products, but it should also be considered when seeking out services. Use your influence wisely when choosing banks, credit card companies, and even cell-phone providers. Think of them the same way you think of going to the farmers' market, where you buy good products from local farmers doing the right thing. Invest in a similar fashion.

SO WHAT CAN BE DONE?

To put your money in banks that have a set of values and a focus that are aligned with yours, begin by searching for an independent bank or a community investment bank. You may run into a neighborhood bank exclusively focused on investing in low-income housing or helping people start small businesses. Read the fine print. HSBC has dubbed itself the world's "local" bank, which is like saying Wal-Mart is a local grocery store. If you cannot find a community bank near you, choose one elsewhere. Most banking can be done by mail, e-mail, and ATMs, so you're not limited by geography. The largest resource for socially and environmentally responsible banks and credit unions, plus financial planners, credit cards, mutual funds, and even retirement options is the Social

Investment Forum (socialinvest.org). Neighborhood groups, parenting boards, and friends and family may also lead you to some good conscious options.

It's arguably easier to find green companies to invest in than it is to find a socially responsible bank; and locating that kind of bank is easier still than finding a holistic insurance provider. The same websites that will help locate a better bank (page 330) can lead to a better insurance provider, though they are few and far between. If you can't find one, ask your current insurance company how it invests its money and see what you think of the answer.

Act Up

✔ Start Small

☐ Move your checking, savings, and mortgage to a socially responsible bank. Ask questions when looking for a new bank, and don't forget to tell your old bank why you're leaving when you close your account.

☐ Green your investments and seek out green credit card and retirement options on socialinvest.org, greenamericatoday.org, and greenmoneyjournal.com.

☐ When buying insurance, be sure to ask providers how they invest policyholders' money.

✔ Get Involved Where You Live

☐ If you're involved with investments at work, as part of a homeowner's association, or through a community group, speak with management or other community members about switching your bank to a more socially responsible one.

✔ Get Involved Beyond Your Community

☐ The following organizations all reach beyond the personal:

Americans for Financial Reform:
ourfinancialsecurity.org
Business for Shared Prosperity:
businessforsharedprosperity.org
Responsible Wealth:
faireconomy.org/issues/responsible_wealth

Community

The true reason we will never live in isolated green bubbles even if we want to is that we're social creatures. All of the constructs of society are communal ones. From family to school to work to group hobbies, community is what sustains human beings. Some of us feel driven by this innate sense to participate civically and take responsibility for our roles in society. But more and more often we don't. This lack of participation can have devastating results. An extreme version of this is that the most toxic facilities and plants built by manufacturers of things like PVC and chlorine bleach tend to be located in the neighborhoods, towns, and cities with the least community involvement. Building community is what's needed for these citizens to fight back, to stop the pollution.

According to the U.S. Census Bureau, about one in six Americans moves each year. We're a pretty mobile society. Before making a move, systematically considering the community you're headed to—if you

have the luxury to do so—is a good idea, and can help you make a difference and lead an impactful life. Take into account schools, water quality, the breadth of recycling programs, access to farm-fresh food via markets or farm shares, local government, availability of bike paths in car communities, the capacity to grow food, and the ease of accessing nature. Ultimately, you want a home that works for both you and your neighbors, if you have a choice.

Even if you're not moving, you can still make an effort to get more involved where you do live. Read local newspapers to stay on top of neighborhood issues. Seek out groups of like-minded people: political, environmental, recreational. It doesn't matter if you're a birder, a jogger, a knitter, or even a misanthrope: human interaction can lead to action for the greater good. Join in to make a difference.

SO WHAT CAN BE DONE?

Be aware of your community and your neighbors no matter where you live. Make an effort to consider the effect of your actions on others as you go about your day. Try to see yourself as part of a greater whole, and remember that the decisions we make today have long-lasting ramifications for us, our neighbors, other citizens of the world, and generations to come.

Act Up

✔ Start Small

☐ Begin at home. Treat your living space with care, remembering that your actions can affect your neighbors and the world.

☐ If moving, carefully consider the community you'll be moving to and, if you have a choice, choose wisely. Factor in everything from public transportation to schools to local politics to manufacturing and power plants.

☐ If building a new home, make it as small, green, and energy-efficient as possible.

✔ Get Involved Where You Live

☐ Don't stand on the sidelines—jump in and get involved. Stand up for something near and dear to your heart that benefits the community, such as clean water, environmental justice, alternative energy, or composting.

☐ Get political. Stay on top of issues where you live. If your town is small enough, get to know your elected officials. If you live in a large city, you can still let government workers know by phone, e-mail, and city hall protests about concerns you and your community might be having.

✔ Get Involved Beyond Your Community

☐ If the Internet has proven anything, it's that community can exist beyond familiar faces. Get involved with environmental groups and organizations working to protect and clean up the world we share. They send action alerts and ask for you to e-mail, write, and call your elected officials. Do your part.

☐ Boycott, protest, and otherwise make noise when necessary.

TOXICITY GUIDE

When you read about something—a product, an ingredient, or a chemical—being "toxic" or a "probable carcinogen," it's not always obvious to the average consumer what exactly that means. Here's the breakdown. The following definitions are based on those used by the United Nations Globally Harmonized System of Classification and Labeling of Chemicals (UNGHS) and the International Agency for Research on Cancer (IARC), part of the World Health Organization. The FDA regulates cosmetic products but doesn't actually define these terms specifically for them. The Consumer Product Safety Commission and the Environmental Protection Agency use similar definitions.

TOXIC: Has a lethal dose of 50–500 mg/kg. In other words, less than 500 mg has a 50 percent chance of causing death in a 2.5-lb animal when given orally. A 110-lb person would have to ingest about 1 ounce to suffer a 50 percent chance of dying.

SLIGHTLY/MODERATELY TOXIC: Has a lethal dose of 500–5,000 mg/kg. In other words, 500–5,000 mg of such a substance has a 50 percent chance of causing death in a 2.5-lb animal. A 110-lb person would have to ingest between 1 ounce and 1 cup to suffer a 50 percent chance of dying.

NONTOXIC: Has a lethal dose of over 5 g/kg. In other words, a 110-lb person would have to ingest about 1 cup of the substance to suffer a 50 percent chance of dying. That said, products labeled "nontoxic" may cause sickness and should not be consumed. If one is swallowed, play it safe and call your doctor.

ACUTE TOXICITY: Has health effects that appear after short-term exposure, such as skin, eye, or respiratory irritation; mild to strong allergic reactions; or death occurring in less than twenty-four hours of exposure.

CHRONIC TOXICITY: Has health effects that appear after long-term or repeated exposure and can result in cancer, neurological or autoimmune disorders, hormone or reproductive effects, tissue damage, or death.

KNOWN TOXICITY: Sufficient evidence to support the idea that the ingredient can cause adverse health effects in humans.

PROBABLE TOXICITY: Known to cause adverse health effects in animals but with limited evidence supporting similar health effects in humans.

POSSIBLE TOXICITY: Sufficient evidence of harm to animals, but no evidence of harm to humans.

SUSPECTED TOXICITY: Used interchangeably with probable.

SEVERELY IRRITATING: Causes continuous, intense, uncomfortable irritation that is intolerable and may persist for more than 21 days. Often corrosive.

IRRITATING: Causes short-term irritation that subsides within a few hours.

SLIGHTLY IRRITATING: Does not cause irritation or causes irritation that passes quickly.

BIOACCUMULATION: Occurs when chemicals accumulate permanently in the blood, tissues, or organs of a living organism, and may lead to adverse health effects.

PERSISTS IN THE ENVIRONMENT: Is non-biodegradable and remains in the environment as a pollutant that will not be broken down or destroyed.

BIOCIDE: A broad term for a chemical substance capable of killing a living organism. Biocides are usually used in selective ways as pesticides or antimicrobials.

PESTICIDE: A chemical substance that is capable of killing, repelling, or preventing pests (rodents, insects, weeds, fungi, and other microorganisms). Consumers are familiar with these being used in agriculture and in gardens, but they're also found in cosmetics, cleaning products, and more.

INGREDIENTS GUIDE

Alkyl phenoxy ethoxylates (APEs, including nonyl phenoxy ethoxylate)

Function:
- Surfactants

Found in:
- Dishwashing and laundry detergents, all-purpose and carpet cleaners, pesticides, and industrial cleaners

Reasons to Avoid:
- Hormone disrupters—may cause such reproductive/developmental issues as birth defects, infertility, and reduced sperm count
- Petroleum-derived
- Slow to biodegrade

Alkanol amines (monoethanolamine [MEA], diethanolamine [DEA], triethanolamine [TEA])

Function:
- pH adjusters (TEA functions as a fragrance ingredient and surfactant as well)

Found in:
- All-purpose cleaners, dishwashing liquids, laundry detergents, liquid hand soaps, sunscreens, moisturizers, facial cleansers, anti-itch creams, shampoos, makeup

Reasons to Avoid:
- May cause adverse blood effects, liver and kidney damage
- May form nitrosamines, which are known to be carcinogenic
- VOCs—contribute to indoor and outdoor air pollution
- Petroleum-derived

Alkyl ammonium chloride (quat 15)

Function:
- Preservative or antistatic agent

Found in:
- Disinfectants, deodorizers, fragrances, detergents, baby shampoos, baby wipes

Reasons to Avoid:
- May cause contact dermatitis (or similar skin allergies) in sensitive people
- Releases formaldehyde, a known human carcinogen

Alkyl dimethyl benzyl ammonium chloride (ADBAC)

Function:
- Disinfecting agent, cosmetic biocide, deodorant, surfactant, or preservative

Found In:
- Disinfecting all-purpose cleaners, bathroom cleaners,

eyedrops, moisturizers, sunscreens, pain relief medications

Reasons to Avoid:
- Gastrointestinal and liver toxin, immuno- and neurotoxin, sensory organ toxin
- May cause reproductive and birth defects
- Highly toxic to fish
- Limited biodegradability

Amyl acetate

Function:
- Solvent or masking fragrance

Found in:
- Deodorizers, fragrances, furniture polishes

Reasons to Avoid:
- Irritating to eyes and lungs
- Toxic to kidneys and nervous system (neurotoxin)
- VOC—contributes to indoor and outdoor air pollution
- Petroleum-derived

Benzene (benzol, phenyl hydride)

Function:
- Solvent, disinfecting agent, or masking fragrance

Found in:
- Oven cleaners, stain removers, carpet cleaners, deodorizers, detergents, furniture polishes

Reasons to Avoid:
- Known human carcinogen, hormone disrupter—may cause such reproductive/developmental effects as birth defects, infertility, or cognitive impairment
- Sensitizer—may trigger allergic reactions in sensitive people
- Petroleum-derived
- VOC—contributes to indoor and outdoor air pollution

p-Dichlorobenzene (paradichlorobenzene, PDCB)

Function:
- Pesticide or deodorant

Found in:
- Moth balls, deodorizers

Reasons to Avoid:
- Known human carcinogen
- Toxic to liver, kidneys, spleen, and blood
- Irritating to lungs and eyes
- VOC—contributes to indoor and outdoor air pollution

Dichloroisocyanurate

Function:
- Disinfecting agent

Found in:
- Disinfectants, tub and tile cleaners, scouring powders, dishwashing detergents, water and sewer treatments

Reasons to Avoid:
- Hormone disrupter—may cause developmental abnormalities

- Immune system disrupter
- Irritating to eyes, skin, and lungs
- Corrosive to skin
- May produce harmful by-products

Dimethicone

Function:
- Anti-foaming agent, skin protectant (as lubricant), or hair conditioning agent

Found in:
- Fabric softeners, silicone-based products, high-efficiency laundry products, moisturizers, foundations, eye shadows, anti-aging creams, nail polishes, sunscreens, lipsticks

Reasons to Avoid:
- Irritating to skin with prolonged exposure
- Promotes tumor growth in liver and lymph nodes
- Non-biodegradable
- Petroleum-derived

Dioxane (1,4-dioxane, diethylene dioxide, diethylene ether, diethylene oxide)

Function:
- None. Dioxane is a by-product of sodium laureth sulfate (SLS) manufacturing (see the sodium laureth sulfate entry).

Found in:
- Glass cleaners, laundry liquids, dishwashing liquids

Reasons to Avoid:
- Known human carcinogen
- Central nervous system depressant (neurotoxin)
- Damaging to liver and kidney
- Non-biodegradable

Ethylene diamine tetra acetate (EDTA)

Function:
- Chelating agent (water softener)

Found in:
- All-purpose cleaners, laundry detergents, dishwashing detergents, bathroom and floor cleaners

Reasons to Avoid:
- Slow to biodegrade
- Petroleum-derived
- Releases heavy metals into the environment

Formaldehyde

Function:
- Preservative or cosmetic biocide

Found in:
- Disinfectants, deodorizers, fragrances, adhesives (including those found in furniture), paints, nail polishes

Reasons to Avoid:
- Known human and animal carcinogen
- Irritating to skin, eyes, and lungs—may cause contact dermatitis and/or trigger asthma in sensitive people

- May cause headaches and chronic fatigue
- VOC—contributes to indoor and outdoor air pollution

Fragrance, Synthetic

Function:
- Mask odor of product ingredients

Found in:
- Deodorizers; air fresheners; all synthetically scented products, including personal care items, perfumes, cleaning products, diapers, and feminine care products

Reasons to Avoid:
- Hormone disrupters—may cause damage to chromosome, thyroid, and sperm cells
- May cause headaches or such asthma or asthma-like symptoms as chest tightness and wheezing
- May cause diarrhea or vomiting in infants
- Irritating to airways and sensory organs (lungs, nose, eyes)—may cause reduced pulmonary function
- Irritating to skin—may cause contact dermatitis or eczema in sensitive people
- Petroleum-derived
- Non-biodegradable
- VOC—contributes to indoor and outdoor air pollution

Glycol and Glycol ethers (2-Butoxyethanol, ethylene glycol, butyl cellosolve, diethylene glycol, triethlene glycol)

Function:
- Solvents

Found in:
- All-purpose cleaners, glass cleaners, spray cleaners, scouring cleaners, perfumes, cosmetics, paints

Reasons to Avoid:
- Reproductive toxins—may cause reduced sperm count and/or infertility
- May cause damage to liver and kidneys, may depress central nervous system
- VOCs—contribute to indoor and outdoor air pollution

Hydrochloric acid

Function:
- pH adjuster
- lime scale remover

Found in:
- Sink and shower cleaners, toilet bowl cleaners, deodorizers, eyedrops, hair coloring and bleaches, dandruff treatments, fertilizers, rubbers, dyes

Reasons to Avoid:
- In high concentrations, corrosive to skin, eyes, and respiratory system

Naphthalene

Function:
- Surfactant, solvent, antifoaming agent, dispersant, or pesticide

Found in:

- Fragrances, deodorizers, toilet bowl cleaners, carpet cleaners, mothballs, synthetic dyes, gasoline, fuels

Reasons to Avoid:

- Known human carcinogen
- Kidney toxin
- Triggers cataracts
- Petroleum-derived
- VOC—contributes to indoor and outdoor air pollution

Optical brighteners

Function:

- Make colors of fabric and paper appear brighter or cause a perceived whitening by reflecting light, not by cleaning

Found in:

- Laundry detergents, shampoos, conditioners, makeup, paper, fabrics

Reasons to Avoid:

- May have reproductive or developmental effects
- Irritating to skin
- Non-biodegradable
- Petroleum-derived

Phthalates

Function:

- Solvent for fragrances, makes plastics flexible

Found in:

- Fragrances, nail polishes and removers, PVC plastics (toys, flooring, food containers, etc.)

Reasons to Avoid:

- Hormone disrupters and reproductive toxins—may cause birth defects or sexual abnormalities
- Probable human carcinogen
- Petroleum-derived
- VOCs—contribute to indoor and outdoor air pollution

Phenols (methylphenols, cresol)

Function:

- Preservatives, fragrances, or disinfecting agents

Found in:

- Fragrances, polishes, mold/mildew removers, face treatments, moisturizers, antiaging products, makeup, sunscreens, shampoos, plastics, herbicides, hair coloring

Reasons to Avoid:

- Kidney and liver toxins
- Central nervous system toxicants
- Severely irritating to skin and eyes
- Petroleum-derived

Phosphoric acid

Function:

- pH adjuster

Found in:

- Grout cleaners, toilet bowl cleaners, sink and shower

cleaners, toothpastes, eyedrops, mouthwashes

Reason to Avoid:

- In high concentrations, corrosive to skin and eyes

Quaternary ammonium compounds (quats)

Function:

- Surfactants, disinfecting agents, fabric softeners, or antistatic agents

Found in:

- Disinfecting all-purpose cleaners, laundry detergents, dishwashing detergents, fabric softeners, disinfectants, bathroom cleaners, makeup, baby lotions, shampoos, conditioners, eyedrops, pain relievers

Reasons to Avoid:

- Irritating to skin, eyes, lungs, and mucous membranes
- Gastrointestinal and liver toxins
- Highly toxic to aquatic life
- Slow to biodegrade
- Petroleum-derived

Sodium hydroxide (caustic soda or lye)

Function:

- pH adjuster

Found in:

- Oven and drain cleaners (in high concentrations) and other products to adjust pH

Reasons to Avoid:

- In high concentrations, corrosive to skin and eyes
- In spray products, may be damaging to lungs if inhaled

Sodium hypochlorite (chlorine beach)

Function:

- Oxidizing agent or bleaching agent

Found in:

- Bleaches, whitening detergents, nail treatments

Reasons to Avoid:

- Corrosive to skin and eyes
- May cause death when mixed with acidic cleaners or ammonia and inhaled
- Produces organochlorines as by-products—toxic pollutants that persist in the environment

Sulfuric acid

Function:

- pH adjuster

Found in:

- Drain cleaners, dyes, hair mousses, hair coloring and bleaches, hair growth inhibitors

Reason to Avoid:

- In high concentrations, severely damaging to skin, eyes, lungs, and digestive tract

Toluene

Function:
- Solvent

Found in:
- All-purpose cleaners, aerosols, air fresheners, nail polishes and removers, paints, rubber, printing inks, glues

Reasons to Avoid:
- Reproductive toxin—may cause birth defects
- May damage liver, kidneys, blood, or central nervous system
- Irritating to lungs, skin, and eyes
- Inhalation may cause headaches, dizziness, confusion, or fatigue
- VOC—contributes to indoor and outdoor air pollution

Triclosan

Function:
- Disinfecting agent, preservative, deodorant, pesticide, or cosmetic biocide

Found in:
- Disinfectants, antibacterial hand soaps, detergents, antiperspirants, facial cleansers, toothpastes, lipsticks, eye shadows

Reasons to Avoid:
- May encourage bacterial resistance to antibiotics
- Reproductive toxicant
- Produces chlorinated dioxins (known human carcinogens) when exposed to sunlight
- Very toxic to aquatic life—may cause long-term adverse effects in the aquatic environment
- Petroleum-derived
- Non-biodegradable
- Persistent in the environment and through the food chain—builds up over time (bioaccumulates) in wildlife

Trisodium nitrilotriacete (NTA)

Function:
- Chelating agent (water softener) or pesticide

Found in:
- Laundry detergents, stain removers, carpet cleaners, dishwashing detergents, facial moisturizers, acne treatments, anti-aging products, pesticides

Reasons to Avoid:
- Suspected human carcinogen
- May release heavy metals into environment

Xylene

Function:
- Solvent or masking fragrance

Found in:
- Degreasers, aerosols, perfumes, nail polishes

Reasons to Avoid:
- Reproductive toxin—may have reproductive effects, including infertility
- Neurotoxin—may cause memory loss on repeated exposure

- Slow to biodegrade
- Petroleum-derived

Some Ingredients With Known Acute or Suspected Chronic Toxicity Used in Both Conventional and "Green" Products

Alcohol (ethanol, ethyl alcohol)

Function:
- Solvent, disinfecting agent, anti-foaming agent, fragrance, thinning agent, or preservative

Found in:
- All-purpose cleaners, dishwashing liquids, glass cleaners, laundry detergents, sanitizers, facial moisturizers, toners, mouthwashes, shampoos, flavorings, gasoline additives

Reasons to Avoid:
- Possibly irritating to eyes and skin
- VOC—contributes to indoor and outdoor air pollution

Reasons to Choose:
- Generally recognized as safe
- Plant-derived
- Biodegrades quickly

Alcohol ethoxylates (fatty alcohol ethoxylates, coceth-7, coceth-4, deceth-5)

Function:
- Surfactants

Found in:
- Laundry detergents

Reason to Avoid:
- Petroleum-derived (may be partially plant-derived)

Reasons to Choose:
- Biodegradable

Alkylbenzene sulfonate (ABS)

Function:
- Surfactant

Found in:
- Dishwashing detergents, fabric softeners, laundry detergents

Reasons to Avoid:
- Slow to biodegrade
- Petroleum-derived

Amine oxides (lauramine oxides, lauramidopropylamine oxide)

Function:
- Surfactants

Found in:
- Laundry detergents, dish liquids, body washes, liquid hand soaps, bubble baths, facial cleansers, conditioners

Reasons to Avoid:
- May contain nitrosamines, impurities that are known to be carcinogenic

Reasons to Choose:
- Plant-derived

Ammonia (ammonium hydroxide)

Function:
- pH adjuster or denaturant

Found in:
- All-purpose cleaners, glass and wood cleaners, disinfectants, hair coloring, bleaches, facial moisturizers, printer inks, industrial cleaners

Reason to Avoid:
- In high concentrations, irritating to skin, eyes, and lungs. (Concentrations typically not high in the products listed.)

Essential Oils

Function:
- Fragrances (some function as disinfecting agents, chelating agents, or insect repellents)

Found in:
- Naturally fragranced products, air fresheners, aromatherapy products

Reasons to Avoid:
- Possibly irritating—may trigger allergies in sensitive people
- VOCs—contribute to indoor and outdoor air pollution

Reasons to Choose:
- Safer alternatives to many synthetic fragrances
- Plant-derived

Hydrogen peroxide

Function:
- Disinfecting agent, oxidizing agent, cosmetic biocide, or oral health care agent

Found in:
- Oxygen bleaches, stain removers, disinfectants, tooth whiteners, mouthwashes, acne treatments, facial cleansers

Reasons to Avoid:
- Irritating to skin and eyes

Reasons to Choose:
- 3-4% concentration is nontoxic (not fatal to humans if swallowed)
- Chlorine bleach alternative
- Safe for the environment
- Biodegradable

Isopropyl alcohol (isopropanol)

Function:
- Solvent, antifoaming agent, or masking fragrance

Found in:
- All-purpose cleaners, glass cleaners, stain removers, carpet cleaners

Reasons to Avoid:
- Petroleum-derived

- VOC—contributes to indoor and outdoor air pollution

Oxalic acid

Function:
- Chelating agent, pH adjuster, disinfectant, pesticide, purifying agent, bleaching agent or waste water treatment

Found in:
- Bathroom and wood cleaners, rust removers, plastics

Reasons to Avoid:
- Irritating to skin and eyes
- May be petroleum-derived

Reason to choose:
- Can be plant-derived

Propylene glycol (PG)

Function:
- Solvent, humectant (keeps products moist), skin-conditioning agent, fragrance agent, or thinning agent

Found in:
- Glass cleaners, deodorizers, floor polishes, dishwashing liquids, laundry detergents, toilet bowl cleaners, toothpastes, low-fat ice cream and sour cream, pharmaceuticals, cosmetics

Reasons to Avoid:
- Long-term exposure may damage central nervous system
- Petroleum-derived

Reasons to Choose:
- Nontoxic to animals
- Biodegradable
- Does not bioaccumulate

Sodium Borate (sodium tetraborate, borax)

Function:
- pH adjuster, antifungal agent, or insecticide

Found in:
- laundry detergents, disinfectants, oven cleaners, eyedrops, moisturizers, bath salts, styling lotions, ceramics, wood glues

Reason to Avoid:
- High-level exposure may cause sperm damage

Reasons to Choose:
- Considered safe—no short-term health effects
- Found in nature

Sodium laureth sulfate
(Sodium lauryl ether sulfate, SLES)

Function:
- Surfactant

Found in:
- Laundry detergents, liquid soaps, shampoos, toothpastes

Reasons to Avoid:
- May be contaminated with 1,4-dioxane (a known human carcinogen) formed during manufacturing
- May be petroleum-derived

The Cosmetics Chart

Chemicals to Avoid	Function	Found in	Health Effects
Coal Tars	Can be a by-product of coal, or more recently a petroleum-derived synthetic, used for dye; also prevents dryness and acts as a biocide, killing living organisms	Hair dyes—some FD&C and D&C colors, PPD (phenlyenediamine) dye; makeup; shampoo; rosacea, dandruff, psoriasis, and eczema treatments; anti-itch/rash cream	Known human carcinogen; irritating to skin and respiratory tract; will persist in environment (i.e., not biodegrade) and is known to accumulate in the blood and tissues of humans and animals to levels of concern
Cocamide DEA (diethanolamine) and its compounds, Cocamide TEA and Cocamide MEA	Creates foam or makes foam last longer. Also increases the viscosity of a product.	Shampoo; sunscreen; antifungal, acne, and wound treatments; anti-itch/rash cream; moisturizer	Excess diethanoamine in Cocamide DEA can react to form diethanolnitrosamine, a known human immune system toxicant; linked to liver and kidney cancer; Cocamide MEA and Cocamide TEA are much less likely to form nitrosamines
PEGs and other ethoxylates (look for "eth-" in ingredient names, like polyethylene glycol)	Petroleum-derived surfactants that help water mix with oil and create foam	Foundation/concealer; shampoo; hand soap; facial cleanser; hair coloring and bleaching products; sunscreen	Reproductive toxin; may cause birth defects; process of ethoxylation can create 1,4-dioxane (a carcinogen); can alter or reduce the skin's natural moisture, causing an increase in the appearance of aging and vulnerability to bacteria
Formaldehyde	Used as a polymerization reagent in nail polish or as a preservative	Deodorants; nail treatments and polish; moisturizers; shaving cream; shampoo; conditioner; styling gels; antiaging products; facial cleanser; makeup; and many others; Also a by-product of some preservatives and biocides	Known human carcinogen; known immune system and respiratory toxicant; reproductive/developmental toxicant
Lead	A contaminant, not an ingredient	Makeup; moisturizers; antiaging products; hair spray; hair coloring; diaper cream; sunscreen; toothpaste; acne treatments	Known neurotoxin that can cause learning, language, and behavioral problems; probable human carcinogen; probable endocrine disrupter; may cause damage to the immune system

Chemicals to Avoid	Function	Found in	Health Effects
Mercury	A contaminant, not an ingredient	Eye drops; moisturizer; lip gloss, lipstick, and lip liner; eye- and brow liner; mascara; baby lotion	Poisonous to humans and animals; known human carcinogen; known human nervous system and developmental toxin linked to brain damage, birth defects, infertility, and hypothyroidism; probable endocrine disrupter; known human immune-system toxicant
Parabens (butyl-, propyl-, ethyl-, and methyl-)	Synthetic preservative (petroleum-derived), disinfectant	Very widely used including in acne treatment, conditioner, shampoo, tanning oil, moisturizer, sunscreen, makeup remover, shaving cream, deodorant, hair relaxer, and ointments (antibacterial and others)	Known endocrine disrupter; reproductive/developmental toxin; may cause allergies and skin rashes
Phthalates (diethyl-, diethyl hexyl-, dibutyl-)	Used as a solvent for fragrance, and to improve plasticity	Synthetic perfumes and fragrances, or anything labeled "fragrance" (unless specifically listed as a natural essential oil); bath oils/salts; scented lotions; air fresheners; liquid hand soaps; anything with a long-lasting scent; nail polish	Reproductive toxins (risk of infertility) and endocrine disrupters; may cause birth defects; very toxic to aquatic organisms; some are banned for use in Europe
SLES (sodium laureth sulfate or sodium lauryl ether sulfate)	Used as a surfactant (soil remover)	Both cleaning and personal care products—mainly things that foam, like soap, shampoo, and even toothpaste	Can be a source of 1,4-dioxane (a carcinogen) contamination
Toluene	Solvent used to dissolve soils and stains or to help keep products together	Stain removers; degreasers; nail polish	Reproductive/developmental toxin (risk of abnormal sperm count and mental retardation); may cause damage to human nervous system (cognitive impairment) and nonreproductive organs including kidneys, heart, and ears; lung and skin irritant
Triclosan	Antibacterial (disinfectant), also used as a preservative	Liquid hand soap; disinfecting hand gels; antiperspirants/deodorants; facial cleansers; toothpaste; acne treatments; lipsticks; eye shadow; body washes; tooth whiteners	Irritating to eyes and skin; may cause adverse effects to thyroid hormone; known to accumulate in bodies and has been found in breast milk of almost all American women; bioaccumulates in aquatic organisms and may cause long-term adverse effects in the aquatic environment

RESOURCES GUIDE

Here are some select recommended resources. Some of these products are better for us and the earth we all share. Others are made by responsible companies. The best of the best are both. Reading labels and asking questions are excellent precautions to take, even for items listed here; ingredients, materials, and manufacturers can change, and companies may be bought and sold. For even more resources, check out the list of recommended reading.

KITCHEN

APPLIANCES (REFRIGERATORS, STOVES, DISHWASHERS, ETC.)

Consumer Reports: consumerreports.org
Consumer Reports' Greener Choices:
  greenerchoices.org
Energy Star: energystar.gov

BEVERAGE CONTAINERS

Klean Kanteen: kleankanteen.com

COMPOSTING

Gardener's Supply Company: gardeners.com
NatureMill: naturemill.com

DISHES AND RECYCLED GLASSWARE

Eden Home: edenhome.com
Fiestaware: dinnerwareusa.com
The Green Glass Company: greenglass.com
Viva Terra: vivaterra.com

DISINFECTING HAND SPRAY

CleanWell: cleanwelltoday.com

FOOD STORAGE CONTAINERS

Anchor Hocking Company: anchorhocking.com
Crate and Barrel: crateandbarrel.com
Frigoverre: containerstore.com
Ikea: ikea.com
Preserve: preserveproducts.com
Pyrex: pyrexware.com

POTS AND PANS

De Buyer: debuyer.com
Le Creuset: lecreuset.com
Lodge Cast Iron: lodgemfg.com

TABLE LINENS

Etsy: etsy.com
Gaiam: gaiam.com
Rawganique: rawganique.com

FOOD

HOW TO FIND LOCAL GOODS

Eat Well Guide: eatwellguide.org
Local Harvest: localharvest.org
Natural Food Coop Directory: coopdirectory.org

WIDELY AVAILABLE ORGANICS

Annie's Homegrown: annies.com
Applegate Farms: applegatefarms.com
Clif Bar: clifbarstore.com
Earthbound Farm: ebfarm.com
Organic Valley: organicvalley.coop
Stonyfield Farm: stonyfield.com
Whole Foods Market: wholefoods.com

BPA-FREE CANNED GOODS

Eden Organic: edenfoods.com
Vital Choice: vitalchoice.com

BEVERAGES

Appellation Wine & Spirits: appellationnyc.com
Café Alta Gracia: cafealtagracia.com
Fork & Bottle: forkandbottle.com
Green Mountain Coffee: greenmountaincoffee.com
Grgich Hills Estate: grgich.com
In Pursuit of Tea: inpursuitoftea.com
Jenny & Francois Selections: worldwidewine.net

Juniper Green: junipergreen.org
New Belgium Brewing: newbelgium.com
Organic Wine Journal: organicwinejournal.com
Peak Organic Brewing Company: peakbrewing.com
Prairie Organic Vodka: news.prairievodka.com
Shinn Estate Vineyards: shinnestatevineyards.com
Sweet Marias: sweetmarias.com
Tuthilltown Spirits: tuthilltown.com

BEDROOM

AIR FILTERS

AllerAir: allerair.com
Austin Air: austinairpurifiers.com

BEDDING (SHEETS, BLANKETS, PILLOWS, ETC.)

ABC Home: abchome.com
Allergy Buyers Club: allergybuyersclub.com
Anna Sova: annasova.com
Coyuchi: coyuchi.com
Dax Stores: daxstores.com
Gaiam: gaiam.com
Loop Organic: looporganic.com
Organic Mattress Store: organicmattressstore.com
Plover Organic: ploverorganic.com
White Lotus: whitelotus.net

CARPETING AND RUGS

Earth Weave: earthweave.com
Eco by Design: ecobydesign.com
Flor: flor.com
Nature's Carpet: naturescarpet.com
Northern Naturals: northernnaturals.com
Shaw Floors: shawfloors.com

CLOTHING

Bag Borrow or Steal: bagborroworsteal.com
Earth Pledge Future Fashion Project:
   earthpledge.org/ff
Edun: edun.com
Eileen Fisher: eileenfisher.com
Etsy: etsy.com
The Green Loop: thegreenloop.com
Kaight: kaightshop.com
Linda Loudermilk: lindaloudermilk.com
Loomstate: loomstate.org
Patagonia: patagonia.com

ECO SEX PRODUCTS

Earth Erotics: eartherotics.com

The Sensual Vegan: thesensualvegan.com

FURNITURE (*See Furniture in Family Rooms*)

HARDWOOD BEDS AND BOX SPRINGS

Furnature: furnature.com
The Organic Mattress: theorganicmattress.com
Pacific Rim Woodworking:
   pacificrimwoodworking.com
Vermont Tubbs: vermonttubbs.com
Vivavi: vivavi.com

MATTRESSES

Englander: englander.com
Ikea: ikea.com
Natura: naturaworld.com
Omi: organicpedicbyomi.com

SHADES AND CURTAINS

Earthshade: earthshade.com
Ikea: ikea.com

VACUUMS WITH HEPA FILTERS

Dyson: dyson.com
Miele: mieleusa.com
Sebo: sebo-vacuums.com

NURSERY AND KIDS' ROOMS

ART SUPPLIES

Clementine Art: clementineart.com
Eco-Kids: eco-kidsusa.com
Stockmar: stockmar.de

BABY BLANKETS (*Also see Bedding under Bedroom*)

Nui Organics: nuiorganics.com
Satara Baby: satarababy.com
Tiny Birds: tinybirdsorganics.com

BOTTLES

BornFree: newbornfree.com
Evenflo: evenflo.com
Klean Kanteen: kleankanteen.com
Lifefactory: lifefactory.com
Silikids: silikids.com
Weego: weegobaby.com

BREAST-FEEDING CARE (NIPPLE CREAM, NURSING PADS)

Motherlove: motherlove.com
Organic Essentials: organicessentials.com
Under the Nile: underthenile.com

CARRIERS, STROLLERS, AND SLINGS

Didymos: didymos.com
ErgoBaby: ergocarrierbaby.com
Orbit: orbitbaby.com
Maya Wrap: mayawrap.com

CHANGING PADS (IN-HOUSE)

Ikea: ikea.com
Naturepedic: naturepedic.com

CHANGING PADS (TRAVEL)

Patemm: patemm.com

CLOTHING

Green Babies: greenbabies.com
Hanna Andersson: hannaandersson.com
Kate Quinn Organics: katequinnorganics.com
Kee-Ka: kee-ka.com
The Little Seed: thelittleseed.com
Under the Nile: underthenile.com

CRIB MATTRESSES

Englander: englander.com
Ikea: ikea.com
Natura: naturaworld.com
Omi: organicpedicbyomi.com

CRIBS

Pacific Rim Woodworking:
    pacificrimwoodworking.com
Q Collection Junior: qcollectionjunior.com

KID-SPECIFIC PERSONAL CARE PRODUCTS (LOTION, SOAP, SHAMPOO, ETC.)

Dr. Bronner's: drbronner.com
Erbaviva: erbaviva.com
Weleda Baby: usa.weleda.com

LEAD SWAB KITS

Lead Check: leadcheck.com
Lead Test Toys: leadtesttoys.com

PACIFIERS

Natursutten: natursutten.dk
Soothie: soothie-pacifier.com

TOYS

Fair Trade Sports: fairtradesports.com
Healthy Stuff: healthystuff.org
MiYim Organics: miyim.com
Nova Natural: novanatural.com
Oompa: oompa.com
Peace Toys: peacetoys.com
PlanToys: www.plantoys.com
Rosie Hippo: rosiehippo.com
Tree Blocks: treeblocks.com

FAMILY ROOMS

FURNITURE

Forest Stewardship Council: fscus.org
Green America: greenamericatoday.org
Greenguard Environmental Institute:
    greenguard.org
Haworth: haworth.com
Herman Miller: hermanmiller.com
Q Collection: qcollection.com
Steelcase: steelcase.com
Sustainable Furnishings Council:
    sustainablefurnishings.org
Vermont Farm Table: vermontfarmtable.com

ELECTRONICS (STEREOS, TELEVISIONS, ETC.)

Consumer Reports' Greener Choices:
    greenerchoices.org
Greenpeace's Guide to Greener Electronics:
    greenpeace.org

FABRIC/UPHOLSTERING

Etsy: etsy.com
NearSea Naturals: nearseanaturals.com
Organic Cotton Plus: organiccottonplus.com
Q Collection: qcollection.com

FLOORS

EcoTimber: ecotimber.com
GreenFloors: greenfloors.com
USFloors: naturalcork.com

LIGHTING

American Environmental Products: sunalux.com
American Scientific Lighting: asllighting.com
Enlux Lighting: enluxled.com
Herman Miller: hermanmiller.com
LEDTronics: ledtronics.com
Mule: mulelighting.com
Steelcase: steelcase.com

NO- OR LOW-VOC FLOOR STAINS

AFM Safecoat: afmsafecoat.com

NO-VOC PAINT

AFM Safecoat: afmsafecoat.com
Anna Sova Food Paint: healthyzerovocpaint.com
Bioshield: bioshieldpaint.com
Ecoprocote: ecoprocote.com
Green Depot Color Collections: greendepot.com
Ivy Coatings: ivycoatings.com
Yolo Colorhouse: yolocolorhouse.com

PET FOOD, TREATS, TOYS, LITTER, AND GEAR

DogBedWorks: dogbedworks.com
Earth Dog: earthdog.com
Feline Pine: felinepine.com
Fetch Dog: fetchdog.com
GreenPets: greenpets.com
Heidi's Homemade: heidisbakery.com
Natura Pet: naturapet.com
Mountain Meadows: mtnmeadowspet.com
Nature's Paws: naturespaws.com
Only Natural Pet Store: onlynaturalpet.com
PetGuard: petguard.com
PetHabitats: pethabitats.com
Taraluna: taraluna.com
West Paw Design: westpawdesign.com

PVC-FREE YOGA MATS AND OTHER EQUIPMENT

The Harmony Natural Yoga Mat: jadeyoga.com
Kulae: kulae.com

RENOVATIONS (GENERAL MATERIALS AND INFORMATION)

Eco Haus: ecohaus.com
Green Building: greenbuilding.com
Green Depot: greendepot.com
Greenguard Environmental Institute: greenguard.org
Healthy Building Network: healthybuilding.net
IceStone: icestone.biz
The Pharos Project: pharosproject.net
U.S. Green Building Council: usgbc.org

BATHROOM

PERSONAL CARE PRODUCTS AND SUNSCREEN

Badger: badgerbalm.com
Dr. Alkaitis: alkaitis.com
Dr. Bronner's: drbronner.com
Dr. Hauschka: drhauschka.com
Erbaviva: erbaviva.com
Intelligent Nutrients: intelligentnutrients.com
John Masters Organics: johnmasters.com
New Chapter: newchapter.com
Pangea Organics: PangeaOrganics.com
Soléo Organics: soleousa.com
Suki: sukiskincare.com
Terressentials: Terressentials.com
True Body Soap: truebodyproducts.com
Weleda: weleda.com

SHOWER CURTAINS AND SHOWERHEAD FILTERS

Green Depot: greendepot.com
Pristine Planet: pristineplanet.com
Rawganique: rawganique.com

TOWELS AND BATH MATS

Anna Sova: annasova.com
Gaiam: gaiam.com
Loop Organic: looporganic.com

TUB TOYS (WOODEN BOATS, PVC-FREE RUBBER DUCKIES, ETC.)

Maple Landmark: www.maplelandmark.com
Our Green House: ourgreenhouse.com

UTILITY ROOMS

PEST CONTROL

Beyond Pesticides: beyondpesticides.org
Pesticide Action Network: panna.org

RADON TEST KITS

Radon Zone: radonzone.com

ROOFING

Green Roofs: greenroofs.com

LAUNDRY ROOM

RACKS, LINES, AND AIR-DRYING GEAR

Project Laundry List: laundrylist.org

WASHERS/DRYERS

Consumer Reports: consumerreports.org
Energy Star: energystar.gov

HOME OFFICE

BUSINESS CARDS

Barefoot Press: barefootpress.com
Green Printer: greenprinter.com

BUSINESS COMMUNICATION

TextID: textid.com

ELECTRONICS (COMPUTERS, PHONES, ETC.)

Consumer Reports' Greener Choices:
   greenerchoices.org
Greenpeace's Guide to Greener Electronics:
   greenpeace.org

OFFICE BUSINESS SERVICES

BetterWorld Telecom: betterworldtelecom.com
New Resource Bank: newresourcebank.com
Working Assets/CREDO: workingassets.com

OFFICE FURNITURE (See Furniture in Family Rooms)

OFFICE SUPPLIES

The Green Office: thegreenoffice.com
Green Home: greenhome.com
New Leaf Paper: newleafpaper.com

WASTE-FREE LUNCH CONTAINERS

Reuseit: reuseit.com
Kids Konserve: kidskonserve.com
Laptop Lunches: laptoplunches.com

FURTHER READING

BOOKS

Biomimicry, by Janine M. Benyus
Capitalism as if the World Matters, by Jonathon Porritt
The Complete Organic Pregnancy, by Deirdre Dolan and Alexandra Zissu
The Conscious Kitchen, by Alexandra Zissu
Do One Green Thing, by Mindy Pennybacker
Feeding Baby Green, by Alan Greene
Green, Greener, Greenest, by Lori Bongiorno
Healthy Child Healthy World, by Christopher Gavigan
Presence, by Peter M. Senge
Raising Baby Green, by Alan Greene
The Real Wealth of Nations, by Riane Eisler
Thinking in Systems, by Donella H. Meadows

WEBSITES

Care2: care2.org
The Daily Green: thedailygreen.com
Environmental Health News:
   environmentalhealthnews.org
The Environmental Working Group: ewg.org
GoodGuide: goodguide.com
Grist: grist.org
Healthy Child Healthy World: healthychild.org
The Networker: sehn.org/thenet.html
NRDC's Simple Steps: simplesteps.org
Organic Consumers Association: organicconsumers.org
Planet Green: planetgreen.com
Safer Chemicals, Healthy Families: saferchemicals.org
Seventh Generation News: seventhgeneration.com
Treehugger: treehugger.com

GET INVOLVED

WAGES (Women's Action to Gain Economic Security) is a nonprofit organization based in California that works to create new jobs and empowers low-income women by organizing environmentally-friendly cleaning cooperatives (with telltale names like Natural Home Cleaning Professionals). To get active with WAGES or to help develop similar cooperatives in your area, go to WAGEScooperatives.org.

INDEX

A

abrasives, 16
acetic acid, 24
acids, 16, 24, 192, 215, 229
activated carbon filters, 316
acute toxicities, 22–23, 334
AFM Safecoat Safe Seal, 137
air fresheners, 26, 35, 193, 210
air purifiers, 108, 129, 135
air quality
    basements, 241
    family rooms, 163–165
    nursery/children's rooms, 128
    political activism, 323
    systems, 320–323
    See also ventilation
alarm clocks, 111
alkalis, 16–17
alkylphenol ethoxylates (APEs), 215
alkyl polyglucoside (APG), 24
allergies, 128, 320–321
all-purpose cleaners, 26, 60
aluminum cookware, 38
American Academy of Pediatrics, 130
American Medical Association, 59
American Society for Testing
    and Materials (ASTM), 152
animal-welfare approved, 83
antibacterial hand soaps, 59
antifreeze, 233
appliances, 48–52, 54–55, 63
art supplies, 152–153
asbestos insulation, 229, 241
asbestos vinyl tiles, 56
asphalt shingles, 231
attics, 228–231, 242
automotive fluids, 233

B

baby wipes, 141
baking soda, 28, 214, 216, 258
bamboo, 106, 137, 204
basements, 236–239, 241, 242, 243
bathing water, 200
bath mats, 203
bathrooms
    accessories, 204
    cleaning, 216–217
    cleaning products, 190–193, 214–215
    conscious living, 187–189
    cosmetics, 218–223
    feminine care, 210–211
    fixtures, 212–213
    materials and maintenance,
        212–213
    moisture reduction, 198–199

renovations, 212, 213
resources, 346
sinks, 208, 216
systems, 207
toilets, 206–209, 212, 215, 216
ventilation, 190–199, 230
water, 206–207, 209, 210
batteries, 234, 280, 305
bedding, 106–107, 121, 137, 155, 262
bedrooms
    bedding, 106–107, 121, 137, 155, 262
    beds, 98–103
    cleaning, 120–121
    closets, 116–117
    conscious living, 95–97
    curtains, 109
    floors, 114–115
    intimate products, 104–105
    lighting, 112
    resources, 343–344
    setting up, 110–111
    systems, 113, 119
    ventilation, 108, 113
beer, 91
beeswax, 28, 136, 210
Berthold-Bond, Annie, *Better Basics*
    for the Home, 67, 263
BeyondPesticides.org, 66
birth control, 105
black mold, 196
blankets, 107, 121, 137, 155
bleaches, 17, 192, 193, 256
borax, 28, 179, 258
boric acid, 229
bottled goods, 90–91
bottle-feeding, 130–131
box springs, 103
BPA (bisphenol-A), 42, 44, 88,
    130–131, 132, 180
breast-feeding, 130, 132, 133
breast pumps, 132
builders, 17, 18
butoxyethanol, 193

C

Campaign for Safe Cosmetics, 143,
    221
candles, 113, 165, 210
carpets
    basements, 241
    bathrooms, 213
    bedrooms, 115
    home-made stain removers, 26
    nursery/children's rooms, 146–147
    pets, 179
car seats, 146
cast-iron cookware, 37–38
cation exchange softeners, 316
caulk, 202

cedar shingles, 231
cell phones, 280
cellulose, 229
Center for Health, Environment
    and Justice, 131
ceramics
    for cookware, 38–39
    for food storage, 41
    for plates, 46
certified humane raised and handled,
    83
changing tables, 144
cheese, 85
chelating agents, 17, 18
chicken, decontamination of, 65
children
    diapers, 140–141
    education and responsibility, 154
    food for, 130–133
    tableware for, 46
    See also nursery/children's rooms;
        toys
chlorine bleach, 193, 211, 256, 260
chronic toxicities, 22, 23, 334
cigarette smoke, 129, 164
citric acid, 24, 201
cleaner energy, 296–297
cleaning products
    bathrooms, 190–193, 214–215
    chemicals in, 13, 14, 192, 193, 207
    household ingredients for, 28–29
    ingredients in green products,
        24–25
    kitchens, 35, 60, 61, 67
    labels, 14, 15, 23, 192
    making at home, 26–29, 214
    nursery/children's rooms, 156–157
    pH scale, 16, 20–21
    safety, 19, 61, 190, 192
    storage, 19, 61
    toxicity of, 22–23, 334
    types of, 16–18
    ventilation, 35, 190–193
cleaning timelines
    bathrooms, 216–217
    bedrooms, 120–121
    family rooms, 182–185
    home offices, 288–289
    kitchens, 62–64
    laundry rooms, 269
    nursery/children's rooms, 154–157
    utility rooms, 242–243
cleaning water, 201
CleanWell, 69
cloth diapers, 140–141
clothing, 116–117, 119, 148, 155,
    262–263, 275
clutter, 10, 288
coffee, 91

phosphates, 17, 52
pH scale, 16, 20–21
pillows
    bedrooms, 106, 121
    nursery/children's rooms, 155
plants, 26, 276
plastics
    avoiding use with microwaves, 41, 54
    bottle-feeding, 130–131
    food storage, 40–44
    recycling, 40, 93, 304
    toys, 150
    water filters, 317
plates, 46
political activism
    air quality, 323
    community, 333
    conscious living, 11
    energy sources, 298–299
    money, 330
    outdoor spaces, 327
    systems, 291, 293
    waste, 308–309
    water, 319
polybrominated diphenyl ethers (PBDEs),
    99, 101, 134, 163, 179
PP (polypropylene), 42
Precautionary Principle, 9–10
prescriptions, 222, 318
pressure cookers, 55
Product Look Up (PLU) code, 79
Project Laundry List, 264
PS (polystyrene), 42
pumice stones, 215
PVC (polyvinyl chloride), 42, 43, 104, 115,
    149, 177, 204

R

radon, 36, 229, 315
rags, kitchen, 60
Rainforest Alliance Certified, 91
recycling
    batteries, 234, 280, 305
    education for children, 154
    electronics, 176, 279, 280
    packaging, 15, 93, 261
    plastics, 40, 93, 304
    systems, 302–305
    washing machines, 251
reduction
    in amount of stuff, 10, 124, 288
    in garbage, 301, 303, 308
refrigerators, 48–49, 63
renovations
    bathrooms, 212, 213
    family rooms, 162, 166–169
    kitchens, 36
    nursery/children's rooms, 127
retrofitting toilets, 208–209

ReusableBags.com, 43
reverse osmosis filters, 132, 317
rockers, 145
roofs, 231
root cellars, 238–239
rugs
    bedrooms, 115, 121
    home offices, 283
    mudrooms, 243
    nursery/children's rooms, 127,
       146–147, 156
rust stains, 215

S

Safer Chemicals, Healthy Families
    coalition, 14, 131
safety
    attics, 228
    basements, 236
    cleaning products, 19, 61, 190, 192
    conventional drying, 266, 267
    fireplaces, 165
    garages, 232–233
    home office, 274–275
    laundry detergents, 252
    plastics, 41–43
    toys, 149
seafood, 87–89
sea salt, 29
The Secret Life of Germs (Tierno), 210
Seventh Generation, 15, 141, 257, 261
sheets, 106–107, 121, 137, 155
shoes, 119, 148, 163, 235, 243
shopping bags, reusable, 78
shower curtains, 191, 203
SIDS, 124, 147
Silent Spring Institute, 120
silver, for flatware, 46, 47
Silverstone, 39
sinks, 208, 216
Skin Deep Cosmetic Safety Database, 221
skin treatments, making at home, 223
Snack-Taxi, 43
soaps
    hand soaps, 59
    liquid soaps, 59
soda ash, 17, 25, 29
sodas, 90
sodium bicarbonate, 25, 28
sodium carbonate, 17, 25, 29, 259
sodium lauryl sulfate (SLS), 25
Soil Association, 221
solar panels, 231, 297
solid food, 132–133
solvents, 18
sponges, kitchen, 61
stainless steel
    for bottle-feeding, 130
    for cookware, 38

    for flatware, 46
    for food storage, 41
    for water bottles, 314
sticky notes, 286
storage
    attics, 230
    basements, 236
    cleaning products, 19, 61
    food storage, 40–44
    garages, 232–233
The Story of Stuff (Leonard), 106
stoves, 50–51, 62, 63
stove vent, 35
stuffed animals, 135
sugar, 92
sunlight, 156, 171, 175, 264
sunscreens, 143, 222
surfactants, 18, 215, 252–253, 257
sustainability, food, 72, 74
Sustainable Cotton Project, 210
Sustainable Forestry Initiative (SFI),
    170–171
systems
    bathrooms, 207
    bedrooms, 113, 119
    community, 292, 293, 331–333
    conscious living, 291
    defined, 292
    energy sources, 294–297
    food, 77
    garages, 240
    home offices, 277
    kitchens, 53, 65
    laundry and laundry rooms, 260
    money, 328–330
    nursery/children's rooms, 135
    outdoor spaces, 324–327
    political activism, 291, 293
    waste, 300–307
    water, 310–318

T

table settings, kitchen, 45–47
talc, 143
tampons, 210–211
tea, 91
tea tree oil, 214, 216
teething toys, 149
Teflon, 39
telephone headsets, 280
telephone providers, 287
telephones, 278, 280, 289
television, 173–177, 184
Thornton, Joe, 256
thymol, 58, 157, 185, 191, 216, 289
Tierno, Philip, 210
toilet paper, 207, 209
toilets, 206–209, 212, 215, 216
toner, 284